Adverse Impact and Test Validation

Adverse Impact and Test Validation

A Practitioner's Guide to Valid and Defensible Employment Testing

Second Edition

DAN BIDDLE

Routledge
Taylor & Francis Group

LONDON AND NEW YORK

First published in paperback 2024

First published 2006 by Gower Publishing

4 Park Square, Milton Park, Abingdon, Oxon OX14 4RN
605 Third Avenue, New York, NY 10158

Routledge is an imprint of the Taylor & Francis Group, an informa business

First issued in hardback 2019

British Library Cataloguing in Publication Data
Biddle, Dan
    Adverse impact and test validation: a practitioner's guide
    to valid and defensible employment testing
    1. Employment tests
    I. Title
    658.3'1125

Library of Congress Cataloging-in-Publication Data
Biddle, Dan.
    Adverse impact and test validation: a practitioner's guide to valid and defensible
employment testing/ by Dan Biddle.
        p. cm.
    Includes bibliographical references and index.
    ISBN 978-0-566-08778-3
    1. Employment tests. I. Title.
    HF5549.5.E5B53 2005
    658.3'1125--dc22

                                                                                    2004027183

ISBN: 978-0-566-08778-3 (hbk)
ISBN: 978-1-03-283869-4 (pbk)
ISBN: 978-1-315-26329-8 (ebk)

DOI: 10.4324/9781315263298

Contents

List of Figures	*vii*
List of Tables	*ix*
Definition of Terms	*xi*
About the Authors	*xv*
Foreword – Richard E. Biddle	*xvii*
Dedications	*xx*
Introduction – James E. Kuthy	*xxi*

Chapter 1: Adverse Impact — **1**
Overview — 1
Types of adverse impact analyses — 5
The concept of statistical significance — 6
Selection rate comparison for a single event — 13
Selection rate comparisons for multiple events — 17
Availability comparison for a single event — 20
Availability comparisons for multiple events — 24

Chapter 2: Selection Procedure Development and Validation — **27**
Validation defined — 27
Overview of the mechanics of content and criterion-related validity — 27
Benefits of the validation process — 28
Professional standards for validation — 29
Uniform Guidelines requirements for validation — 31
Blending the professional and government validation standards
  into practice — 31
Steps for completing a content validation study — 33
Eight steps for completing a job analysis — 34
Developing a selection plan — 44
Content validation requirements for "work sample" and "KSAPC"
  types of selection procedures — 47
Criterion-related validity — 50

Chapter 3: Developing, Validating, and Analyzing Written Tests — **57**
Step 1: Determine the KSAPCs to be measured by the test — 58
Step 2: Develop a test plan for measuring the selected KSAPCs — 58

Step 3: Develop the test content 63
Step 4: Validate the test 64
Step 5: Score and analyze the test 66

Chapter 4: Developing, Validating, and Analyzing Structured Interviews 81
Methods for improving the interview process 81
Types of questions to include in structured interviews 83
Steps for developing situational questions 86
Administering and scoring an interview 90

Chapter 5: Developing, Validating, and Analyzing Training, Education, and Experience Requirements 93
Uniform Guidelines criteria regarding TEE requirements 95
Professional standards regarding TEE requirements 96
Using TEE requirements in open selection/promotional processes 97
Using TEE requirements in closed selection/promotional processes 100

Chapter 6: Using Selection Procedures: Cutoff Scores, Banding, Ranking, and Weighting 105
Developing valid cutoff scores 105
Banding 111
Ranking 112
Weighting selection procedures into combined scores 115

Chapter 7: Using Multiple Regression Analysis to Examine Compensation Practices by Jim Higgins, Ed.D 121
How does Multiple Regression (MR) Analysis work? 122
Steps for conducting Multiple Regression (MR) Analysis 124

Chapter 8: Internet Applicant Regulations: Recordkeeping, Adverse Impact, and Basic Qualifications by Patrick Nooren, Ph.D 149
Internet Applicant Regulations 150

Appendix: Seven Steps for Developing a Content Valid Job Knowledge Written Test by Stacy L. Pilchard 165

References 177
List of Cases 181
Index 185

List of Figures

2.1	Job Expert sample size guidelines	35
3.1	SEM by score level	76
5.1	Sample TEE survey	99
5.2	TEE rating guidelines	100
7.1	Setting up an Excel File for Use in Multiple Regression	140
7.2	Excel Data Analysis Dialogue Box	141
7.3	Excel Regression Window	141
7.4	Excel Input Y Range Window	142
7.5	Excel Input Range Window	142
7.6	Interpreting Multiple Regression Analysis Output	143

Supplementary Resources Disclaimer

Additional resources were previously made available for this title on CD. However, as CD have become a less accessible format, all resources have been moved to a more convenient online download option.

You can find these resources available here: https://www.routledge.com/9780566087783

Please note: Where this title mentions the associated disc, please use the downloadable resources instead.

List of Tables

1.1	2 X 2 contingency table	15
1.2	Simpson's Paradox example	17
2.1	Selection plan example	46
2.2	Content validity requirements for work sample and KSAPC tests	48
2.3	Guidelines for interpreting correlations	54
3.1	Bloom's Taxonomy for item writing	62
3.2	Guidelines for interpreting test reliability	74
7.1	SPSS Model Summary Report	133
7.2	SPSS ANOVA Report	134
7.3	SPSS Coefficients Report	135
7.4	SPSS Collinearity Diagnostics Report	137
8.1	Basic Qualification (BQ) Development Survey	157
A.1	Firefighter Certification Test Development Survey	173
A.2	Process-by-Content Matrix: Police Sergeant	174

Definition of Terms

ADA – Americans with Disabilities Act. An Act passed by the US Congress in 1990 designed to establish a clear and comprehensive prohibition of discrimination on the basis of disability.

Adverse impact – A substantially different rate of selection in hiring, promotion, or other employment decision which works to the disadvantage of members of a race, sex, or ethnic group (see the Definitions section of the *Uniform Guidelines*). Adverse impact is sometimes referred to as "disparate impact".

DCR – Decision Consistency Reliability. A type of test reliability that estimates how consistently the test classifies "masters" and "non-masters" or those who pass the test versus those who fail.

DIF – Differential Item Functioning. A statistical analysis that identifies test items where a focal group (usually a minority group or women) scores lower than the majority group (usually whites or men), after matching the two groups on overall test score. DIF items are therefore potentially biased or unfair.

EEO – Equal Employment Opportunity. The collective set of US laws that prohibit discrimination in hiring, promotion, termination, compensation, and other terms and conditions of employment because of race, color, sex, national origin, or religion.

EEOC – Equal Employment Opportunity Commission, a US governmental organization established in 1964 charged with the mission of eliminating illegal discrimination from the workplace.

GOJA – Guidelines Oriented Job Analysis. The job analysis strategy proposed herein for developing thorough and defensible job analyses.

JAS – Job Analysis Survey. A survey used for gathering ratings on job analysis data from job experts in the field.

Job Expert – An incumbent or supervisor in a target position who provides input (e.g., through interviews, workshops, or surveys), on-the-job analysis or test development process for their position.

KSAPCs – Knowledges, Skills, Abilities, and Personal Characteristics. Job knowledges refer to bodies of information applied directly to the performance of a work function; skills refer to an observable competence to perform a learned psychomotor act (e.g., keyboarding is a skill because it can be observed and requires a learned process to perform); abilities refer to a present competence to perform an observable behavior or a behavior which results in an observable product (see the Definitions section of the *Uniform Guidelines*). Personal characteristics typically refer to traits or characteristics that may be more abstract in nature, but include "operational definitions" that specifically tie them into observable aspects of the job. For example, dependability is a personal characteristic (not a knowledge, skill, or ability), but can be included in a job analysis or content validation process if it is defined in terms of observable aspects of job behavior. For example: "Dependability sufficient to show up for work on time, complete tasks in a timely manner, notify supervisory staff if delays are expected, and regularly complete critical work functions."

OFCCP – Office of Federal Contract Compliance Programs. This is the US government agency responsible for the monitoring of EEO-related issues for US employers that contract with the Federal Government.

PCT – Physical capacities test.

SED – Standard Error of Difference. A statistical unit (calculated by multiplying the SEM by the square root of 2, or 1.41421) that can be used for grouping applicants into "substantially equally qualified" score bands by determining scores in a test distribution that represent meaningfully different ability levels. For example, assume a test with an SED of 4. If the highest scoring applicant obtained a score of 99, subtracting 1 SED from this score (99 – 4) arrives at a score of 95, which can be considered the next meaningful stopping place in the distribution. That is, the applicant who scored 99 and the applicant who scored 94 have different ability levels, but the applicant who scored 99 and the applicant who scored 96 do not. Using 1 SED provides 68% confidence that the "true ability levels" of the applicants in the band do not significantly differ from the true ability level of the top score in the band. Using 2 SEDs provides about 95% confidence.

SEM – Standard Error of Measurement. A statistic that represents the likely range of a test taker's "true score" (or speculated "real ability level") from any given score. For example, if the test's SEM is 3 and an applicant obtained a raw score of 60, their true score (with 68% likelihood) is between 57 and 63, between 54 and 66 (with 95% likelihood), and between 51 and 69 (with 99% likelihood). Because test takers have "good days" and "bad days" when taking tests, this statistic is useful for adjusting the test cutoff to account for such differences that may be unrelated to a test taker's actual ability level. Both *traditional* (based on the overall test reliability and standard deviation) and *conditional* (based on the reliability and variance at certain score levels) SEMs are discussed in this text.

Selection procedure – Any measure, combination of measures, or procedure used as a basis for any employment decision. Selection procedures include the full range of assessment techniques from traditional paper and pencil tests, performance tests, training programs, or probationary periods and physical, educational, and work experience requirements through informal or casual interviews and unscored application forms (see the Definitions section of the *Uniform Guidelines*).

TEE – Training, Experience, and Education.

WHE – Work History Evaluation. A method of using work history data in a scored promotional process for closed promotional process (one that is only open to internal employees).

About the Authors

Dan A. Biddle, Ph.D. is the CEO of Biddle Consulting Group, Inc., (BCG) a consulting firm specializing in the areas of test development/validation, Equal Employment Opportunity compliance, and Human Resource software development. Dan is also CEO of sister companies, Firefighter Selection, Inc. and Public Safety Testing Solutions, Inc. – firms dedicated to providing fair and defensible testing solutions to the protective services industry. BCG has consulted with numerous Fortune 500 companies and hundreds of public sector agencies in matters pertaining to these areas, and maintains over 1000 software or service clients worldwide. BCG also provides expert witness/consulting services in state and federal litigation matters, or in response to government audits.

Dan obtained his undergraduate degree in Organizational Behavior from the University of San Francisco and masters and doctorate degrees in Organizational Psychology from Alliant University located in California. He resides in Folsom California with his wife and four children.

Jim Higgins, Ed.D. Jim has worked in the field of human resources and applied human services research for over 16 years. Currently a Senior Consultant at Biddle Consulting Group, he regularly conducts multiple regression analyses to help employers evaluate their compensation practices. He has taught applied behavioral statistics at the college level, where he wrote a textbook geared toward making applied statistical analysis easy to understand for the non-mathematical professional.

James E. Kuthy, M.A. Jim holds a Masters Degree in Industrial and Organizational Psychology and is a doctoral candidate in the same field. He is the author of CritiCall® Dispatcher/Call-Taker Pre-Employment Testing Software, which is used by over 450 public-safety agencies including the U.S. Department of Homeland Security. He has also assisted in the development of validated selection and promotion processes nationwide.

Stacy L. Pilchard is the Director and Principal Consultant of Fire & Police Selection, Inc. (FPSI) a consulting firm specializing in the development and validation of testing instruments used in the protective services industry.

Stacy has 10 years experience in the field and has completed her Masters level coursework in Industrial/Organizational Psychology. She is currently completing her thesis.

Patrick Nooren, Ph.D. is the Executive Vice President of Biddle Consulting Group, Inc. and retains over 12 years experience in the EEO/HR field and has invested thousands of hours in EEO-related cases and projects. His primary focus at BCG is oversight of the EEO/AA division and development of related software products.

Contact information for Biddle Consulting Group, Inc. is provided below:

Biddle Consulting Group
193 Blue Ravine, Suite 270
Folsom, CA 95630
USA
800-999-0438

www.biddle.com

 Biddle Consulting Group, Inc.

Foreword

Reviewing this book for me was a pleasant surprise. It showed me how far the field has grown since I started working in it during the mid-1960s, shortly after the 1964 Civil Rights Act said it was illegal to discriminate with a test. It took a few more years after that for the Supreme Court to tell us what a test was (i.e., any practice, procedure or test) and what discrimination means (i.e., use of a test that adversely impacts a protected group and is not valid or job related). The Equal Employment Opportunity Commission (EEOC) and the Office of Federal Contract Compliance (OFCC) published some guidelines in the late 1960s, attempting to tell us how to validate a test. But there were some conflicts between the two sets of guidelines and adverse impact was not defined. It was not until 1972, that the California Technical Advisory Committee on Testing attempted to resolve differences between the two guidelines in terms of validation requirements for California employers and put an operational definition on the term adverse impact. The courts later refined this early definition of adverse impact as well as the legal requirements for validity.

The first thing that impressed me about this book was the table of contents. The author has not dodged sensitive areas. This is indeed a handbook. While I am sure there probably will be future editions with revisions, especially as court cases shape various topics, this book right now offers a great overview as well as practical steps in doing the work of test validation. The first chapter can be used to identify problems with adverse impact. Chapters 2–5 can be used to determine whether the practice, procedure or test causing the adverse impact is valid. If it is not valid, developers can use the techniques described to make it valid. Chapter 6 provides guidance on using selection procedures. With the proper use of a practice, procedure, or test causing adverse impact, the adverse impact may be eliminated or substantially reduced while not compromising validation. Chapter 7 provides recommendations for conducting a multiple regression analysis to analyze employer's pay practices for possible inequities between various groups. Chapter 8 includes direction for adhering to US Department of Labor (OFCCP) standards for tracking internet applicants, and for analyzing such tracking systems for adverse impact. It also includes guideance for setting up basic qualifications under these standards.

Adverse impact and test validation – why should we be concerned about either? Who should be concerned about these topics? Is adverse impact or test validation a problem? If so, to whom? If either is a problem, what does this book do to help?

Adverse impact is a term of art. Test validation is a term of art. Both terms mean something different than you will find in Webster's dictionary. Adverse impact occurs when an employer uses a practice, procedure, or test in a selection process which disproportionately excludes members of a group protected by a law. The amount of the difference between the two groups is measured with statistical significance formulae and practical significance procedures that have been approved in court cases. The history of adverse impact, the statistical formulae, and practical significance procedures can be found in this book.

As you know by now, the word test in test validation does not mean just a written test. The word test means practice, procedure, or test. The definition expansion of the word test to mean practice, procedure, or test was done for us by the United States Supreme Court in a unanimous decision the book will tell you about. Validation, another term of art, is a process of demonstrating that the practice, procedure, or test at issue is job-related and consistent with business necessity. The book gives step-by-step procedures on how to go about the validation process.

Practices, procedures, and tests are used in decisions involving hiring, firing, promotion, demotion, layoff, transfer, training, raises, bonuses, and other employment decisions. The cumulative effect of these decisions can cause adverse impact regardless of whether or not we intend any discrimination. For example, an interview may exclude more Hispanics than whites. A physical ability test may exclude more women than men. A severance process may have the result of retaining more of one group than another. When this happens to the point that adverse impact occurs, then the president of the company in which this is occurring, the chief executive officer of the organization, the head of human resources, and others who have any responsibility for the effect of the selection process need to be concerned for several reasons. Putting the entire moral question aside, these people need to be concerned because the adverse impact could cost the employer hundreds of thousands of dollars in litigation costs, huge amounts of time defending the practice, procedure, or test causing the adverse impact, and the potential is real for back pay, front pay, and injunctions, along with someone being appointed by the court to monitor your selection practices, procedures, and tests for a while.

I served as a monitor in a Federal court case for 11 years, where each step the employer took had to be reviewed and approved. Many times, court battles ensued over technical issues. The employer did not have the freedom to use any practice, procedure, or test that they wanted to use. All of these problems were the result of a test that adversely impacted a group protected by the Civil Rights Act, and the test was not properly validated.

During my career, I testified as an expert in numerous testing and selection cases in the Equal Employment Opportunity field, usually in a Federal court. Often my testimony was given before a jury, as well as a judge. A jury is supposed to be composed of one's peers. However, it was an unusual event to find anyone on the jury who had taken any testing, measurement, or statistical courses. Yet this jury was to decide such issues raised by plaintiff and defense experts. I can recall only one Federal judge who had any prior statistical training. Therefore, the decision-makers (judges and juries) are making decisions based upon testimony from experts and papers submitted. Quite often, plaintiffs or defendants would have two categories of experts: one to testify about adverse impact (sometimes a statistician, an economist, a psychomotrist, or someone trained in the statistical applications required for adverse impact analyses) and the other to testify about validation (sometimes an industrial psychologist, behavioral scientist, or someone trained in the validation process). The author of this book has been qualified in various courts as an expert in both adverse impact and validation and has worked for plaintiffs and defendants during his career, so he possesses an important balance in these sensitive areas.

The thousands of court cases in the employment discrimination field, the millions of dollars spent on litigation, the time spent in preparing these cases, the emotional costs of winning and losing all have yielded results that can be found in this book. You will find in this book how to do the things necessary to see if there is adverse impact and how to validate.

Richard E. Biddle

Dedications

To my supportive wife, Jenny, and our four children, Makaela, Alyssa, Matthew, and Amanda, who invested greatly in this work. They mean the world to me.

To my father, Richard E. Biddle, who gave me opportunities galore and a huge head start in life.

To my co-workers at Biddle Consulting Group: Patrick Nooren, Leigh Bashor, Jim Kuthy, and Stacy Bell who contributed greatly to the completion of this project, and are a joy to work with.

To my friends and colleagues at Seattle City Lights who taught me the importance of converting theory into what actually works and who contributed greatly to the refinement of the tools discussed herein.

To my mentors, Dr Frances Campbell-Lavoie, who strengthened me; Dr Shelly Zedeck, who set a professional standard; and to Mr R. Lawrence Ashe Jr, who taught me that what doesn't kill me can only make me stronger.

Most of all, I want to acknowledge and thank my Savior and Lord, Jesus Christ, for the many miracles He has performed in my life. This book is truly the result of His grace.

This is the Lord's doing; it is marvelous in our eyes.

Psalm 118:23

D.A.B.
2005

Introduction

James E. Kuthy

One of the most difficult challenges a human resource professional faces is effectively applying legal and academic theory to the "real world." The motivation in writing this book was to provide human resource professionals with something more than a textbook that explains only the concepts, theories, and ideas behind adverse impact and test validation. Regarding adverse impact, the aim of this book is to describe the actual tools and procedures for calculating adverse impact that have the backing of the U.S. courts. The compensation analysis and Internet applicant content in this book is provided for similar reasons. The goal regarding test validation is to bridge the gap between theory and practice, and provide a guidebook for actually taking steps to validate some of the most common selection procedures: written tests, interviews, and Training, Experience, and Education (TEE) requirements.

Since 1974, our firm has worked with hundreds of clients and has been involved in over 200 Equal Employment Opportunity (EEO)-related cases that involved adverse impact and/or test validation matters. The challenge we encounter most frequently with clients and cases is that clients often know what to do, but not necessarily how to do it. Because of this, litigants and government agencies often find that employers are "sitting ducks" in the area of EEO liability, with exposure on all sides.

Adverse impact analyses and test validation, in the way they are presented in this text, promote social justice and equity while maintaining value. Employers who are unknowingly using invalid tests that have adverse impact are reducing minority and/or female representation in their workforce, unfairly screening out qualified workers and, worst of all, just plain discriminating.

Using the adverse impact analyses described in this book will allow employers to be informed about which of their selection procedures might have an adverse impact. The compensation analysis techniques described in this book will assist employers in the process of identifying pay practices that have resulted in pay inequities between various groups. Following the validation steps described herein will enable the employer to decide whether to retain the selection procedure because it is valid, change it, or stop using it altogether. The payoff can be great. In many instances, replacing invalid selection procedures with ones that are fair and valid have led to increased productivity and greater employee satisfaction. They have also decreased time to train newly-hired workers, and reduced turnover and absenteeism. Using formally-validated selection procedures also drastically reduces the potential for EEO-related litigation. It just makes good business sense to conduct a job analysis and validation study of all of the selection procedures used by an employer.

Finally, a brief word about terminology. A great deal of confusion seems to exist in the human resource community over when and how "competencies" can be measured during an employment selection process. Unfortunately, there appears to be no universally-accepted definition for the word "competency" in either the field of Industrial and Organizational Psychology or in the courts. With that in mind, the courts would be unlikely to accept the validity of selection procedures based on generic and overly-broad competencies, unless those competencies were operationally defined in accordance with Section 14C4 of the federal Uniform Guidelines on Employee Selection Procedures (Uniform Guidelines) or have been empirically demonstrated to be job-related using other types of validity evidence.

Interestingly, an operationally-defined competency that is used during a content validation study must be, according to the Uniform Guidelines, a knowledge, skill, or ability that is operationally defined in terms of how it is actually used in the job. In addition, the Uniform Guidelines require that criteria examined in a criterion-related validity study should represent important or critical work behaviors, or work outcomes. Renaming knowledge, skills, abilities, work behaviors, or outcomes using the less-precise term of "competency" could possibly dilute the quality of a validation study. For that reason, this book does not use the term "competency," but instead uses the terminology that the courts are familiar with, and which the courts are more likely to accept.

Since the federal Uniform Guidelines were originally published in 1978, the proposition has been put forth that instead of there being different types of validity (i.e., content, criterion, and construct), there are only different kinds of evidence for determining validity. This updated concept has been incorporated into much of the literature, including the Standards (1999), which refer to content-related evidence, criterion-related evidence, and construct-related evidence of validity. The authors of this book recognize and support the proposition that validity is a unitary concept. However, since the Uniform Guidelines play such an important role in employment testing as it is performed in the "real world," the more traditional content validity, criterion validity, and construct validity terminology is used throughout this book as shorthand for content-related evidence, criterion-related evidence, and construct-related evidence of validity.

EVALUATION CD

The CD included in the back cover of this book includes tools (that can be used on a trial evaluation basis) that will complete several of the functions described in this book. The tools included are described below.

ADVERSE IMPACT TOOLKIT®

This program can be used to evaluate an employer's practices, procedures, and tests for adverse impact. The program consists of a Microsoft® Excel® workbook that includes numerous features that use embedded programming and macros to complete various adverse impact calculations that have been approved in court, including:

- selection rate comparison for a single event (including the 80% Test, Statistical Significance Tests, and Practical Significance Tests);

- selection rate analysis for multiple events (including Pattern Consistency Tests and Statistical Significance Tests);

- availability comparison for a single event (including Descriptive Statistics and Statistical Significance Tests); and

- availability comparisons for multiple events (including Pattern Consistency Tests and Statistical Significance Tests). Microsoft Excel was chosen as a development platform for this program to allow the user to readily import and export data and relevant analysis results.

TEST VALIDATION & ANALYSIS PROGRAM® (TVAP®)

TVAP can be used to validate and analyze written tests. Because this program uses a content validity approach for validation (see Section 14C and 15C of the Uniform Guidelines), it is most appropriate for validating tests designed to measure Knowledges, Skills, Abilities, and Personal Characteristics (KSAPCs) that can be validated using this method. Once a test is administered, TVAP can be used to analyze responses to dichotomously scored test items, such as true/false or multiple-choice questions, in which a single response to a test item is either correct or incorrect.

TVAP was developed by integrating concepts and requirements from professional standards, the Uniform Guidelines, and relevant court cases into a system that is relatively automated. While efforts were made to automate these processes as much as possible, professional judgment should be used when operating this program and evaluating its results.

TVAP includes two separate workbooks: the Test Validation Workbook and the Test Analysis Workbook. Used in sequence, the workbooks provide a complete set of tools to validate written tests (entry level or promotional), analyze item-level and test level results (after administration), and set job-related and defensible cutoffs using court-approved methods.

The Test Validation Workbook includes the tools for validating a test before it is administered to applicants. This Workbook includes a survey that is printed and given to a panel of Job Experts. The Job Experts use the survey to rate each question on the draft written test. These ratings are then entered into the Test Validation Workbook and analyzed using the program to evaluate which items to include on the final test (and which items to discard, or save for re-evaluation by Job Experts after revision). After the surviving items are identified using this Workbook, part of the Job Expert ratings (the item difficulty – or "Angoff" ratings) are exported to the Test Analysis Workbook for the remaining steps in the process. These difficulty ratings are later used by the Test Analysis Workbook to automatically determine defensible job-related cutoff scores for the test.

The Test Analysis Workbook is used to analyze the test results (at both an item and overall test level), modify and improve the test based on these results, and then set job-related cutoffs using methods that have been previously endorsed by the courts. There are seven steps included in this workbook, all of which should be completed the first time a new test is administered and only some of which are used to analyze test data for subsequent administrations.

The TVAP User Manual includes three attachments that can be used by practitioners in the test development and validation process:

- Attachment A: Instructions for Completing the Test Item Survey (a survey included in TVAP that can be used for validating written tests).

- Attachment B: An explanation of the Conditional Standard Error of Measurement (SEM), statistic useful for determining valid cutoff scores.

- Attachment C: Test Item Writing Guidelines that provide information for working with Job Experts and Human Resources staff to write effective written test items.

GUIDELINES ORIENTED JOB ANALYSIS® (GOJA®) MANUAL

This manual enables practitioners to develop job analyses using the court-approved GOJA Process. The GOJA Process can be used for developing job analyses that can specifically be used to develop validated selection procedures and determine job duties that should be classified as "essential functions" under the 1990 Americans with Disabilities Act (ADA).

Because the GOJA Process results in the identification of critical job duties, KSAPCs, and physical requirements, it lays the necessary foundation for a content validity study, and may also be used for gathering other forms of validity evidence (including criterion-related validity, construct validity, and other forms of validity). The ADA requires providing "qualified individuals with disabilities" with "reasonable accommodations" to perform the essential functions (or "job duties") of a given position. The GOJA Process addresses the ADA requirements because it investigates the frequency and importance of duties, the percentage of time that current job holders spend completing duties, whether a duty constitutes a fundamental part of the job, and the extent to which duties can readily be assigned to other employees, the GOJA Process is designed to distinguish between the essential and non-essential duties of a position (these are some of the primary ways that duties can be deemed essential).

In addition to using the GOJA Process for developing fair and validated selection processes and determining the essential functions of a position, it can help in the creation of Job Descriptions, Selections Plans, Supplemental Application Forms, and Performance Appraisal Forms.

However, while the GOJA manual does provide a step-by-step "cookbook method" for performing a job analysis, it is not written in stone. Those who use the GOJA manual for conducting job analyses would be well served to also employ their training and professional judgment to determine which of the specified procedures are required and how those procedures are to be carried out, based on the needs of the employer and the job being analyzed.

CONTENT VALIDITY CHECKLISTS

A selection device is never valid in and of itself. Instead, it is the inferences regarding the specific uses of a selection device that are either valid or not. One way to insure that the inferences being made are valid is to make certain that the Uniform Guidelines are being addressed when a test is being created and validated.

To help insure that the Uniform Guidelines are being addressed during key stages of a "typical" selection process, the evaluation CD contains easy-to-follow Content Validity Checklists for Written Tests, Interviews, and Training, Experience, and Education (TEE) requirements. Validating these types of selection procedures can be a time-consuming and confusing process, especially for those who do not specialize in this area of human resources. These three checklists distill the knowledge obtained from over 30-years of experience in the field to guide users when addressing the federal Uniform Guidelines sections relating to the content validation of selection procedures.

CHAPTER 1

Adverse Impact

OVERVIEW

Not long after the passage of the 1964 US Civil Rights Act (commonly known as Title VII), the legislative and judicial fields began hammering out the concept of *adverse impact*. Now, 40 years later, after thousands of cases and arbitrations and well over one billion dollars[1] spent by employers, government enforcement agencies, special interest plaintiff groups, and law firms, the concept has been highly refined. It has also expanded to apply to settings other than that for which it was first designed (e.g., some US circuit courts have recently approved of using adverse impact calculations for age discrimination cases).

While the courts still struggle for a definitive explanation of what constitutes a "finding of adverse impact," the term started out and has ended up today with much the same meaning: a *substantially different rate of selection* in hiring, promotion or other employment decision which works to the disadvantage of members of a race, sex or ethnic group (Uniform Guidelines Questions & Answers #10).[2] The three most common methods for determining adverse impact are the 80% Test, statistical significance tests, and practical significance tests. Each will be discussed in this chapter.

WHY DOES ADVERSE IMPACT EXIST?

It is not uncommon for public sector employers to have one or more entry-level positions with adverse impact in the testing process. Written tests typically have the highest degree of adverse impact, with the high level of impact against blacks, then Hispanics, and sometimes Asians (Sackett, 2001; Neisser, 1996). Physical ability tests typically have adverse impact against women, especially when they measure upper body strength. Robert Guion (1998, p. 445) cites several reasons why adverse impact can occur:

1.   chance;

2.   measurement problems inherent to the test (e.g., poor reliability);

3.   the nature of test use (e.g., ranking versus pass/fail);

4.   differences in distribution sizes (e.g., a selection process with 100 men and only 10 women);

5.   reliable subgroup differences in general approaches to test taking; and

6.   true population differences in distributions of the trait being measured.

Test bias is another possible reason why adverse impact can occur, but this can only be a valid reason if one or more of the first five reasons above exist and the sixth is rejected. Genuine discriminatory intent and actions can be yet another reason that adverse impact can occur in a selection process.

Adverse impact has become a loaded term, fraught with suggestions of ill intent on the part of the employer. It should, however, be noted that adverse impact simply describes differences between groups on a testing process. It is not a legal term that implies guilt or a psychometric term that implies unfairness or test bias. Many employers that test for relevant job skills will generate adverse impact in a testing process in one way or another, and most studies show that adverse impact is not normally due to forms of bias inherent to the tests (Sackett, 2001; Neisser, 1996).

HISTORY AND DEVELOPMENT

The US government treatise that first mentioned the concept of adverse impact was the Equal Employment Opportunity Commission (EEOC) Guidelines on Employment Testing Procedures (issued on August 24, 1966). This document, however, offered no indication on how to determine (by calculation or otherwise) if adverse impact existed in an employer's selection practices. The government had defined some of the "what" but not the "how" of adverse impact. This left the higher circuit or supreme courts with the burden of using key legal cases to make judicial findings that provided insight into what is really meant by adverse impact.

The first major case where this took place was the infamous Griggs v. Duke Power Company (1971). Duke Power was using a high-school diploma and an off-the-shelf intelligence test as screening devices, both of which had adverse impact against blacks. Since the jobs being tested did not appear to really require a high school diploma to be performed successfully, the court held that the employer had to show a "business necessity" for these two requirements, or Duke Power would be in violation of Title VII. Responding to the adverse impact that these two requirements had on blacks, the court only stated a few words: "… they operated to disqualify blacks at a *substantially higher rate* than white applicants." Once again, the Equal Employment Opportunity (EEO) field had only a "what" but not a "how" regarding adverse impact.

Exactly what is a "substantially higher rate?" Wanting to answer this question (and many others pertaining to personnel testing) and build a set of criteria that employers could use for determining exactly *how* "adverse" a testing process needed to be to represent "adverse impact," an advisory committee called the Technical Advisory Committee on Testing (TACT)[3] was assembled by the State of California Fair Employment Practice Commission (FEPC) in 1971. TACT was charged with compiling the State of California Guidelines on Employee Selection Procedures (which were published in final form in October, 1972). Some content from these California Guidelines were designed to "supersede and enlarge upon" (Section 3 preamble) the earlier set of Guidelines on Employment Testing Procedures, issued by the US EEOC on August 24, 1966. Some content from these California Guidelines was later incorporated into the Federal Uniform Guidelines on Employee Selection Procedures (1978), a document still in force at the time of writing.

TACT included 32 specialists from various labor, employment, and technical fields, who deliberated the specific techniques and steps that would be taken to evaluate adverse impact. It was out of these deliberations that the (now infamous) 80% Test was born (in short, the 80% Test is calculated by dividing the focal group's (the focal group is typically minorities or women) passing rate on a selection procedure by the reference group's (typically whites or men) passing rate, and any value less than 80% is said to violate a "threshold test" for evaluating adverse impact). One of the committee members[4] describes its origin this way:

> *During the negotiations of the FEPC Guidelines (which went on for months), one session had a significant debate on an appropriate statistical tool for determining adverse impact. We wanted to put an operational definition to some words defining what constituted adverse impact. There were about 20 of the committee members in the room. The members agreed that a statistical test was appropriate, but not enough. They also agreed that those who would implement these guidelines (the FEPC consultants) would never have the appropriate training to implement statistical tests (prior to the common use of computers, calculating probability statistics was a difficult task only completed by the technically savvy). Therefore, we needed an administrative guideline as well as a technical one for cases. I recall a heated debate that went on for way too long (as usual) with two camps: a 70% camp and a 90% camp. The 80% Test was born out of two compromises: (1) a desire expressed by those writing and having input into the Guidelines to include a statistical test as the primary step but knowing from an administrative point of view a statistical test was not possible for the FEPC consultants who had to work the enforcement of the Guidelines, and (2) a way to split the middle between two camps, the 70% camp and the 90% camp. A way was found to use both. In the way the 80% Test was defined by TACT, if there was no violation of the 80% Test, then there would be no reason to apply statistical significance tests. This hopefully would eliminate many calculations and many situations where TACT would not be necessary and the decision could be made in the field. So from the practical point of view, the 80% Test became a first step. If there was no 80% Test violation, there was no need to go further and use a statistical test. If there was a violation of the 80% Test, statistical significance was needed and the 80% Test then became a practical significance test for adverse impact.*

These deliberations resulted in the final text used in the 1972 California Guidelines, which constituted an industry-first, concrete definition to these terms by defining "adverse effect":

> *Adverse effect refers to a total employment process which results in a significantly higher percentage of a protected group in the candidate population being rejected for employment, placement, or promotion. The difference between the rejection rates for a protected group and the remaining group must be statistically significant at the .05 level. In addition, if the acceptance rate of the protected group is greater than or equal to 80% of the acceptance rate of the remaining group, then adverse effect is said to be not present by definition (Section 7.1).*

Prior to the publication of the California Guidelines, there were no government-endorsed *mathematical* guidelines for proving adverse impact. The EEOC Guidelines issued on August 1, 1970 (replacing the earlier August 24, 1966 version), had discrimination broadly defined in section 1607.3 without providing mathematical guidance. The Office of Federal Contract Compliance (OFCC) Guidelines (issued October 2, 1971) had discrimination defined in section 60-3.3, also without specific guidance. The EEOC used the term "adversely affects" while the OFCC used the term "adversely affected." Neither of these two documents defined just exactly how adverse impact was to be actually calculated.

The TACT committee agreed that statistical significance testing for "adverse effect" should be paramount, as a matter of policy, even if the FEPC consultants were not likely to implement that part. So the FEPC Guidelines present the concept of statistical significance first ("The difference between the rejection rates for a protected group and the remaining group must be statistically significant at the .05 level."). They wrote the 80% Test as a *practical significance* test ("In addition, if the acceptance rate of the protected group is greater than or equal to 80% of the acceptance rate of the remaining group, then adverse effect is said to be not present by definition.").

After the 1972 FEPC Guidelines were published, the Equal Employment Opportunity Coordinating Council (EEOCC) issued some drafts in August 23, 1973, and June 24, 1974. The Ad Hoc Industry Group found them unworkable as reported in the Daily Labor Report on October 24, 1974. The next attempt at developing an acceptable set of Guidelines was the Federal Executive Agency (FEA) Guidelines published on November 19, 1976. These FEA guidelines applied the 80% Test in section 60-3.4(b) in the same way the current 1978 Uniform Guidelines apply the 80% Test in Section 4D. The 1978 Uniform Guidelines may have been the first to specifically refer to the 80% Test as a "rule of thumb" (Section II, paragraph 2 on page 33291, Federal Register, Vol. 43, No. 166).

The FEPC used the 80% Test as a *practical significance* test in a technical sense, but only as a rule of thumb in a practical sense. The 80% Test as a rule of thumb was given greater power by the FEA and the 1978 Federal Uniform Guidelines because a literal reading could interpret adverse impact under some circumstances resulting in an 80% rule of thumb violation, but with no statistical significance.

TYPES OF ADVERSE IMPACT ANALYSES

Generally speaking, there are two primary types of adverse impact analyses: Selection Rate Comparisons and Availability Comparisons. Each is briefly described in this chapter.

A Selection Rate Comparison evaluates the selection rates *between two groups* on a selection procedure. It can also be used to compare the selection rates of two groups in layoffs, promotions, or placements. This type of analysis always involves two groups: a focal group (typically women or minorities) and a reference group (typically men or whites). Selection Rate Comparisons are most typically used in litigation settings, as they relate specifically to the type of adverse impact analysis called for in the Uniform Guidelines. There are four variables that are entered into an adverse impact analysis of this type: (1) the number of focal group members who were selected, (2) the number who were not selected, and (3) the number of reference group members who were selected and (4) the number who were not selected.

An Availability Comparison evaluates one group's representation in a position (e.g., 13% of the incumbents in the Manager II position are Hispanic) to their availability for that position (e.g., 15% of the qualified applicants available for the Manager II position are Hispanic). It is useful for showing the extent to which one group may be *underutilized* (e.g., 15% Hispanics available compared to 13% currently in the position shows a 2% underutilization). There are three variables that are entered into an adverse impact analysis of this type: (1) the total number of incumbents in a position, (2) the number of focal group members in the position, and (3) the percentage of qualified focal group members who are available for the position.

There are major differences between these two types of analyses regarding the extent to which they constitute legitimate finding of adverse impact that could potentially bring an employer to court. Generally speaking, the Selection Rate Comparison is the only type that can be used alone to demonstrate adverse impact in the classical sense; whereas the Availability Comparison only shows a prima facie reason to investigate further into an employer's practices to see why a "gap" may exist.

There are *descriptive statistics* and *statistical significance* tests that can be applied to both types of adverse impact analyses. Descriptive statistics merely show the mathematical difference relevant to the comparison being made. For Selection Rate Comparisons, this is the difference in selection rates between two groups (e.g., focal group members had a 70% selection rate; reference group members had a selection rate of 80%, which constitutes a 10% difference between the two groups). For Availability Comparisons, the extent of underutilization is the relevant descriptive statistic (e.g., 2% underutilized). Statistical significance tests are the most relevant for adverse impact analyses because they show whether the descriptive statistic is statistically meaningful and whether they can be regarded as a "beyond chance" occurrence.

For each of these types of statistical tests, adverse impact can be analyzed for a single event (e.g., one selection test given during a single year) or multiple events (e.g., one selection test administered over several years and aggregated into a combined analysis). The techniques for conducting each type of analysis will be discussed later in this chapter.

THE CONCEPT OF STATISTICAL SIGNIFICANCE

Karl Pearson (one of the founders of modern statistical theory) formed the foundation of statistical significance testing as early as 1901, and now (a century later) researchers are still applying the concept as the acid test for deciding whether the results of their studies are "onto something meaningful." While the concept of statistical significance can be applied to literally hundreds of different types of statistical analyses, the meaning is essentially the same: If the result of a statistical test (i.e., the final product of its calculation) is "statistically significant," it is unlikely to have occurred by chance. Said another way, a "statistically significant finding" is one that raises the eyebrows of the researcher and triggers the thought, "I think I've found something here, and it is not likely due to chance." Obtaining a finding of statistical significance in a research study signifies a point at which the researcher is capable of stating that a legitimate trend, and not a chance relationship, actually exists (with a reasonable level of certainty).

Statistical significance tests result in a p-value (for probability). P-values range from 0 to +1. A p-value of 0.01 means that the odds of the event occurring by chance is only 1%. A p-value of 1.0 means that the there is essentially a 100% certainty that the event is "merely a chance occurrence," and cannot be considered as a "meaningful finding." P-values of .05 or less are said to be "statistically significant" in the realm of EEO analyses. This .05 level (or 5%) corresponds with the odds ratio of "1 chance in 20."

The use of statistical tests to identify whether statistical significance exists in a data set is highly contingent on whether the analysis has sufficiently high levels of statistical power to find it. The important concept of statistical power is reviewed next.

STATISTICAL POWER

When a statistical test is calculated to evaluate whether the event being analyzed is "statistically significant," there is always a "power" associated with the test which can be used to describe its *ability to reveal a statistically significant finding if there is one to be found*. Thus, a powerful adverse impact analysis is one that has a high likelihood of uncovering adverse impact if it really exists. When applying the statistical power concept specifically to adverse impact analyses, there are three factors that impact the statistical power of the analysis:

1. Effect size: For Selection Rate Comparisons, this pertains to the size of the "gap" between the selection rates of the two groups (e.g., if the male passing rate on a test is 80% and the female passing rate is 60% there is a 20% "gap" or effect size between the two groups). For Availability Comparisons, effect size means the size of the difference between a group's representation in the workplace versus their availability (e.g., qualified applicants).

2. Sample size: The number of focal and reference group members plays a key role in adverse impact analyses.

3. The type of statistical test used: This includes the actual formula of the adverse impact analyses (some tests are more powerful than others) and whether a one-tail or a two-tail test for significance is used (see discussion on one-tail versus two-tail tests later in this chapter).

Because the effect size is outside the practitioner's control when analyzing adverse impact, only the latter two factors will be discussed here.

SAMPLE SIZE

Amassing a large sample size is perhaps the single most effective way to increase the power of an adverse impact analysis. There are at least five ways this can be accomplished (see section 4D of the Uniform Guidelines):

1. Widen the timeframe of the events being analyzed. For example, rather than analyzing a selection process for just one year, several administrations from previous years can be included to make an overall historical analysis. In EEO litigation settings, including several events into a single analysis requires the plaintiff to successfully argue a "continuing violation" of the employer's practices over a longer timeframe than just the single at-issue event (e.g., a written

test administered in a certain year) or that the sample size in the case is simply too small to conduct a meaningful analysis.

2. Combine various geographic areas together into a "regional" analysis, when appropriate. For example, a plaintiff group could challenge all of the employer's sites in a particular state and demonstrate that these sites operated under similar policies or hiring/promotion strategies.

3. Combine events from several jobs, job groups, or divisions. Combining jobs or divisions into an overall adverse impact analysis is a complicated issue that requires considering several factors. Some of these factors are: the similarity in work behaviors between jobs, job groups, or divisions; statistical homogeneity (discussed later in the Multiple Events section of this chapter); and the consistency and similarity of the patterns and practices.

4. Combine various selection procedures. Under some circumstances the courts will allow combining various selection procedures into a combined "overall selection process" analysis. While this type of analysis may sometimes yield meaningful results, an event-by-event analysis should be the primary comparison in most circumstances (the 1991 Civil Rights Act requires that a "particular employment practice" needs to be identified as the source of adverse impact for a plaintiff to establish an adverse impact case, unless the results are not capable for separation for analysis – see Section 2000e-2[k][1][A][i]).

5. Combine different ethnic groups together for analysis purposes. Some EEO litigation circumstances allow plaintiff groups to form a class of two or more ethnic groups who share similar allegations (e.g., "total minorities").

It is important to note that the first four of the five aggregation techniques described above require using the appropriate multiple events type of adverse impact analyses because statistical anomalies can occur when combining data across multiple strata (see the Multiple Event analyses discussed later). In litigation settings, it is almost always more favorable to the employer to *limit* the sample size used in the adverse impact analysis (because this limits statistical power and makes it more difficult to identify significant findings) and almost always more beneficial for the plaintiffs to *increase* the sample size (for the reverse reason). The courts will typically have the final say on the nature of the sample used.

WHEN IS A SAMPLE "TOO SMALL" FOR ADVERSE IMPACT ANALYSIS?

Despite years of debate among statistical practitioners, there is no absolute, bottom-line threshold regarding the minimum sample size necessary for conducting statistical investigations. In particular, the courts frequently take the stance that there is no clear minimum sample size. For example, in Bradley v. Pizzaco of Nebraska, Inc. (1991), the court stated "There is no minimum sample size prescribed either in federal law or statistical theory."

If one had to pick a firm minimum number for adverse impact analyses, it would be 30 with at least 5 expected for selection (i.e., hired, promoted, etc.) (OFCCP, 1993). The Uniform Guidelines Questions & Answers (#20) state that a sample of 20 is too small. In some circumstances, however, it can be argued that a sample with fewer than the "30 requirement" from OFCCP or the "20 requirement" from the Uniform Guidelines can still allow a meaningful statistical analysis to be conducted. For example, consider a testing situation where only five men and five women applied for a position and all five of the men passed and none of the women. A statistical significance test of this example reveals a probability value of .008 (or odds of 1 chance in 126, well beyond the 1 chance in 20 required for statistical significance). Below are a few examples of how some US courts have addressed the issue of small samples in adverse impact calculations:

- The courts have provided several rulings in situations where zero (0) focal group members are selected or represented. Such circumstances have been referred to as the "inexorable zero," and almost always result in the court finding adverse impact (e.g., Association Against Discrimination in Employment, Inc. v. City of Bridgeport (1979); Franks v. Bowman Transportation Co. (1974, 1976)).

- In Watson v. Fort Worth Bank & Trust (1977, 1988), the court stated, "Our formulations, which have never been framed in terms of any rigid mathematical formula, have consistently stressed that statistical disparities must be sufficiently substantial that they raise an inference of causation."

- In Shutt v. Sandoz Corp. (1991), the court stated that it is sometimes necessary to rely on statistics derived from small samples, however, when it is not completely necessary, it is better to base the statistics on a larger sample (the appeals court in this case reversed the district court's ruling which used a sample of 21 employees working in one of two merged companies instead of 106 employees total). This court also referenced two other cases where sample sizes of 30 and 28 were considered too small.

- In Cicero v. Borg Warner Automotive (1999), the court stated that "... statistical evaluations ('disparate impact analysis') of an employer's subjective decisions are permissible in a disparate treatment case brought under Michigan law ... However, the United States Supreme Court has repeatedly warned courts to be wary of simplistic percentage comparisons based on small sample sizes (see Watson, 487 US at 1000, 108 S.Ct. 2777: 'It may be that the relevant data base is too small to permit any meaningful statistical analysis.')."

- A sample size of six was found to be too small in Gault v. Zellerbach (1998).

- A sample size of seven or 11 was insufficient to demonstrate a pretext in Martin v. United States Playing Card Co. (1998).

- A sample size of 13 was too small in Tinker v. Sears, Roebuck & Co. (1997).

- A sample of eight was insufficient in Anderson v. Premier Industrial Corp. (1995).

- An eight-person sample was too small to support a discrimination case in Osborne v. Brandeis Machinery & Supply Corp. (1994).

While the courts will provide only general guidelines on sample size requirements (almost always evaluating this issue on a case-by-case basis), one characteristic is common, however, to all statistical analyses where small numbers are involved: they suffer from having a higher "sampling error" than analyses involving larger data sets. Analyses with "high sampling error" are prone to change in ways that would likely lead to different statistical outcomes if the event hypothetically occurred again.

For example, consider a situation where ten men and ten women applied for a job and eight men were hired (80%) and four women were hired (40%) (a substantially different, however not statistically significant, selection rate of 40% between men and women). It is very likely that subsequent selection processes would have different results. A difference of just a few hires could change the 40% selection rate difference to 10%, 20%, or 30%. In fact, the very next selection process could result in the complete opposite extreme (e.g., 80% selection rate for women and 40% for men). For this reason, adverse impact analyses that are based on small numbers should be viewed as "less stable" than analyses that involve larger sample sizes. The Uniform Guidelines offers some specific guidance regarding this problem with small data sets:

> *Where the user's evidence concerning the impact of a selection procedure indicates adverse impact but is based upon numbers which are too small to be reliable, evidence concerning the impact of the procedure over a longer period of time and/or evidence concerning the impact which the selection procedure had when used in the same manner in similar circumstances elsewhere may be considered in determining adverse impact (Section 4D).*

TYPES OF STATISTICAL TESTS

"Exact tests" are considered the most powerful statistical tests to use for adverse impact calculations. These are tests that calculate the precise probability value and require mathematical formulas and iterations that typically can only be completed using computer software. The key exact statistical tests are discussed later in this chapter.

The other factor to consider when determining the statistical significance levels of a statistical test used for adverse impact analysis is a one-tail versus a two-tail test. A one-tail statistical test investigates the possibility of discrimination occurring in just one direction (e.g., against women when making a men versus women comparison). A two-tail test takes the assumption that discrimination *could have* occurred in either direction (e.g., against men or against women) and hence *spends its statistical power* investigating discrimination in both directions. A one-tail test is more powerful than a two-tail test when investigating discrimination cases because it requires only a 5% level of significance level in one direction in the probability distribution, whereas the two-tail test allows 2.5% on each end of the probability distribution (i.e., it assumes that the at-issue group's selection rate could have been either more or less than the comparison group's).

Mathematically speaking, the probability value for the first tail is calculated by summing the probability values obtained from the original data set and all more extreme cases against the disadvantaged group. The probability value for the second tail is calculated by summing the probability values from all iterated cases (where the passing numbers in each group are hypothetically changed) that are just as or more extreme than the original data set, but in the opposite direction (in favor of the disadvantaged group, starting with the first set that has a selection ratio that is equal to or more extreme than the original) (Agresti, 1990, p. 62). For example, the probability value of a case where 14 men passed, six failed (a 70% passing rate), and one woman passed and four failed (a 20% passing rate) is .059 (notice the difference in passing rates is 70% − 20% = 50%).

The next "iteration" in this same direction (making it less favorable for women) is 15 men passing and five failing, and 0 women passing and all five failing (a probability of .005). Adding these two values together produces the total one tail probability value of .064 (.059 + .005). The second tail probability is calculated by iterations going the other direction (increasing the number of women passing while decreasing the number of men passing, one at a time until 0 is reached for one group, while keeping the total passing and failing the same), and only summing probability values of iterated cases with selection ratios that are at least as extreme as the original data set (i.e., 50% or more). The only iteration that is at least as extreme as the original case (i.e., 50% or more) is where ten men pass and ten fail, and 5 women pass and 0 fail, which results in a probability value of .057. Adding this value to the total first tail probability results in a total, two-tail probability value of .121. Notice that this value is different than just doubling the one tail probability value (.064 x 2 = .128, which is slightly higher than the exact value of .121), a technique often applied by practitioners.

Thus, because a one-tail test is focused on finding discrimination against only one group, it will always find statistical significance before a two-tail test. For this reason, a one-tail test is a more plaintiff-oriented test than a two-tail test. While statisticians sometimes disagree on the validity of the one-tailed test in discrimination cases,[5] the courts have been almost totally consistent in their requirement of using a two-tail test for significance. The cases cited below have discussed the one-tail versus two-tail issue (and some rather extensively – e.g., Palmer v. Shultz (1987)), and they almost unanimously agree that a two-tail test is the technique they prefer for adverse impact cases:

- Brown v. Delta Air Lines, Inc. (1980);

- Chang v. University of Rhode Island (1985);

- Csicseri v. Bowsher (1994);

- EEOC v. Federal Reserve Bank of Richmond (1983);

- Hoops v. Elk Run Coal Co., Inc. (2000);

- Moore v. Summers (2000);

- Mozee v. American Commercial Marine Service Co. (1991);

- Palmer v. Shultz (1987).

While these cases and the OFCCP[6] have clearly endorsed the two-tail method,[7] two cases have allowed a one-tail investigation under certain circumstances:

- Ottaviani v. State University of New York at New Paltz (1988): this case did not involve a typical adverse impact analysis, but rather involved using regression analysis for evaluating differences in salary.

- Police Officers for Equal Rights v. City of Columbus (1985).

The courts obviously prefer using a two-tail test because it mirrors the philosophy of Title VII, which is to evaluate a disparity against any group, not just one group. It would seem allowable to use a one-tail test for adverse impact analyses if the plaintiff could make a showing that the employer's actions were overtly discriminatory. Such actions on the part of the employer would justify a one-tail test because the researcher would have good cause to suspect that the overt discriminatory actions lead to some unequal outcome, hence the use of a one-tail test would only look for what was suspected to exist based on credible evidence.

SELECTION RATE COMPARISON FOR A SINGLE EVENT

This type of analysis can be regarded as the "most typical" type of adverse impact analysis, and is specifically explained in the Uniform Guidelines as a "rates comparison" (Section 4D) that compares the passing rates between two groups (e.g., men and women) on a selection procedure. This type of analysis can also be used to analyze the outcome of layoffs, demotions, or other similar personnel transactions where there are only two possible outcomes (e.g., promoted/not promoted; hired/not hired, etc.) (see Table 1.1).

This type of analysis should not be used to analyze combined sets of data (e.g., analyzing the passing rates of men and women in several years combined). The Multiple Events Selection Rate Comparison (discussed later in this chapter) is necessary when multiple years or tests are placed into a combined analysis. This is because statistical anomalies can occur when combining data across multiple strata.

There are several types of statistical tests that can be used for this type of analysis. The primary types include the 80% Test, statistical significance, and practical significance.

SELECTION RATE COMPARISONS: THE 80% TEST

Much of the historical development regarding this test has been discussed previously. This section will limit the discussion of this test to the mechanical aspects, and how this test is sometimes used in litigation settings.

The 80% Test is an analysis that compares the passing rate of one group to the passing rate of another group (e.g., men vs. women). An 80% Test "violation" occurs if one group's passing rate is less than 80% of the group with the highest rate. For example, if the male pass rate on a test is 90% and the female pass rate is 70% (77.7% of the male pass rate), an 80% Test violation has occurred. The 80% Test is described by the Uniform Guidelines as:

> ... a "rule of thumb" as a practical means for determining adverse impact for use in enforcement proceedings ... It is not a legal definition of discrimination, rather it is a practical device to keep the attention of enforcement agencies on serious discrepancies in hire or promotion rates or other employment decisions (Overview, Section ii).

It is also described by the Uniform Guidelines as having some limitations:

> ... a selection rate for any race, sex, or ethnic group which is less than four-fifths (4/5) (or eighty percent) of the rate for the group with the highest rate will generally be regarded by the Federal enforcement agencies as evidence of adverse impact, while a greater than four-fifths rate will generally not be regarded by Federal enforcement agencies as evidence of adverse impact. Smaller differences in selection rate may nevertheless constitute adverse impact, where they are significant in both statistical and practical terms ... (Section 4D, emphasis added).

The 80% Test has been scrutinized in Title VII litigation because it is greatly impacted by small numbers and does not consider the "statistical significance" of the passing rate disparity between the two groups (see, for example, Bouman v. Block (1991); and Clady v. County of Los Angeles (1985)). More typically, courts consider the statistical significance of the passing rate disparity between groups:

- "Rather than using the 80 percent rule as a touchstone, we look more generally to whether the statistical disparity is 'substantial' or 'significant' in a given case" (Bouman v. Block (1991), citing Contreras v. City of Los Angeles (1981), at 1274–75).

- "There is no consensus on a threshold mathematical showing of variance to constitute substantial disproportionate impact. Some courts have looked to Castaneda v. Partida (1977), which found adverse impact where the selection rate for the protected group was 'greater than two or three standard deviations' from the selection rate of their counterparts" (Clady v. Los Angeles County (1985)).

Notice in the above cases that standard deviations are used to represent the extent of the adverse impact against a group. Because standard deviations sometimes present a more straightforward interpretive tool for the courts to use when discussing statistical significance and probability values, they have widely adopted the common "two or three standard deviations" as a criteria for establishing statistically significant adverse impact. To be exact, however, a standard deviation that equates to the .05 level of statistical significance is 1.96 (see below for further explanation).

SELECTION RATE COMPARISONS: STATISTICAL SIGNIFICANCE TESTS

There are two categories of statistical significance tests that can be used for analyzing adverse impact for Selection Rate Comparisons: exact and estimated. Exact tests provide the precise probability value of the analysis. Estimated techniques approximate the exact results without requiring lengthy calculations. The exact statistical significance test to use for Selection Rate Comparisons is a two-tail Fisher Exact probability statistic for 2 X 2 contingency tables (Mosteller et al., 1970, pp. 315–318; Agresti, 1990, pp. 60–62; see Table 1.1).

Table 1.1   2 X 2 contingency table

	Men	Women
Pass	50	40
Fail	50	50

These 2 X 2 contingency tables will always have *two groups* and *two categories*. The two-tail Fisher Exact Test is the "precise" statistical procedure most frequently used in litigation for establishing "statistically significant" levels of adverse impact for 2 X 2 tables.

Any probability value that is less than .05 is statistically significant and indicates a difference in passing rates between two groups that is not likely occurring by chance. A probability value of .05 corresponds with a likelihood of 1 chance in 20, a probability value of .01 to a likelihood of 1 chance in 100, etc. A probability value can also be interpreted as a standard deviation unit, with a probability value of .05 corresponding to a (two-tail) standard deviation value of 1.96. A standard deviation of 2.58 corresponds with a probability value of .01, and a likelihood of 1 chance in 100.

SELECTION RATE COMPARISONS: PRACTICAL SIGNIFICANCE TESTS

The concept of practical significance for Selection Rate Comparisons was first introduced by Section 4D of the Uniform Guidelines ("Smaller differences in selection rate may nevertheless constitute adverse impact, where they are *significant in both statistical and practical terms* ..."). Generally, practical significance tests are applied to adverse impact analyses to evaluate the "practicality" or "stability" of the results. For Selection Rate Comparisons, this analysis has been applied in at least four litigation settings.

Two different practical significance tests were evaluated in Contreras v. City of Los Angeles (1981, Footnote #4). A different type of practical significant test was applied in US v. Commonwealth of Virginia (1978), and similarly was applied in Waisome v. Port Authority (1991). While there are a few other cases[8] that discuss the need for practical significance, these three cases will be discussed here.

The first of the two Contreras methods for assessing practical significance can be conducted by evaluating the additional number of test takers (from the group with the lowest rate) who would need to pass the test to eliminate the 80% Test violation. Footnote 4 of the Contreras case explains that if three or more persons from the group with the lowest pass rate had passed the test, the 80% Test would not have been violated (i.e., it would have changed from "violated" to "not violated"). Since small changes such as this are often likely to occur by chance (especially when small samples are being evaluated), the court indicated that the 80% Test violation was not practically stable.

The second of the two methods used in the Contreras case for assessing practical significance can be conducted by evaluating the additional number of test takers (from the group with the lowest rate) who would need to pass the test in order to bring the passing rates between the two groups *very close* (in the Contreras case, to within 2.1% of each other). Footnote 4 of the Contreras case explains that if four or more persons from the group with the lowest pass rate had passed the test, the passing rates of the two groups would have narrowed to only 2.1% of each other (hence the results were not practically significant).

The Virginia/Waisome method for assessing practical significance is conducted by evaluating the additional number of successful (passing) group members (from the group with the lowest rate) who would need to pass to eliminate the statistical significance finding (i.e., to bring the probability value from $<.05$ to $\geq.05$). The Virginia and Waisome cases explain that if two or fewer persons from the group with the lowest pass rate were hypothetically changed from "failing" to "passing" status, and this resulted in eliminating the statistical significance finding, the results were not to be considered practically significant.

MAKING A FINAL DETERMINATION OF ADVERSE IMPACT FOR SELECTION RATE COMPARISONS

Under most circumstances a Selection Rate Comparison analysis should result in a firm finding of both statistical and practical significance to constitute a solid finding of adverse impact. However, the myriad of factors involved in litigating adverse impact cases will often lead to differing judicial findings based on the circumstances involved. For this reason, when practices, procedures, or tests show signs of adverse impact (or may show adverse impact if greater sample sizes were evaluated), the employer should consider either conducting validation studies or using alternative employment practices that have less adverse impact (see Section 2000e-2[k][1][A][i]-[ii] of the 1991 Civil Rights Act). For this reason it is a good idea for employers to keep track of the results of their testing, so that they might consider adjusting the process if adverse impact does occur.

SELECTION RATE COMPARISONS FOR MULTIPLE EVENTS

This section discusses the proper methodology for comparing the passing rates of gender and ethnic groups on several combined "events" or administrations of various practices, procedures, or tests. This technique may also be used to complete an overall adverse impact analysis on several jobs or groups of jobs with similar skill sets, or for comparing group passing rates on an overall selection or promotion process for multiple years, although an event-by-event analysis should be the primary comparison in most circumstances (the 1991 Civil Rights Act requires that a "particular employment practice" needs to be identified as the source of adverse impact for a plaintiff to bring establish a adverse impact case, unless the results are not capable for separation for analysis – see Section 2000e-2[k][1][A][i]).

SIMPSON'S PARADOX: THE REASON FOR CAUTION WHEN COMBINING DATA

Statistical anomalies can occur when combining data across multiple strata. While it may be tempting to simply aggregate several years of a particular testing practice into an overall, combined adverse impact analysis, the results will sometimes be misleading unless a special "multiple events" technique is used. A statistical phenomena called "Simpson's Paradox"[9] shows why this can be a problem. Consider the data presented in Table 1.2.

Table 1.2 Simpson's Paradox example

Testing Year	Group	# Applicants	# Selected	Selection Rate %
2004 Test	Men	400	200	50.0%
	Women	100	50	50.0%
2005 Test	Men	100	20	20.0%
	Women	100	20	20.0%
2004 + 2005 Tests Combined	Men	500	220	44.0%
	Women	200	70	35.0%

Notice that the selection rate for men and women in the table is *exactly the same* for each of the two years individually. Thus, a year-by-year analysis of the selection rates between men and women would reveal no differences in passing rates. No

80% Test, statistical significance, or practical significance occurred. However, when the two years are simply added together for a combined analysis, there is an enormous gap of 9% between men and women! Because the application ratio (the number of men compared to women for each year) has not remained constant for the two years, the combined analysis shows that women have a lower selection rate when the years are combined. When evaluating the data in Table 1.2 statistically, the following results are calculated:

- When calculating the adverse impact for each year individually, no statistical significance exists (the selection rates are exactly equal for each year).

- When calculating the adverse impact for both years aggregated (i.e., simply adding the passing and failing values together for both years into a single analysis), the probability value is statistically significant (p = .034, or odds of about 1 chance in 30).

- However, when calculating adverse impact for both years combined, using the proper technique (the Multiple Events technique discussed herein), the probability value is appropriately not significant (the probability value exceeds .90).

Because of limitations like Simpson's Paradox, proper aggregation techniques need to be used in place of simple aggregation techniques.

PROPERLY AGGREGATING DATA FOR SELECTION RATE COMPARISONS

Unlike the Selection Rate Comparison test used for single events, two steps are necessary for evaluating multiple event Selection Rate Comparisons. The first step is to calculate the pattern consistency of the events to evaluate whether the events can be combined into a single analysis; the second is to calculate and interpret the statistical significance test.

Step 1: Evaluate the events for pattern consistency

Before data sets can be combined into an overall analysis, they must first be analyzed to see whether they are similar enough statistically to be combined together. This first step involves a test called a *pattern consistency* test, or in technical terms, a *homogeneity of odds ratios* test. While there are several different tools and techniques that can be used to accomplish this, the end goal of these test is the same: to evaluate whether the "trend" in the passing rate difference between groups is consistent between "events" (e.g., years, tests, etc.).

When one group continually maintains a passing rate that is lower than the other group, the probability value resulting from this test will be close to 1.0 – indicating there are no significant fluctuations between the events in the combined data set. When there are flip-flops between events (e.g., when one group's selection rates are below the other group's for four years in a row, but reverse dramatically in the fifth year), the value will approach 0. When the result of this test is below .05, a statistically significant flip-flop of one or more events has been detected, and conducting separate analyses for these events (or removing them altogether) should be considered.

There are at least two frequently used statistical tests available for analyzing pattern consistency. The first test uses the "Treatment by Strata Interaction" test (Mehrotra & Railkar, 2000); the second is a widely used test called the "Breslow-Day" (1980) with Tarone's (1988) Correction. If the output from these test results is .05 or higher, no significant flip-flops in the selection rates (between events) have been detected and the results can be safely included in an overall analysis.

Step 2: Calculate statistical test results

If the events can safely be combined into an overall analysis, the next step is to evaluate whether adverse impact occurred in the overall analysis. There are three statistical tests that can be used to investigate adverse impact. The Mantel-Haenszel[10] Test is the most commonly used test for multiple 2 X 2 data sets (such as the data required for Selection Rate Comparisons, where there are two outcomes for the two groups being evaluated).

While the Mantel-Haenszel Test is not an exact statistical test (but rather an estimator) for the precise probability value, it comes very close. For large data sets, it will match the exact test results almost precisely. The mathematical iterations necessary for calculating the exact test are highly sophisticated and require advanced statistical software.[11]

Two versions of the Mantel-Haenszel estimator formula are included in the Adverse Impact Toolkit Demo Version on the Evaluation CD. Version 1 is likely to be closest to the "exact" probability value, and only uses a modest (.125) continuity correction.[12] Version 2 uses a conventional correction (.5) and will typically overestimate the probability value (especially with small data sets). These tests assess whether the selection rate difference between two groups (e.g., men v. women) for *all events combined* is extreme enough to be considered "beyond chance." Values less than .05 are statistically significant; values between .05 and .10 should be considered "close to significance." Both versions use the Cochran version of the Mantel-Haenszel statistic, which weights each event according to its sample size.

Another statistical analysis called the Minimum Risk Weights Test (Mehrotra and Railkar, 2000) can be used for multiple Selection Rate Comparisons. This test does not weight the events by sample size and can sometimes provide a "more powerful" analysis than the Mantel-Haenszel Test (above). The test uses a moderate correction for continuity (.375) and can be interpreted using the same guidelines proposed for the Mantel-Haenszel.

While the courts have applied practical significance tests to Single Event Selection Rate Comparisons (as of the time of this writing). One such practical significance test would be to evaluate whether hypothetically changing two focal group applicants from failing to passing status in *any* of the events eliminated a statistical significance finding.

THE MULTIPLE EVENTS TEST IN LITIGATION

This type of analysis has been applied in numerous EEO litigation settings. A partial list is provided below:

- Arnold v. Postmaster General (1987);

- Covington v. District of Columbia (1995);

- Dees v. Orr, Secretary of the Air Force (1983);

- Dennis L. Harrison v. Drew Lewis (1983);

- Hogan v. Pierce, Secretary, Housing and Urban Development (1983);

- Johnson v. Garrett, III as Secretary of the Navy (1991);

- Manko v. US (1986);

- McKay v. US (1985);

- Paige v. California Highway Patrol (1999);

- Trout v. Hidalgo (1981).

AVAILABILITY COMPARISON FOR A SINGLE EVENT

This type of adverse impact analysis is designed for comparing one group's representation (i.e., the percentage of incumbents in a given position who belong to the gender or ethnic group) to that group's availability in the relevant labor market (using availability data from inside or outside the organization). This type of comparison is useful for determining whether a group is underutilized in a particular position, or group of positions.

This analysis should be differentiated from the Selection Rate Comparison because (under most circumstances) a statistically significant finding (meaning the at-issue group is significantly underutilized) does not automatically constitute a finding of adverse impact.[13] The reason for this is straightforward: a Selection Rate Comparison directly evaluates how two groups fared on a particular selection procedure, so if one group significantly outperforms the other, direct evidence is amassed regarding the impact of a *particular* employment practice on a *specific* group when *compared to another group*. Then the attention can shift toward evaluating that particular selection procedure for job relatedness (i.e., validity).

By contrast, the Availability Comparison does not (necessarily) consider the impact of a single employment practice. Because the comparison is an overall evaluation that considers one group's makeup in a given position compared to their availability outside of that position, it does not individually consider all of the selection procedures that may have been used to select or promote individuals for that position. Further, it does not take into consideration other factors such as "job interest" or qualification levels of the at-issue group.

For example, if outside availability data shows that men are statistically significantly underutilized for a group of clerical jobs at a given employer, the underutilization could possibly be explained by either lack of interest on the part of men to pursue these positions, or the fact that men performed poorly on the multitude of qualification screens required for entry into the position (or, more likely, some combination of these two factors and/or others). For these reasons, the Availability Comparison should be considered as a "threshold" or "initial inquiry test."

TYPES OF STATISTICAL ANALYSES FOR AVAILABILITY COMPARISONS

While the 80% Test is sometimes used by government enforcement agencies for evaluating underutilization of various groups, it will not be discussed here for two reasons: it has already been discussed in the previous sections relevant to the Selection Rate Comparisons and it is not regularly used in litigation to assess adverse impact on groups.[14] In addition, the 80% Test is not endorsed by the Uniform Guidelines as a valid adverse impact analysis (it is only referenced as a "rule of thumb" for comparing the selection rates of two groups).

The concept of practical significance, while it may be highly relevant in some cases, is also not discussed here because it has not been referenced or applied in litigation settings to Availability Comparisons. This leaves only statistical significance as the relevant test for Availability Comparisons.

Like the Selection Rate Comparison, calculating adverse impact for Availability Comparisons can be done using exact or estimator techniques. The exact test provides the precise probability value of the analysis. The estimator techniques can approximate the exact results without requiring lengthy calculations. The estimator technique can readily be calculated in Microsoft Excel by using the BINOMDIST function and doubling the value to obtain an estimated two-tail probability value. The proper exact test is a (two-tail) Exact Binomial Probability Test. This test requires sophisticated iterations that require programming or advanced computer software (this calculation is available on the Evaluation CD). The same conventions used for the Selection Rate Comparison can also be used for this test (e.g., any value below .05 constitutes a statistically significant finding).

MAKING A FINAL DETERMINATION OF ADVERSE IMPACT FOR AVAILABILITY COMPARISONS

Because this test compares one group's representation to its availability (rather than comparing the selection rates of two groups, such as the test used for the Selection Rate Comparison), statistically significant findings (without other evidence) should not be considered as direct evidence of adverse impact (because both discriminatory and non-discriminatory reasons can possibly account for the group's underutilization). Rather, results that yield probability values of less than .05 should be regarded as "statistically significant underutilization," but not necessarily as adverse impact.

These findings are sometimes called a "manifest imbalance" or "statistically significant underutilization" in litigation, which simply means that there is a "statistically significant gap" between the comparison group's availability for employment or promotion (typically derived from a group's representation in the qualified applicant pool for entry-level positions and the "feeder" positions for promotional positions[15]) and the group's current representation in the at-issue job or group of jobs. When such a statistically significant "imbalance" or "underutilization" exists, any of the five circumstances listed below can possibly lead to a court's finding of adverse impact:

1. The employer failed to keep applicant records (sometimes referred to as an "adverse inference" – see Section 4D of the Uniform Guidelines). If an employer fails to keep applicant data, the government has reserved the right to infer adverse impact on the selection or promotion process if the agency has an imbalance in a job or group of jobs.

2. The employer failed to keep adverse impact data on the selection or promotional processes (Section 4D of the Uniform Guidelines). Similar to #1 above, if employers have an imbalance in a job (or group of jobs) and do not have information regarding the adverse impact

of the various practices, procedures, or tests used in the selection or promotion process, an "adverse inference" can be made. Employers should maintain passing rate data for their various selection and promotional processes, and practices, procedures, or tests that have adverse impact should be justified by evidence of job relatedness and business necessity.

3.   The employer's recruiting practice was discriminatory toward the protected group (see Section 4D of the Uniform Guidelines and Hazelwood School District v. United States, 1977). For example, if the employer recruits for certain jobs only by "word of mouth," and the only applicants who are informed about the job opportunities are a certain race and/or gender group, the employer could be held liable in a discrimination lawsuit. Plaintiff groups may also argue that minorities and/or women were "funneled" by the employer's systems and processes into filling only certain position(s) in the organization.

4.   The employer maintained a discriminatory reputation that "chilled" or "discouraged" protected group members from applying for the selection process (Section 4D of the Uniform Guidelines). This argument has successfully been made in several discrimination cases,16 and is a viable argument for plaintiffs to make in some circumstances.

5.   The employer failed to conduct a formal selection process for the position and instead hired or promoted individuals through an "appointment only" process. This "promotion by appointment" practice would certainly lend itself to a viable plaintiff argument because the practice was exclusionary to qualified individuals who were not allowed an equal opportunity to compete for a position. Further, this type of promotional practice could make the use of conventional adverse impact analyses impossible (because there are no clear "promotional processes" or "events" that can be analyzed by comparing the passing rates between two groups), which could limit the adverse impact analysis to a comparison between the disadvantaged group's representation in the promotional position to their availability in the "feeder" positions. While informal selection procedures are not directly prohibited under the various civil rights laws, they are much more difficult to defend against claims that they were used unfairly than are more standardized selection processes.

Unless one of these five situations exists, a plaintiff group will be required to pinpoint the specific selection procedure that caused the adverse impact (using the 80% Test, statistical significance tests, and/or practical significance tests). The only exception is if the employer's practices cannot be "separated for analysis purposes."

AVAILABILITY COMPARISONS FOR MULTIPLE EVENTS

Availability Comparisons can be made for several different jobs (or groups of jobs) or for the same job across multiple years (the reader is referred to the Availability Comparison for a Single Event section of this chapter for several caveats that apply to these types of analyses). This technique is useful for many personnel assessments, such as:

- employment trends of specific groups over time;

- utilization rates of groups in various departments at one employer;

- utilization rates of specific groups across different geographic regions of one employer.

PROPERLY AGGREGATING DATA FOR AVAILABILITY COMPARISONS

Like the Selection Rate Comparison analyses, analyses for the Availability Comparisons should first be assessed for *pattern consistency* or *homogeneity across events* before they are combined into an overall analysis. Thus, there are also two steps for completing stratified (multiple event) Availability Comparison analyses.

Step 1: Evaluate the events for pattern consistency

These statistical tests evaluate whether the "trend" in the Availability Comparisons is consistent between events. When the at-issue group is continually underutilized across events, the result of this test will be close to 1.0. When there are flip-flops between events (e.g., when the at-issue group changes from over- to underutilized across events), the value will approach 0. One statistical technique for assessing the pattern consistency of the events is the Breslow-Day (1980) with Tarone's (1988) Correction (adapted for binomial distributions). When the result of this test is below .05, a statistically significant flip-flop of one or more events has been detected, and conducting separate analyses for these events (or removing them altogether) should be considered.

Step 2: Calculate statistical test results

If the "Pattern Consistency" test (above) is not violated (i.e., statistically significant), the second step can be completed. This step allows for the independent "events" to be combined into an overall analysis to see if the combination of all events results in statistical significance. There are two statistical tests to investigate adverse impact in this step.

The first test (and perhaps the most robust) is Fisher's Method with Lancaster's Correction.[18] This (two-tail) test evaluates whether the Focal Group's continual (i.e., across multiple events) underutilization is statistically significant. Values less than .05 are "statistically significant"; values between .05 and .10 are "close" to significance. Fisher's method is known for being the most reliable test when small data sets are being evaluated.

The second test is the Generalized Binomial Test.[19] This test uses the binomial probability formula across multiple strata and typically outputs values that are very similar to Fisher's method. It should not be relied upon when small samples are included.

THE MULTIPLE EVENTS AVAILABILITY COMPARISON IN LITIGATION

This type of analysis has been applied in several EEO litigation settings. A partial list is provided below:

- Cooper v. University of Texas at Dallas (1979);

- EEOC v. United Virginia Bank (1980);

- Vuyanich v. Republic National Bank (1980).

NOTES

1. The EEOC filed 710,928 Title VII charges against various employers between 1992 and 2003. These charges resulted in $1.16 billion in monetary benefits to plaintiffs. While only about 5% of Title VII cases are based on adverse impact claims, the 1 billion estimate should still be regarded as conservative because it does not include monetary benefits obtained through litigation, cases filed by private law firms, and the costs associated with defending against such lawsuits. In fact, the author's consulting firm has worked on over 200 EEO cases since 1974; and the cases directly relating to adverse impact claims exceed the 200 million mark (when combining plaintiff and defense costs).
2. The Uniform Guidelines on Employee Selection Procedures and the related Questions & Answers can be found at www.uniformguidelines.com.
3. DeGroot, M. H., Fienberg, S. E., Kadane, J. B. (1985), *Statistics and the Law*, New York, NY: John Wiley & Sons (p. 30).
4. Personal communication (August, 2004) with Richard E. Biddle, member of the subcommittee on Guidelines Preparation, and Mary Tenopyr, Special Consultant to TACT.

5. For example, compare Harper, G. (1981), Statistics as evidence of age discrimination, *Hastings L.J.*, **32**, 1347–1375 & n. 65 with Kaye, D. (1982), The numbers game: Statistical inference in discrimination cases, *Mich.L.Rev.*, **80**, 833–836.

6. The "Pooled Two-Sample Z-Score" test specified in Chapter 3 of OFCCP's Compliance Manual (October 13, 2004 on-line Internet version) outputs a Z-score value that is a two-tail Z value.

7. Title VII protects everyone from discrimination, which is why a two-tail test has been determined to be more appropriate.

8. In Frazier v. Garrison I.S.D. (980 F.2d 1514, 5th Cir., 1993), the Court stated that the selection rates were within 4.5% of each other, which was insufficient for a finding of adverse impact, even with statistically significant rate differences. In Moore v. Southwestern Bell (593 F.2d 607, 5th Cir., 1979), the court found that a 7.1% difference in selection rates was not enough for a finding of adverse impact, even though the standard deviations were above 3.0.

9. See Finkelstein, M. O. & Levin, B. (2001), *Statistics for Lawyers* (2nd ed.). New York, NY: Springer (p. 237).

10. The Mantel-Haenszel technique was originally developed for aggregating data sets for cancer research. See Mantel, N. & Haenszel, W. (1959), Statistical aspects of the analysis of data from retrospective studies of disease. *Journal of National Cancer Institute*, **22**, 719–748.

11. At the time of this writing, only one commercially available software program is available for calculating the exact version of the Mantel-Haenszel: StatXact® from Cytel Software Corporation (Version 4.0 and higher).

12. A correction to a discrete probability distribution to approximate a continuous probability distribution. This correction adjusts the estimator formula to better approximate the exact probability value. Correction values typically range between 0 and 0.5.

13. A statistically significant finding on a Selection Rate Comparison analysis does not necessarily automatically constitute adverse impact either. Practical significance should usually be considered as well.

14. A more commonly applied technique is called a "gross under-representation" or "gross disparity", which evaluates the gap between focal and reference group representation using the statistical significance tests described herein for the Availability Comparison analysis.

15. If the target position is not underutilized when compared to the relevant feeder position(s), yet the relevant feeder position(s) is underutilized when compared to those with the requisite skills in the relevant labor area (called an "outside proxy group"), it can be argued that the proxy group can be used to compare to the target position. This process is referred to as a "barriers analysis."

16. See Donnel v. General Motors Corp. (576 F2d 1292, 8th Cir 1978); Dothard v. Rawlinson (433 US 321, 1977); Williams v. Owens-Illinois, Inc. (665 F2d 918, 9th Cir.; Cert. denied, 459 US 971, 1982).

17. 1991 Civil Rights Act (42 U.S.C. §2000e-2[k][ii][B]).

18. This test uses a procedure described in Louv, W. C. & Littell, R. C. (1986), Combining one-sided binomial tests. *Journal of the American Statistical Association*, **81**, 550–554.

19. Gastwirth, J.L. & Greenhouse, S.W. (1987), Estimating a common relative risk: Application in equal employment. *Journal of the American Statistical Association*, **82**, 38–45.-

CHAPTER 2

Selection Procedure Development and Validation

VALIDATION DEFINED

Let's begin the journey of validation with three distinct but related definitions of the concept. This will include practical, legal, and academic definitions of validity.

Practically speaking, a valid selection procedure is one that accurately measures the actual requirements of the job in a fair and reliable way. A valid selection procedure is one that "hits the mark," and does it consistently, with the mark being the core, essential requirements for a given position that are targeted by the selection procedure. A valid selection procedure effectively measures the net qualifications that are really needed for the job, and not much more or less.

In the legal realm, a selection procedure is valid if it can be proven by an employer in litigation that it is "... *job related and consistent with business necessity*" (to address the requirements of the 1991 Civil Rights Act, Section 703[k][1][A][i]). This standard is usually met (or not) by arguing how the selection procedure first addresses the Uniform Guidelines[1] (1978), followed by professional standards (i.e., the Standards and Principles, discussed below), then by parallel or lower courts that have applied the standard in various settings.

Academically, the Principles (2003) and Standards (1999) have adopted the same definition for validity: "The degree to which accumulated evidence and theory support specific interpretations of test scores entailed by proposed uses of a test."

OVERVIEW OF THE MECHANICS OF CONTENT AND CRITERION-RELATED VALIDITY

Subsequent chapters in this book describe in detail how to validate various selection procedures, so only a cursory overview of validation mechanics is provided here, and this is provided only as a primer to the subsequent, more advanced discussions.

How is a content validation study conducted? What are the mechanistic parts involved? What are the basic elements of a criterion-related validity study? Mechanically speaking, content and criterion-related validity are very different. Let's take a look at how they differ based on how they are constructed.

A content validity study is conducted by *linking* the essential parts of a job analysis (the job duties and/or knowledges, skills, abilities and personal characteristics – or KSPACs) to the selection procedure. Thus, content validity is formed by creating a *nexus* between the job and the selection procedure. It relies on a process that requires Job Experts (incumbents or immediate supervisors) to provide judgments (usually by providing ratings on surveys) regarding *if* and *how well* the selection procedure represents and measures the important parts of the job.

A word processing test that measures skills in using word processing software to edit and format business correspondence would likely be content valid for a clerical worker's job if they perform these functions. An entry-level physical ability test measuring fire scene physical performance uses a content validity approach for the position of firefighter.

Criterion-related validity is statistical. This type of validity is achieved when a selection procedure is statistically correlated with important aspects of job performance at a level that is "statistically significant" (with a probability value less than .05). One interesting benefit of this type of validity is that the employer is not pressed to define exactly what the selection procedure is measuring! While it is always a very good idea to know and describe to applicants the KSAPCs that are measured by the selection procedure, it is not a requirement to do so because the selection procedure is scientifically related to job performance. By contrast, content validity has specific requirements for the employer to show and describe exactly what KSAPCs are being measured by the selection procedure and how they related to the job (see 15C4 – 5 of the Uniform Guidelines).

Criterion-related validity can be achieved by correlating selection procedure scores to several different types of job performance measures, including both subjective and objective measures. The most typical subjective performance measures include supervisor ratings and/or peer ratings of work products (quality and/or quantity) or job performance, and performance review scores.[2] Objective measures can include quantifiable work output measures (e.g., number of widgets produced per hour), quality-related measures (e.g., number of widgets returned because of defects), absenteeism, turnover, disciplinary actions, safety incidents, and other aspects of performance that are gathered and recorded in a uniform and consistent manner.

BENEFITS OF THE VALIDATION PROCESS

Now that validation has been briefly defined, what is the value for the employer? Why validate selection procedures? "Validation is expensive" and "We are only required to validate a selection procedure if it has adverse impact" (a true statement) are statements that personnel consultants hear frequently. With formal validation studies sometimes costing in the tens of thousands of dollars, these are all legitimate concerns.

Validation generates two major benefits for the employer. First, validation helps insure that the selection process is measuring key, relevant job requirements in a reliable and consistent manner. This, of course, helps screen better workers into the workforce. Even if the validation process increases the effectiveness of a selection process only slightly, the results over years and hundreds of applicants can sometimes be astounding. Second, the validation process generates evidence (for use in litigation) that the selection procedures are "… job related and consistent with business necessity" (to address the requirements of the 1991 Civil Rights Act, Section 703[k][1][A][i]).

Related to this benefit, validated selection procedures can also dissuade potential plaintiffs from even beginning the lawsuit process if the relationship between the selection procedure and the job is sometimes self-evident (called "face validity"). Applicants are much less likely to challenge a selection procedure if it "smells and looks like the actual job." Likewise, plaintiff attorneys will be discouraged to gamble the time and money necessary to wage a "validation war" if the employer has conducted good-faith validation studies.

PROFESSIONAL STANDARDS FOR VALIDATION

In the early 1950s, three different aspects of validity were discussed – content, criterion-related, and construct (Principles, 2003, p. 5). From the 1950s to the publication of the 1978 Uniform Guidelines, these three remained as the concrete, "tried and true" validation strategies (especially in litigation settings). While the Uniform Guidelines set down these validation ground rules in 1978, the government foretold that the educational and personnel testing fields would continue to advance the science and art of validation, so it left a loophole for their future developments in framing the criteria that will be used for validating selection procedures:

> For the purposes of satisfying these guidelines, users may rely upon criterion-related validity studies, content validity studies or construct validity studies, in accordance with the standards set forth in the technical standards of these guidelines, section 14 of this part. New strategies for showing the validity of selection procedures will be evaluated as they become accepted by the psychological profession (Section 5A).

Fulfilling this expectation, the psychological community authored the 1985 version of the *Standards for Educational and Psychological Testing* (published by the American Educational Research Association, the American Psychological Association, and the National Council on Measurement in Education) and

Division 14 of the American Psychological Association (the Society for Industrial and Organizational Psychology, or SIOP) published the *Principles for the Validation and Use of Personnel Selection Procedures* (1987).

These two documents advanced the testing field to the current state of validation at that time. Fourteen years later (in 1999), the Standards were substantially updated. Following suit, the Principles received a major update 16 years later in 2003. While published by different associations, the Principles and Standards are virtually in agreement regarding the key aspects of validity (Principles, 2003, p. 4). Part of the motivating factor behind the publication of the new Principles was to provide an update to the earlier (1987) version based on the newly published Standards (1999).

At the heart of these two documents is how they define validity. Both the Standards and the Principles share the same voice on this matter, stating their current definition of validity as no longer the three conventional types of validity (like those discussed in the Uniform Guidelines, below), but moving to "... validity as a *unitary concept* with different sources of evidence contributing to an understanding of the inferences that can be drawn from a selection procedure" (Principles, 2003, p. 4).

The Standards and Principles allow five different "sources of evidence" to generate validity evidence under this "unitary concept" umbrella:

1.   relationships between predictor scores and other variables, such as selection procedure–criterion relationships;

2.   content (meaning the questions, tasks, format, and wording of questions, response formats, and guidelines regarding administration and scoring of the selection procedure. Evidence based on selection procedure content may include logical or empirical analyses that compare the adequacy of the match between selection procedure content and work content, worker requirements, or outcomes of the job);

3.   internal structure of the selection procedure (e.g., how well items on a test cluster together);

4.   response processes (examples given in the Principles include (a) questioning test takers about their response strategies, (b) analyzing examinee response times on computerized assessments, or (c) conducting experimental studies where the response set is manipulated); and

5.   consequences of testing (Principles, 2003, p. 5).

The Principles explain that these five "sources of evidence" (used for showing validity under the unitary validity concept) are not distinct types of validity, but rather "… each provides information that may be highly relevant to some proposed interpretations of scores, and less relevant, or even irrelevant to others" (p. 5).

UNIFORM GUIDELINES REQUIREMENTS FOR VALIDATION

The current government treatise for validation is the 1978 Uniform Guidelines. This document was assembled by a mutual effort by the US EEOC, Civil Service Commission, Department of Labor, and Department of Justice. The goal of publishing the Uniform Guidelines was to provide an objective standard by which testing and adverse impact concepts could be defined and used for government enforcement, arbitration, and litigation. Numerous earlier texts and enforcement guidelines existed prior to the Uniform Guidelines, but it is safe to say that the Uniform Guidelines constituted the most definitive treatise when published in 1978. The Uniform Guidelines remain mostly unchanged (only a few minor updates are pending at the time of this writing, which will constitute the first change since their original publication).

Three primary forms of validation are presented in the Uniform Guidelines: content, criterion-related, and construct (listed in the order most frequently used by employers):

- Content validity: Demonstrated by data showing that the content of a selection procedure is representative of important aspects of performance on the job. See section 5B and section 14C.

- Criterion-related validity: Demonstrated by empirical data showing that the selection procedure is predictive of, or significantly correlated with, important elements of work behavior. See sections 5B and 14B.

- Construct validity: Demonstrated by data showing that the selection procedure measures the degree to which candidates have identifiable characteristics which have been determined to be important for successful job performance. See section 5B and section 14D.

BLENDING THE PROFESSIONAL AND GOVERNMENT VALIDATION STANDARDS INTO PRACTICE

How are the professional standards different from the government standards? How are they similar? All three types of validation described in the Uniform

Guidelines are also contained in the professional standards (the Principles and Standards):

- The content validity described in the Uniform Guidelines is similar to the "validation evidence" source #2 and #5 (to a limited degree) of the professional standards.

- The criterion-related validity described in the Uniform Guidelines is similar to #1 and #5 of the professional standards.

- The construct validity described in the Uniform Guidelines is similar to #1, #3, and #5 of the professional standards.

When conducting a validation study, which set of standards should a practitioner be most concerned about? The Principles? Standards? Uniform Guidelines? The conservative answer is all three. If one had to choose a "primary set" of criteria, here are a few reasons to consider using the Uniform Guidelines:

- They have the backing of the US government (the EEOC, OFCCP, Department of Labor, Department of Justice, and nearly every state fair employment office).

- They are regularly used as the set of criteria for weighing validity studies during enforcement audits conducted by the OFCCP and numerous other state fair employment offices.

- They have been afforded "great deference" by the courts and have consistently been used as the measuring stick by the courts for assessing the merit of validity studies. They have been referenced thousands of times in judicial documents. By contrast, as of the year 2000, the Principles have only been referenced in 13 published federal court cases; the Standards have been referenced in ten, and they have sometimes been viewed as "lower on the totem pole" than the Uniform Guidelines.3

- If practitioners seek to address only the criteria in the Uniform Guidelines when conducting a validation study, there is a high likelihood that the key elements of the Standards and Principles will also be addressed (the reciprocal is also true, but only for some "sources of validation evidence" espoused by the professional standards).

This endorsement is provided with some hesitation, because the Principles and Standards offer a far more exhaustive set of guidelines and regulations than the Uniform Guidelines, and provide more complete guidance for many unique situations that emerge in testing situations.

Nonetheless, for these reasons stated above, the Uniform Guidelines are the primary set of criteria that will be addressed throughout this text as the standard for completing validation studies. Of the three validation types proposed in the Uniform Guidelines, only content and criterion-related validity will be reviewed. Construct validity will not be discussed further for a few key reasons. First, the author is not aware of any EEO-related case where a judge has endorsed a validation study based solely on construct validity. Because the concept is highly academic and theoretical, it is difficult for even advanced practitioners to build selection procedures based solely on construct validity. With this being the case, expert witnesses will find themselves hard-pressed to explain such concepts to a judge! Second, if one were to ask 100 validation experts to define construct validity, 50 or more unique definitions would probably emerge. Some would even contradict each other. Third, most forms of construct validity require some type of criterion-related validity evidence. This begs the question: why not just use criterion-related validity in the first place? For these reasons, the reader is referred to other texts if they desire to review the concept in more depth (see Cascio, 1998, pp. 108–111; Gatewood & Feild, 1994 [1986], pp. 220–221).

STEPS FOR COMPLETING A CONTENT VALIDATION STUDY

There are four steps for conducting a conventional content validation study: job analysis, selection plan, selection procedure development, and selection procedure validation. The first two steps form the essential foundation of a professionally conducted content validation study, and are the same regardless of the type of selection procedure that will be validated (e.g., a written test, physical ability test, interview, etc.). The steps and requirements for completing the last two steps are highly contingent on the type of selection procedure used.

A job analysis consists of a thorough analysis of the job duties and knowledges, skills, abilities, and personal characteristics (KSAPCs) required for a position. A selection plan extracts from the job analysis the key, essential KSAPCs and/or job duties that should be measured by the selection process. The steps for completing each are provided below in this chapter, and the following chapters describe how to develop and validate content valid selection procedures that can be linked back to the job analysis and selection plan components.

EIGHT STEPS FOR COMPLETING A JOB ANALYSIS

Developing a thorough and accurate job analysis is the most important step in a content validation study (it is also important for criterion-related validity, but less so). It is analogous to framing and pouring the foundation of a house – without a strong foundation, the rest of the building does not matter. The rest of the house will be either upright and stable, or crooked and shaky, based on the quality of the foundation.

There are numerous ways to complete a solid job analysis. While there is no "one right way," the steps below are provided as a template for developing a job analysis designed to provide a foundation for validation. This process is adopted from the Guidelines Oriented Job Analysis (GOJA) Process, which has been supported in numerous EEO cases[4] and reviewed in several textbooks and articles.[5] An evaluation copy of the full GOJA Manual is included on the Evaluation CD.

STEP 1: ASSEMBLE AND TRAIN A PANEL OF QUALIFIED JOB EXPERTS

Job Experts are qualified job incumbents who perform or supervise the target position. The following criteria are presented as guidelines for selecting the members of the panel. The Job Experts chosen should:

1.   Collectively represent the demographics of the employee population (with respect to gender, age, race, years of experience, etc.). It is a good idea to slightly over-sample gender and ethnic groups to insure adequate representation in the job analysis process.6

2.   Be experienced and active in the position they represent (e.g., Job Experts should not be on probationary status or temporarily assigned to the position). While seasoned Job Experts will often have a good understanding of the position, it is also beneficial to include relatively inexperienced Job Experts to integrate the "newcomer's perspective." However, at least one-year job experience should be a baseline requirement for Job Experts selected for the panel.

3.   Represent the various "functional areas" and/or shifts of the position. Many positions have more than one division or "work area" or even different shifts, where job duties and KSAPCs may differ.

4.   Include between 10% and 20% supervisors for a given position. For example, if a seven-to-ten-person Job Expert panel is used, include one to two supervisors on the panel.

How many Job Experts are necessary to include in the job analysis process to produce reliable results? Some courts have relied on as few as seven to ten Job Experts[7] for providing judgments and ratings about job and selection procedure characteristics. Figure 2.1 provides some guidance regarding the number of Job Experts necessary to obtain a statistically reliable and accurate estimate regarding job information.

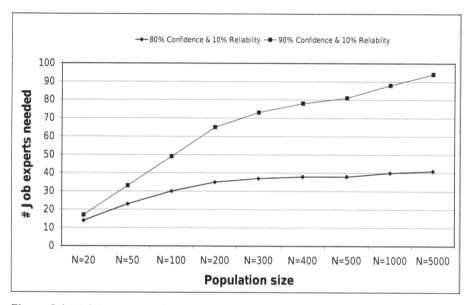

Figure 2.1   Job Expert sample size guidelines

For example, if there are currently 200 employees in a position and the employer desires to be 80% confident (with 10% "margin of error") that the collective opinions of a Job Expert panel will accurately represent the larger population of 200 employees, about 35 Job Experts are required. Using a 90% confidence level requires about 60 Job Experts.[8] Using 10 Job Experts provides about 66% (with 10% margin). While this figure and some court cases have provided guidance on this issue, practical judgment and workforce availability should be considered when assembling a panel of Job Experts.

It should be noted that there is a large "diminishing effect" that can be observed in Figure 2.1. For example, including 80 Job Experts in a population of 400 yields very similar levels of accuracy when compared to including 100 Job Experts for a population of 5000! The time and money that can be saved by using a "smart" rather than "huge" sampling strategy is very significant. It is not uncommon to find situations where employers unnecessarily involve hundreds and hundreds of "extra" subjects in a survey when a much smaller sample would have provided nearly identical results!

It should be noted that the GOJA Process described herein involves conducting a workshop with a Job Expert panel including seven to ten employees who currently hold the job. Based on the experience level of the researcher, the nature and type of the position being studied, and the Job Experts who are available, other job analysis methods may also be very useful. These include conducting structured interviews (of individual Job Experts or Job Expert panels), reviewing diaries, logs, or other work records, conducting time study analyses, administering questionnaires, or using checklists.

After designating the Job Experts who will participate in the job analysis process, they should be trained on the overall process and be informed that their responses should be both *independent* and *confidential* (i.e., not disclosed to anyone outside the job analysis Job Expert panel). Because each Job Expert's opinion should be counted equally regardless of rank or functional job area, it is often useful to explain to the Job Experts that the job analysis workshop is a meeting "without rank." It is important that each Job Expert's opinion be treated with equal weight. It is also useful for the group to be aware of the limitations of possible "group think." They should be encouraged to think independently.

STEP 2: JOB EXPERTS WRITE JOB DUTIES

In this step, Job Experts independently write job duties performed in the target position without providing any ratings (e.g., frequency, importance). Having Job Experts independently identify duties is an important first step in the job analysis process. This independent work – without a group or "paired" discussion – helps insure that the final combined list of duties (which is the next step) is as complete as possible. Job duties should usually begin with an action word, include the process (tasks) for completing the duty, and include the work product or outcome of the duty. For example: "Prepare correspondence using word processing software and reference documents and deliver to clients using e-mail."

Allowing multiple, independent opinions typically allows a final duty list to be created that, after being consolidated, includes two to three times the number of duties that any individual Job Expert recorded. Depending on the complexity of the job, providing Job Experts with one to two hours to record their job duties is usually sufficient.

STEP 3: CONSOLIDATE DUTIES INTO A MASTER DUTY LIST

After the Job Experts have independently recorded the duties of the target position, a facilitator should convene the panel and develop a master, consolidated list that reflects the majority opinion of the group. Using a 70%

consensus rule (e.g., 7 out of 10) for this step is suggested or a lower ratio may be used if the job analysis results will be sent in survey form to a larger Job Expert sample. At this step, job duties from pre-existing job descriptions and other suggestions or data from management should be integrated into the discussion and added to the master list if the majority of the Job Experts agree.

STEP 4: WRITE KSAPCs, PHYSICAL REQUIREMENTS, TOOLS & EQUIPMENT, OTHER REQUIREMENTS, AND STANDARDS

Have the Job Experts repeat the process described in Step 2, but for the KSAPCs, Physical Requirements, Tools & Equipment, Other Requirements, and Standards. The following definitions can be helpful for this step:

- Knowledges: A body of information applied directly to the performance of a duty. For example: Knowledge of construction standards, codes, laws, and regulations.

- Skill: A present, observable competence to perform a learned physical duty. For example: Skill to build basic wood furniture such as bookcases, tables, and benches from raw lumber, following written design specifications.

- Ability: A present competence to perform an observable duty or to perform a non-observable duty that results in a product. For example: Training ability to effectively present complex technical information to students in a formal classroom setting, using a variety of approaches as needed to maximize student learning.

- Personal Characteristics: These are characteristics that are not as *concrete* as individual knowledge, skills, or abilities. Examples include "dependability," "conscientiousness," or "stress tolerance." The Uniform Guidelines do not permit measuring *abstract traits* in content-validated selection process (see Section 14C1) unless they are clearly *operationally defined* in terms of observable aspects of job behavior.9 For example, while the characteristic "dependability" (if left undefined) is too abstract to directly measure in a selection process, if it can be defined as "promptness and regularity of attendance," which is an observable work behavior, it can be measured. "Stress tolerance," if not clearly operationally defined, is also too abstract for inclusion in a selection process under a content validity approach. However, if defined as "the ability to complete job duties in a timely and efficient manner while enduring stressful or adverse working conditions," it is converted into an essential work ability that is readily observable on the job. So, if one desires to include personal characteristics in the selection process, turn them from abstract ideas to concrete, observable skills and abilities that are job related.

Physical Requirements, Other Requirements, and Standards will vary greatly between jobs. Several existing taxonomies are available – see the GOJA Manual included in the Evaluation CD for several examples of each.

STEP 5: CONSOLIDATE KSAPCs, PHYSICAL REQUIREMENTS, TOOLS & EQUIPMENT, OTHER REQUIREMENTS, AND STANDARDS INTO A MASTER LIST

For this step, the Job Experts repeat the process described in Step 3, but for the KSAPCs, Physical Requirements, Tools & Equipment, Other Requirements, and Standards. As in Step 3, the KSAPCs, Physical Requirements, Tools & Equipment, Other Requirements, and Standards from pre-existing job descriptions and other suggestions or data from management can be included in the process.

STEP 6: HAVE JOB EXPERTS PROVIDE RATINGS FOR DUTIES, KSAPCs, AND PHYSICAL REQUIREMENTS

The Job Experts and supervisors can provide ratings now that a final list of duties and KSAPCs has been compiled. For job duties, Job Experts can provide the following ratings (see the GOJA Manual for sample rating scales):

- Frequency of Performance: How frequently is the job duty performed? Daily? Weekly? This is not a requirement under the Uniform Guidelines for *content validity*, but it is useful for several practical reasons. (Note, however, that *it is required* for criterion-related validity studies!) One of the useful purposes for this rating is for determining which job duties constitute *essential functions* under the Americans with Disabilities Act (Section 1630.2[n][3][iii]).

- Importance: How important is competent performance of the job duty? What are the consequences if it is not done or done poorly? The importance rating is perhaps one of the most critical ratings that Job Experts provide. Section 14C2 of the Uniform Guidelines states that the duties selected for a selection procedure (e.g., a work sample test) "... should be *critical* work behavior(s) and/or *important* work behavior(s) *constituting most of the job*." Thus, the Uniform Guidelines are clear that when using content validity for a work sample test, the selection procedure can be linked to a single critical duty ("critical" is later defined by the Uniform Guidelines as "necessary"), or several important duties that constitute most of the job.

For KSAPCs and Physical Requirements, Job Experts can rate:

- Links to Duties: Where is this KSAPC/Physical Requirement actually applied on the job? What are the job duties (by duty number) where it is used? This step is key for establishing content validity evidence. By linking the duties to the KSAPCs and Physical Requirements, a nexus is created showing where actual job skills (for example) are actually applied on the job. Completing this step addresses Section 14C4 of the Uniform Guidelines.

- Frequency: How often is this KSAPC/Physical Requirement applied on the job? While it is a good idea to obtain a direct rating from Job Experts on this factor, this question can also be answered by determining the job duty with the highest frequency rating to which the KSAPC/Physical Requirement is linked.

- Importance: How important is the KSAPC/Physical Requirement to competent job performance? This is perhaps the most important rating in a content validity study because the Uniform Guidelines require that a selection procedure measuring a KSAPC/Physical Requirement should be shown to be a "necessary prerequisite" of "critical or important work behaviors" and shown to be "used in the performance of those duties" (Sections 14C4 and 15C5). Because the Uniform Guidelines make this clear distinction between *only* "important" and "critical or necessary," the importance rating scale should take this into consideration by making a clear demarcation in the progression of importance levels between *important* and *critical*. A selection procedure measuring KSAPCs/Physical Requirements should be linked to critical and/or important work duties, and should be rated as "critical" or "necessary" by Job Experts.

All Job Experts who participated in the job analysis process can provide ratings; however, in Step 7, using only two supervisors is sufficient for providing the supervisor ratings. Calculating inter-rater reliability and removing outliers[10] from the data set can be a useful step for insuring that the raters are providing valid ratings.

After all ratings are collected, they should be reviewed for accuracy and completeness, and then averages for each job duty and KSAPC rating should be calculated. This should be performed before proceeding further because supervisors will consider the rating averages in subsequent steps.

OPTIONAL STEP FOR POSITIONS WITH A LARGE NUMBERS OF INCUMBENTS: DISTRIBUTE A JOB ANALYSIS SURVEY TO ADDITIONAL JOB EXPERTS FOR RATINGS

Completing the six steps above results in a completed job analysis that represents the collective and majority opinions of the seven to ten Job Experts included in the process. While including seven to ten Job Experts in the process is likely to provide accurate and reliable information about a position for many employers, increasing the Job Expert sample size will increase the accuracy and reliability of the information about the position (if there are more than ten Job Experts in the position).

Obtaining the opinions of additional Job Experts can be completed using a Job Analysis Survey (JAS). A JAS can be prepared by providing the duties, KSAPCs, and Physical Requirements in survey form to the Job Experts and having the Job Experts rate the "content" of each, in addition to all other standard "job-holder ratings." For example, Job Experts can use the following scale in a JAS for rating each duty:

This duty is (select one option from below) a duty that I perform.

1.   Not at all similar to (does not describe)

2.   Somewhat similar to (some of the objects listed and actions described in the duty are somewhat similar to the objects and actions in the duty performed in your job)

3.   Similar to (most of the objects listed and actions described in the duty are similar to the objects and actions in the duty performed in your job)

4.   The same as (extremely similar or exactly like)

Job Experts can use the following scale to rate each KSAPCs and Physical Requirements:

This KSAPC/Physical Requirement is (select one option from below) a KSAPC/Physical Requirement I apply on the job.

1.   Not at all similar to (does not closely describe)

2.   Somewhat similar to (somewhat describes)

3.   Similar to (closely describes)

4.   The same as (very accurately describes)

One potential benefit of providing the additional Job Expert group with a JAS is that the additional Job Experts may know of other legitimate job duties, KSAPCs, or Physical Requirements that are required for the position, but were not identified by the original Job Expert group. It is suggested to provide extra space on the JAS where the additional Job Experts can record and rate additional duties, KSAPCs, and/or Physical Requirements they identify while completing the JAS.

It is recommended to use 3.0 as the minimum average rating criteria for these two ratings when deciding whether to include a duty or KSAPC/Physical Requirement in a final job analysis.

STEP 7: HAVE TWO SUPERVISORS REVIEW THE COMPLETED JOB ANALYSIS AND ASSIGN SUPERVISOR RATINGS

After the final job duty, KSAPC, and Physical Requirements have been rated by the Job Experts and the ratings have been averaged, convene two supervisors (these supervisors may have participated in the first six steps of the process, or can be new to the GOJA Process) to assign the "Supervisor Only" Job Expert ratings. The ratings that supervisors should provide for job duties include:

- Percentage of Time: When considering all job duties, what percentage of a typical incumbent's time is spent performing this job duty? Evaluating the percentage of time that incumbents spend on a particular duty is one of several factors that should be considered when making essential function determinations under the 1990 Americans with Disabilities Act (Section 1630.2[n][3][iii]). While helpful, it is not absolutely required for content validation studies.

- Best Worker: What job duties distinguish the "minimal" from the "best" worker? Job duties that are rated high on the Best Worker rating are those that, when performed above the "bare minimum," distinguish the "best" performers from the "minimal." For example, lifting boxes and occasionally helping guests with luggage may be necessary for a hotel receptionist position. However, performing these job duties at a level "above the minimum" will not likely make any difference in a person's overall job performance. It would likely be other job duties such as "greeting hotel guests and completing check-in/check-out procedures in a timely and friendly fashion" that would distinguish between the "minimal" and the "best" workers for this job. The average rating on this scale can provide guidance for using a *work sample* type of content validity selection procedure on a pass/fail, ranking, or banding basis (see Section 14C9 of the Uniform Guidelines). It is not necessary to obtain this rating for job duties unless the employer desires to validate a *work sample* type of selection procedure (i.e., a selection procedure that relies on linkages to job duties and not necessarily KSAPCs).

- Fundamental: How fundamental is this job duty to the purpose of the job? Would the position be fundamentally different if this job duty was not required for performance? Handcuffing suspects is fundamental to the job of police officer. Rescuing victims is fundamental to the firefighter job. Fundamental job duties are duties that constitute "essential functions" under the 1990 Americans with Disabilities Act (this rating is helpful, but not necessary for validation). A job duty may be considered fundamental to the job in any of the following ways:

  - the duty is frequently performed (check the Frequency rating) and/or the proportion of work time spent on it is significant (check the average Percentage of Time rating); or

  - the consequence to the purpose of the job is severe if the job duty is not performed or if it is performed poorly (check the average Importance rating); or

  - removing the job duty would fundamentally change the job – in other words, the duty is fundamental because the reason the job exists is to perform the duty; or

  - there are a limited number of employees available among whom the performance of this job duty can be distributed; or

  - the duty is so highly specialized that the incumbent was placed in the job because of their expertise or ability to perform this particular job duty.

- Assignable (Assignable to Others): Can this job duty be readily assigned to another incumbent without changing the fundamental nature of the position? In such instances, the job duty should not be considered as an "essential function" under the 1990 Americans with Disabilities Act. For example, a job duty can be determined to be fundamental (using the "fundamental duty" rating) and hence also "essential" under the Americans with Disabilities Act; however, if such job duty can be readily assigned to another employee without changing the fundamental nature of the job, the job duty can be re-designated as not essential. Job duties which are frequently performed or which take up a large proportion of work time and which are important or critical, probably are not easily assigned to others. Duties which occur infrequently and/or which require a small percentage of work time can sometimes be assumed by others, regardless of how important or unimportant they are.

For KSAPCs and Physical Requirements, supervisors can rate:

- Minimum v. Helpful Qualifications: Is this KSAPC/Physical Requirement a necessity for the position? Or, while possibly helpful to the performance of the job, is it an absolute requirement? This rating can help determine which KSAPCs/Physical Requirements should be included in a selection process. Minimum qualifications are those that the applicant or candidate must have prior to entry into the position; helpful qualifications can still be included in the selection process (if they meet the other requirements discussed herein), but are not absolute necessities prior to entry.

- Level Needed for Success (for Job Knowledges Only): What level of this job knowledge is required on the first day of the job? Total, complete mastery? General familiarity? The data from these ratings are useful for choosing the job knowledges that should be included in a written job knowledge test (see Section 14C4 of the Uniform Guidelines for specific requirements for measuring job knowledge in a selection process).

- Level Needed Upon Entry: How much of this KSAPC/Physical Requirement will be required on the first day of the job? All? Some? None? Will some on-the-job training be provided, or will candidates be required to bring all of this KSAPC/Physical Requirement with them on the first day of the job, with no additional levels attained after hire? This rating provides direction on which KSAPCs/Physical Requirements to screen in a selection process. This is a requirement of the Uniform Guidelines (Section 14C1).

STEP 8: PREPARE FINAL JOB ANALYSIS DOCUMENT, INCLUDING DESCRIPTIVE STATISTICS FOR RATINGS

After compiling the Job Expert and supervisor rating data, a report should be compiled that provides descriptive statistics (e.g., means and standard deviations) for each rated item. The final data (e.g., job duties, KSAPCs, etc.) can be entered directly into the job analysis document, along with the means and standard deviations that accompany each, to compile a final job analysis for a position.

DEVELOPING A SELECTION PLAN

Now that a thorough job analysis has been developed, a selection plan is the next step in the content validation process. Completing a selection plan is the step in the validation process where the key, measurable KSAPCs and Physical Requirements are laid out as targets to be assessed by the selection process. A selection plan distills the complete list of KSAPCs and Physical Requirements into only those that can and should be tested by one or more selection procedures in the overall selection process. Thus, it begins with every KSAPC/Physical Requirement produced through the job analysis, and ends with a list of fewer KSAPCs/Physical Requirements after running each through the stepwise "selection plan screening process." This process uses the average KSAPC/Physical Requirement ratings provided by Job Experts, as shown below:

1. Importance: Select only the KSAPCs/Physical Requirements that are above a certain level on the Importance rating scale. It is usually sufficient to draw the line at one-half (0.5) a rating point above the level on the rating scale that distinguished between the "important" versus "critical and necessary" (e.g., require an average rating of 3.5 if 3.0 is "important" and 4.0 is "critical"). This is important because the KSAPCs/Physical Requirements selected for measurement should be those that are most critical for success on the job (see Section 14C4 of the Uniform Guidelines). It is possible to develop a valid selection procedure for measuring only "important" (not necessary) KSAPCs if they "constitute most of the job" (see Section 14C4 of the Uniform Guidelines).

2. Level Needed Upon Entry: Select only the KSAPCs/Physical Requirements that are above a certain level on this rating scale. Establish the point on the rating scale where more than one-half (51% +) of the level needed is required on the first day of the job. This step is important because the KSAPCs/Physical Requirements selected for measurement should be those needed upon entry to the job (see Sections 5F and 14C1 of the Uniform Guidelines).

3. Level Needed (Knowledges only): Select only the job knowledges that are required (on the first day of the job) at a "working" or "mastery" level. This step helps avoid measuring job knowledges that are not critical for job success, or can easily be looked up without a negative impact on the job. This step is only required if job knowledge tests will be included in the selection process, and is required to address Section 14C4 of the Uniform Guidelines.

4.   Minimum/Helpful Qualification (MQ/HQ): While it is possible to measure KSAPCs/Physical Requirements that are Helpful Qualifications and not absolutely "minimum" (if they meet the other steps above), it is typically a good idea to focus primarily on those that are absolutely necessary for the job (i.e., are MQs).

5.   Best Worker: Rank order the remaining KSAPCs/Physical Requirements (i.e., those that met the criteria above) from highest to lowest using the average Best Worker rating. This will place the "best predictors" for selecting the best workers at the top of the list.

After this five-step process has been used to filter the KSAPCs/Physical Requirements, conduct a meeting with the Job Experts and the Supervision/Management staff and discuss the selection procedures that have been used in previous selection processes and those that can possibly be used for future selection processes. Next, allow them input to choose which selection procedures will be used in the next selection process and how each will be used (pass/fail, ranked, or weighted and combined with other selection procedures – see Chapter 6 for a discussion of the various criteria for each). At a minimum, rank only on selection procedures that are among the highest on the Best Worker ratings, or those that received absolute ratings that were sufficiently high to justify ranking).

The following factors should be discussed when deciding which selection procedures to use, and how to use them (listed in priority order):

1.   Which selection procedures were most effective in selecting the most qualified incumbents? While a criterion-related validity study is required to answer this question definitively, management judgment can be used in most situations. Which proposed (but not yet used) selection procedures do we believe are most likely to screen in the best workers? What have similar employers used successfully? The reliability of the selection procedures can also be considered at this step (see Chapter 3 for a discussion on reliability).

2.   What degree of adverse impact did the previous selection procedures have against women and minorities? How does this weigh against the perceived level of effectiveness of these selection procedures? Are there alternatives that would have less adverse impact, but be substantially equally valid? (Section 3B of the Uniform Guidelines requires that employers make this consideration when using a selection procedure that has adverse impact.)

3.   Which selection procedures are easiest to administer? Which take the longest time to complete and score? For example, a written test can be administered to 1000 applicants with much less time and administrative effort than an interview involving multiple rater panels.

4.   What are the costs of the selection procedures? Notice that this factor is last on the list. When making selection decisions that impact the overall performance of an employer, the careers and livelihoods of individuals, and impact the social community as a whole, other factors should be considered above cost whenever possible.

Table 2.1 provides an example of what this five-step process will produce. Notice that the KSAPCs in Table 2.1 are ranked from top to bottom based on their average Best Worker rating assigned by Job Experts. Reproducing all of the relevant KSAPC ratings allows management to make informed decisions on if and how each will be assessed in the selection process.

Table 2.1   Selection plan example

KSAPC/ Physical Req.	KSAPC/Physical Requirement Rating					Selection Procedure and Use (_P_ass/_F_ail, _R_ank, or _C_ombine*)			
Knowledge, Skill, Ability, Personal Characteristic, or Physical Requirement	Best Worker (1–5)	Level Needed Upon Entry (1–4)	Level Needed (Knowledges only) (1–4)	Importance (1–5)	Minimum/Helpful Qualification (MQ/HQ)	Application Form	Written Test	Structured Interview	Background Check
Interpersonal and teamworking skills	4.2	3.2	N/A	4	MQ			R	
Verbal communication skills	3.9	3.5	N/A	3.7	MQ			R	
Knowledge of State vehicle code	2.6	3.5	3.4	3.9	MQ		P/F		
Upper body strength	1.9	3.9	N/A	3.4	MQ				
Basic math skills	1.4	3.5	N/A	3.1	MQ				

* The score from this selection procedure will be combined with scores from other selection procedures in the selection process.

CONTENT VALIDATION REQUIREMENTS FOR "WORK SAMPLE" AND "KSAPC" TYPES OF SELECTION PROCEDURES

The Uniform Guidelines present different criteria for validating "work sample" tests (i.e., tests that attempt to directly mirror or replicate one or more job duties) and KSAPC tests (i.e., tests that measure KSAPC without necessarily directly mirroring or replicating the job). Table 2.2 shows these requirements by type of test.

Section 14C1 of the Uniform Guidelines states:

> *Selection procedures which purport to measure knowledges, skills, or abilities may in certain circumstances be justified by content validity, although they may not be representative samples, if the knowledge, skill, or ability measured by the selection procedure can be operationally defined as provided in paragraph 14C(4) of this section, and if that knowledge, skill, or ability is a necessary prerequisite to successful job performance.*

This clarification is needed because sometimes content valid selection procedures that measure KSAPCs do not necessary resemble or "closely approximate" the job. Consider reading ability, for example. Reading ability might be a critical, "needed on day one" requirement for the position of police officer, but reading ability can be measured in a valid way without having the applicant read and take a written test on police-related information. In fact, the reading ability of applicants applying for the police department could be measured by having the applicants read a ten-page narrative (written at a grade level needed for success as a police officer) about basket weaving and answer questions to demonstrate adequate comprehension. While basket weaving has absolutely nothing to do with the job of police officer, consider how such a test measures up to the KSAPC test requirements shown in Table 2.2:

Does the basket weaving reading comprehension test:

1. Measure an ability (reading) that is defined in terms of observable aspects of work behavior? Yes, provided that the reading ability in the job analysis (to which this test is linked) is linked to job duties that are observable.

2. Measure the intended KSAPC (reading ability)? Yes, provided that the test measures reading ability at the level necessary for the job.

3. Represent a sample of the KSAPC (reading ability)? Yes, provided that the sentence structure and reading level are similar. Police Table officers are likely to read ten pages or less with certain necessary levels of comprehension.

Table 2.2   Content Validity requirements for work sample and KSAPC tests

Requirements for work sample tests	Requirements for KSAPC tests
Test must be a **representative sample** of the **behavior** measured, or of a **work product** of the job.	Knowledges must be **operationally defined** (as a body of learned information which is (1) used in and (2) a necessary prerequisite for observable aspects of work behavior. SAPCs must be **defined in terms of observable aspects of work behavior**.
The **manner** of the test should **closely approximate** the work situation.	Show that the **test measures the intended KSAPC.**
The **setting** of the test should **closely approximate** the work situation.	Show that the test is a **representative sample** of the KSAPC.
The **level of complexity** of the test should **closely approximate** the work situation.	Show that the KSAPC measured is **used in the performance** of a critical or important work behavior(s).
	Show that the KSAPC measured is a **necessary prerequisite** to performance of critical or important work behavior(s).
	For SAPCs, the SAPC should either **closely approximate** an observable work behavior, or its product should closely approximate an observable work product.

4. Measure a KSAPC that is used in the performance of a critical or important work behavior(s)? Yes, provided that reading ability is linked to critical or important job duties.

5. Measure a necessary prerequisite to performance of critical or important work behavior(s)? Yes, provided that reading ability has been rated sufficiently high on the importance scale used.

6. Closely approximate an observable work behavior, or does its product closely approximate an observable work product? Yes, a police officer can be observed reading and studying new laws, bulletins, etc.

Now, would it be a better idea to administer a reading ability test that used content that was similar in content to the job? Yes, the more closely the content of the test represents the job, the better! This adds to the face validity of the process and helps improve applicants' perception of the fairness of the process as a whole. As such, the example above is provided for illustration purposes only. One could certainly make a case for using sample job material (e.g., sample police policies and procedures, vehicle traffic codes, etc.) because the psychological processes of comprehending this type of material may be slightly different than those used when learning about basket weaving (e.g., especially if one type was more or less abstract or concrete than the other).

Next, consider a test event commonly found in physical ability tests for the position of firefighter called a "Dry Hose Advance." This event is one of several events in a test used to screen applicants for the position of entry-level firefighter. To take the test, applicants are required to wear firefighter protective clothing (including pants, coat, gloves, and a 20-pound breathing apparatus) since this is how the event is performed on the job. This event measures the applicant's ability to take a dry (not charged with water) 1 1/2 inch fire attack hose line from a fire truck and extend the hose 150 feet (which simulates taking the hose line from the truck and deploying it to the position where it will be used to attack the fire).

Does this test event mimic the job? Yes – almost exactly (and as best as can be hoped for without lighting an actual fire). When linking this event back to the job analysis (to complete the essential nexus necessary for content validity), where does it fit? Is this a *work sample* or a *KSAPC* test? It is clearly a work sample test. Consider how this test fares when running it through the criteria shown in Table 2.2 for work sample tests.

Is the Dry Hose Advance test:

1. A *representative sample* of the behavior measured, or of a work product of the job? Yes, clearly. Firefighters perform this exact same event, even for a similar distance, while performing it on the job. The only difference on the job is the fire and the smoke that may be present.

2. Conducted in a *manner that closely approximates* the work situation? Yes, the physical movements and actions in this test event are done in a way that very closely approximates the work situation, and does not require specialized training.

3. Conducted in a way that the *setting* of the test *closely approximates* the work situation? Yes, both the test and the actual job duty it simulates are done outside, by one person, using a "transverse hose bed" and are done in a way where speed is of the essence.

4. Conducted in a way that the *level of complexity* of the test *closely approximates* the work situation? Yes, the test is not too difficult or easy compared to the job. It is about the same.

This example is intended to show that work sample tests – more so than KSAPC tests – need to be specific about such factors as "how long," "how heavy," "how far," "how difficult," etc.

CRITERION-RELATED VALIDITY

OVERVIEW

The Uniform Guidelines define criterion-related validity as, "Data showing that a selection procedure is predictive of, or significantly correlated with, important elements of job performance." How is this different than content validity? First let's consider what criterion-related validity can do that content validity cannot.

The Uniform Guidelines state that a content validity strategy is "… not appropriate for demonstrating the validity of selection procedures which purport to measure traits or constructs such as intelligence, aptitude, personality, common sense, judgment, leadership, and spatial ability" (Section 14C1). It has been mentioned previously that content validity can, in fact, be used to measure some of these "more abstract traits" if they are operationally defined in terms of observable aspects of the job (see Section 14C4 and Questions & Answers #75). That is, if they are converted from "generic abstracts" into concrete, measurable characteristics that are defined in ways they can be observed on the job, they are fair game for measurement under a content validation strategy.

But what if they cannot be converted in this way? Is it permissible to measure these traits *at all*? Yes, and this is where criterion-related validity comes in. Hypothetically speaking, an employer defending a selection procedure that is based on criterion-related validity could stand up in court and say:

> *Your honor, I don't know exactly what this test is measuring, but I do know it works. Applicants who score high on this test typically turn out to be our best workers, and applicants who score low typically do not. We know this because we conducted a study where we correlated test scores to job performance ratings and the study showed a correlation of .35, which is statistically significant at the .01 level – meaning that we are highly assured that the relationship between test scores and job performance is well beyond what we would expect by chance alone.*[11]

It would be nice if the defense of a selection procedure based on criterion-related validity was this simple! This "simple defense," however, is in fact true *in concept*. Content validity battles in litigation are always much more involved, with experts fighting over the complex nuances of what constitutes a "defensible content validity study" that addresses government and professional standards. This is because criterion-related validity is by nature empirical – the employer either has a statistically significant correlation or does not. With content validation, the end decision regarding its merit is typically based on a judgment call regarding the relative degree of content validity evidence that exists based on a job analysis remaining parts of the study.

Criterion-related validity studies can be conducted in one of two ways: using a *predictive* model or a *concurrent* model. A predictive model is conducted when applicant test scores are correlated to subsequent measures of job performance (e.g., six months after the tested applicants are hired). A concurrent model is conducted by giving a selection procedure to incumbents who are currently on the job and then correlating these scores to current measures of job performance (e.g., performance review scores, supervisor ratings, etc.).

Before going into detail regarding the mechanics on how to complete a criterion-related validity study using either of these two methods, a brief caution is provided first: completing a criterion-related validity study is a gamble. If an employer has been using a written test for years, and has never completed any type of study to evaluate its validity, a criterion-related validity study would be the easiest type of validation study to conduct. Just gather selection procedure scores for applicants who have been hired over the past several years and enter them into a column in a spreadsheet next to another column containing their average performance ratings, use the =PEARSON command in Microsoft Excel to correlate the two columns and presto! Instant validity. Or not.

If the resulting correlation value from the =PEARSON command is statistically significant, good news: your selection procedure is valid (providing that a host of other issues are addressed!). But what if the correlation value is a big, round zero (meaning no validity whatsoever)? Even worse, what if the correlation is negative (indicating the best test takers are the worst job performers)?

If this type of "quick correlation study" is conducted, and the employer had a sufficient sample size (see discussion below on statistical power), they just invalidated their selection procedure! The drawback? The employer is now open for lawsuits if the information is exposed, or negative information is now available if a lawsuit is currently pending. The benefit? Now the employer can discontinue using the invalid selection procedure and replace it with something much better. This dilemma is referred to among personnel researchers as the "validator's gamble."

STEPS FOR COMPLETING A CRITERION-RELATED VALIDITY STUDY

Before reviewing the steps to complete a criterion-related validity study, a brief discussion on statistical power and reliability are necessary. The reason for this is simple. Without these two ingredients, the rest of the recipe does not matter! Conducting a criterion-related validity study without sufficiently high statistical power and reliability is like trying to bake bread without yeast.

STATISTICAL POWER

Statistical power is the ability of a statistical test (in this case, a Pearson Correlation) to detect a statistically significant result *if it exists to be found*. In the case of correlations, statistical power highly depends on the size of the correlation coefficient the researcher expects to find in the population being sampled. If the researcher suspects that there is a (decent sized) correlation coefficient of .30 in the sample being researched (and they suspect that this correlation can only be in the favorable direction – positive – which requires a one-tail statistical test), 64 subjects are necessary to be 80% confident (i.e., to have 80% power) that the study will result in a statistically significant finding at the .05 level (if it is exists in the population). If the researcher suspects a smaller, but still significant, correlation of .20 exists in the population, 150 subjects are necessary for the same levels of power.

To avoid a gamble, use at least 200 subjects. Using a large sample will provide the researcher with high levels of power to find a statistically significant finding if it exists and will provide assurance that if the study did not result in a statistically significant finding that it was not because the sample was too small (but rather because such a finding just did not exist in the first place!).

CRITERION AND SELECTION PROCEDURE RELIABILITY

It is noted in the steps below that both the criterion measures (e.g., supervisor ratings) and selection procedures (e.g., a written test in the study) should have sufficiently high levels of reliability (at least .60 for the criterion measures and .70 or higher for the selection procedures). The reason for this can be explained with a simple rational explanation, followed by some easy math.

The rational reason why an unreliable measure (i.e., the criterion measure or the selection procedure) can spoil a criterion-related validation study is this: if a measure is inconsistent (unreliable) by itself, it will also be inconsistent when asked to (mathematically) cooperate with another variable (as in the case of the correlation required for criterion-related validity). A selection procedure that is not sure about what it is measuring by itself will not be any more sure about what it is measuring related to another variable (like the criterion measure)!

Mathematically, this is explained with a concept called the "theoretical maximum," which states that the maximum correlation that two variables can produce is limited by the square root of the product of their reliability coefficients. How does this work out practically? Consider a selection procedure with a reliability of .80 and a criterion measure with a low reliability of .40. The maximum correlation one can expect given the unreliability of these two variables (especially the criterion measure) is .57. If the reliabilities are .50 and .60, the maximum correlation that can be obtained is .55. With reliabilities of

.90 and .60, a maximum of .73 is possible. With this caution, be sure that the criterion measure and the selection procedure have sufficiently high levels of reliability! A researcher will be quite disappointed to go through the steps for completing a criterion-related validation process, only to find out that the study did not stand a chance in the first place of resulting with significant findings!

So, assuming that the researcher has a sufficiently large sample (power), and reliable criterion measures and selection procedures, the following steps can be completed to conduct a *predictive* criterion-related validity study:

1.   Conduct a job analysis (see previous section) or a "review of job information." Unlike content validity, a complete A to Z job analysis is not necessary for a criterion-related validity study (see Sections 14B3 and 15B3 of the Uniform Guidelines).

2.   Develop one or more criterion measures by developing subjective (e.g., rating scales) or objective measures (e.g., absenteeism, work output levels) of critical areas from the job analysis or job information review. A subjectively rated criterion can only consist of performance on a job duty (or group of duties). In most cases it should not consist of a supervisor's or peer's rating on the incumbent's level of KSAPCs (a requirement based on Section 15B5 of the Uniform Guidelines) unless the KSAPCs are clearly linked to observable work behaviors. It is critical that these measures have sufficiently high reliability (at least .60 or higher is preferred).

3.   Work with Job Experts and supervisors, trainers, other management staff, and the job analysis data to form solid speculations ("hypotheses") regarding which KSAPCs "really make a difference" in the high/low scores of such job performance measures (above). Important: if the job analysis for the position included Best Worker ratings, these should provide a good indicator regarding the KSAPCs that distinguish job performance in a meaningful way. These ratings can be used to key in on the prime KSAPCs that are most likely to result in a significant correlation with job performance measures.

4.   Develop selection procedures that are *reliable* measures of those KSAPCs. Choosing selection procedures that have reliability of .70 or higher is preferred.

5.   After a period of time has passed and criterion data has been gathered (e.g., 3–12 months), correlate each of the selection procedures to the criterion measures using the =PEARSON command in Microsoft Excel and evaluate the results.12

To complete a *concurrent* criterion-related validation study, complete steps 1–4 above and replace step 5 by administering the selection procedure to the *current incumbent population* and correlate the selection procedure scores to current measures of job performance.

Let's now assume your study outputs resulted in one or more significant correlations. How can these be interpreted? The US Department of Labor (2000, pp. 3-10) has provided the reasonable guidelines shown in Table 2.3 for interpreting correlation coefficients.

Table 2.3   Guidelines for interpreting correlations

Coefficient value	Interpretation
Above .35	Very beneficial
.21 - .35	Likely to be useful
.11 - .20	Depends on circumstances
Below .11	Unlikely to be useful

ADVANCED CRITERION-RELATED VALIDITY TOPICS

This text is designed to provide a fundamental overview of the key components of a criterion-related validity study. Because this type of validation is statistical in nature, there is a practically endless scope of tools, calculations, and issues related to this topic. Some of these are outlined below:

- Expectancy tables and charts: Once a statistically significant correlation has been identified, there are a vast number of calculations that can be used to practically evaluate the impact of using the validated selection procedure in a selection process. Expectancy tables can show, with mathematical accuracy, the expected increase in job performance that can be obtained by ratcheting up (or down) the cutoff used for the selection procedure. For example, a selection procedure with a high correlation to job performance might show that if the employer uses a cutoff of 65% on the selection procedure that expected job performance levels would be a "6.0" (on a scale of 1–9); whereas a cutoff of 80% might equate to a 7.0, etc. The reader is referred to a statistical program titled Theoretical Expectancy Calculator by Personnel Decisions International Corporation for a useful tool for making these (and other related) calculations.

- Cross validation: This is another important concept related to criterion-related validity studies. Cross validation is a useful tool for determining the transportability or "generalizability" of one study's findings to another setting. This can be done mathematically using formulas that adjust the correlation coefficient found in one study, or empirically by taking the selection procedure to that other setting and evaluating the correlation coefficient found in the new setting. It should be noted that correlation values almost always get smaller when this process is done, which means that the correlation values obtained in a single sample are often inflated due to the unique characteristics of that employer, selection procedure, and the combination thereof.

• Corrections: Statistical correlations are typically repressed (i.e., smaller than they could be) because of a phenomena called *range restriction* (that occurs on the selection procedure and/or criterion measures) and because of the unreliability of the criterion and/or the selection procedure. Range restriction occurs on the selection procedure when some of the applicant scores are not included in the study (because they failed the selection procedure). Range restriction occurs on the criterion measure when some of the job incumbents self-select out of the sample or are terminated (e.g., by finding another job). Range restriction reduces the amount of variance in the correlation study, which lowers the power of the study (an ideal study is one that includes both the low- and high-end of test takers and job performers). Corrections can also be made to adjust for the unreliability of the criterion measure, *but corrections should not be made to the selection procedure* (because this is a real limitation that is present in both the study and in the future use of the selection procedure). Formulas to correct for range restriction and unreliability can be found in Guion, 1998; Cascio, 1998; and Hubert & Feild, 1994.

• Bias: If an adequate sample exists for minorities and/or women (typically a minimum rule of 30 are necessary), a study of bias can be conducted to assess whether the selection procedure is a fair and accurate predictor for both majority and minority groups. The procedures for conducting such studies can also be found in Guion, 1998; Cascio, 1998; and Hubert & Feild, 1994.

NOTES

1. While the Uniform Guidelines do not formally constitute a set of legal requirements, they have consistently been awarded "great deference" starting as early as the Griggs v. Duke Power Company (401 US 424, 1971) case. They have also been unilaterally adopted verbatim as a legal standard in several cases – e.g., Brown v. Chicago (WL 354922, N.D. III, 1998).

2. It is important to note that the Uniform Guidelines require that criterion measures consist of *actual job performance*, not ratings of the overall knowledge, skill, ability or personal characteristics of the incumbents (see Section 15B).

3. For example, in Lanning v. Southeastern Pennsylvania Transportation Authority (181 F.3d 478, 80 FEPC., BNA, 221, 76 EPD P 46,160 3rd Cir.(Pa.) June 29, 1999 (NO. 98-1644, 98-1755), the court stated: "The District Court seems to have derived this standard from the Principles for the Validation and Use of Personnel Selection Procedures ("SIOP Principles") ... To the extent that the SIOP Principles are inconsistent with the mission of Griggs and the business necessity standard adopted by the Act, they are not instructive" (FN20).

4. Some of these cases include: Forsberg v. Pacific Northwest Bell Telephone (840 F2d 1409, CA-9 1988; Gilbert v. East Bay Municipal Utility District (DC CA, 19 EPD 9061, 1979); Martinez v. City of Salinas (DC CA, No. C-78-2608 SW (S.J.); Parks v. City of Long Beach (DC CA, No. 84-1611 DWW [Px]); Sanchez v. City of Santa Ana (DC CA, No. CV-79-1818 KN); Simmons v. City of Kansas City (DC KS, No. 88-2603-0); and US v. City of Torrance (DC CA, No. 93-4142-MRP [RMCx]).

5. Buford, J. A. (1991), *Personnel Management and Human Resources in Local Government*, Alabama: Center for Governmental Services, Auburn University. Gatewood, R. S. & Feild, H. S. (1994 [1986]), *Human Resource Selection*, Orlando, FL: Drydan Press; Buford, J. A. (1985), *Recruiting and Selection: Concepts and Techniques for Local Government*, Alabama: Alabama Cooperative Extension Service, Auburn University; Schuler, R. S. (1981), *Personnel and Human Resource Management*, New York: West Publishing Company; Bemis, S. E., Belenky, A. H., & Soder, D. A. (1984), *Job Analysis: An Effective Management Tool*, Washington, DC: Bureau of National Affairs; Campbell, T. (July, 1982), Entry-level exam examined in Court, *The Western Fire Journal*, 1–5.

6. Employers who have been challenged in court for employment discrimination and who have included only majority group members in the job analysis or validation process typically have a difficult time defending themselves in court.

7. Contreras v. City of Los Angeles (656 F.2d 1267. 9th Cir. 1981) and US v. South Carolina (434 US 1026, 1978).

8. Arkin, H., & Colton, R. R. (1950), *Tables for Statisticians*. New York: Barnes & Noble. Technical note: other sampling techniques can be useful for estimating the sample sizes necessary for estimating the average ratings for the job analysis rating scales; however, because most of the (somewhat continuous) scales are used in a dichotomous fashion (and further because the population standard deviations are unknown in each job analysis study), the population proportion formula was used for estimating these sample size requirements.

9. See Section 14C1 and 14C4 of the Uniform Guidelines and Questions & Answers #75.

10. If there are 3–5 raters or less than 20 ratings provided by each rater, it is recommended to eliminate individual ratings (and not entire raters) that have been identified as outliers using a 1.645 standard deviation rule (all ratings that are 1.645 standard deviations above or below the mean are deleted). If there are more than five raters or the raters are providing more than 20 ratings each, consider removing entire raters from the data set if they are identified as outliers using this same rule. Using this criteria will serve to "trim" the average ratings that are in the upper or lower 5% of the distribution.

11. This hypothetical example, of course, assumes that the employer adequately addressed all of the nuances required for defensible criterion-related validity studies.

12. The reader is cautioned against making too many correlational comparisons because doing so increases the odds of finding statistically significant correlations that are due to chance alone.

CHAPTER 3

Developing, Validating, and Analyzing Written Tests

While many types of selection procedures are frequently litigated, none are as vulnerable as the infamous written test. There are at least two reasons for this. First, written tests typically have higher levels of adverse impact against minorities (Sackett, 2001; Neisser, 1996) than other types of selection procedures, making them eligible for civil rights litigation. Second, they are sometimes only theoretically related to the job, or not sufficiently related to the job. Despite these drawbacks, written tests are frequently valid predictors of job success and are typically not biased against minorities (Principles, 2003, p. 32).

For these reasons, employers should complete validation studies on written tests. Completing a thorough validation process helps insure that the test used for selection or promotion is sufficiently related to the job (and includes only test items that Job Experts have deemed fair and effective) and generates documentation that can be used as evidence should the test ever be challenged in an arbitration or civil rights litigation setting.

It would be difficult if not impossible to create a step-by-step instruction guide for developing and validating all of the different types of written tests that are commonly used by employers. Because test content varies based on the *types* of KSAPCs measured, the *level* they are measured (e.g., entry-level testing versus promotional), and the *purpose* of the test (e.g., employment, licensing, credentialing, etc.) this becomes an even more difficult task.

This chapter is not written to take the weight of this burden. Rather, it is designed to provide a basic blueprint that can be followed for developing and validating some of the most commonly used tests by employers, such as:

- mechanical ability
- cognitive ability
- situational judgment
- reading comprehension
- math skills
- job knowledge
- problem solving/decision making skills.

The chapter assumes that the reader will be using a conventional written test format (e.g., multiple choice questions) to measure KSAPCs that are necessary for entry-level or promotional testing purposes. While some of the content herein is relevant for educational and/or credentialing or licensure tests, it is not designed to specifically address these testing situations. See the Appendix for a document describing seven specific steps that can be followed for developing a content valid job knowledge written test.

The steps below can be followed to develop and validate most written tests that will measure KSAPCs needed for the job.

STEP 1: DETERMINE THE KSAPCs TO BE MEASURED BY THE TEST

The selection plan described in Chapter 2 can be used for selecting the KSAPCs that can be measured by the written test. If a selection plan has not been completed, consider using the criteria below (as baselines). The KSAPCs selected for the written test should be:

1. "needed day one" on the job;

2. important or critical (necessary) for the performance of the job;[1]

3. linked to one or more critical (necessary) job duties; and

4. *for job knowledges only*, rated sufficiently high on the "Level Needed for Success" rating (see the Job Analysis section in Chapter 2 and the Appendix). This is necessary for insuring that the job knowledge domains measured by the test are needed (on the first day of hire) at a level that requires the applicant to have the information in memory (written tests should not measure aspects of a job knowledge that can simply be looked up or referenced by incumbents on the job without serious impacting job performance).

It is important to note the KSAPC selected for measurement on the written test should meet these criteria both *generally* (i.e., as defined in the job analysis) and *specifically* (i.e., the *separate facets or aspects* of the selected KSAPCs should also meet these criteria). For example, if "basic math" is required for a job and it meets the criteria above, test items should not be developed for measuring *advanced* math skills.

STEP 2: DEVELOP A TEST PLAN FOR MEASURING THE SELECTED KSAPCs

There are three areas that should be addressed for developing a solid written test plan:

- *general components* of a test plan;

- choosing the *number* of test items; and

- choosing the *types* of test items.

Each of these areas is discussed below.

GENERAL COMPONENTS OF A TEST PLAN

The elements and steps necessary for a written test plan will vary based on the types of KSAPCs measured by the test. The components below should therefore be regarded as general requirements:

- What is the purpose for the test? Will it be used to qualify only those who possess mastery levels of the KSAPC? Advanced levels? Baseline levels?

- Will the test be scored in a multiple hurdle or compensatory fashion? Multiple hurdle tests require applicants to obtain a passing score on each section of the written test. Compensatory tests allow an applicant's high score in one area to compensate for an area in which they scored low. A multiple hurdle strategy should be used if certain, baseline levels of proficiency are required for each KSAPC measured by the test; a compensatory approach can be used if the developer will allow higher levels of one KSAPC to compensate for another on the test. Evaluating how the KSAPCs are required and used on the job is a key consideration for making this decision.

- What is the target population being tested? Has the applicant population been pre-screened using minimum qualification requirements?

- Will the test be a *speeded* test or a *power* test? A test is considered a speeded test when time is considered an element of measurement on the test (for reasons that are related to the job) and it is not necessary to allow the vast majority of applicants to complete the test within the time limit (some tests based on criterion-related validity are designed with speed as an essential component of the test). A power test allows at least 95% of the applicants to complete the test within the allotted time. Most written tests are administered as power tests.

- What reading level will be used for the test? Most word processing programs include features for checking the grade reading level of the test, which should be slightly below the reading level required at entry to the job.

- What will be the delivery mode of the test (e.g., paper/pencil, oral, computer-based testing)?

- What scoring processes and procedures will be used?

- Will a test preparation or study guide be provided to applicants? Test preparation and study guides can be developed at many levels, ranging from a cursory overview of the test and its contents to an explicit description of the KSAPCs that will be measured.

- Will test preparation sessions be offered to the applicants?

CHOOSING THE NUMBER OF TEST ITEMS

Some of the key considerations regarding selecting the number of items to include on the written test are:

- Making an *adequate* sampling of the KSAPCs measured. A sufficient number of items should be developed to effectively measure each KSAPC at the desired level. Note that some KSAPCs will require more items than others for making a "sufficiently deep" assessment of the levels held by the applicants. Be sure that the important aspects of each KSAPC are included in the test plan (see the Appendix for a sample test plan for job knowledge tests).

- Making a *proportional* sampling of the KSAPCs. This pertains to the number of items measuring each KSAPC compared with others. The test should be internally weighted in a way that insures a robust measurement of the relevant KSAPCs (this is discussed in detail below). Special consideration should be given to this proportional sampling requirement when developing job knowledge tests (see the TVAP® User Manual on the Evaluation CD for a sample test plan for job knowledge tests).

- Including a sufficient number of items to generate high test reliability. While there are numerous factors that impact test reliability, perhaps the single most important factor is the number of test items per relevant KSAPC and in the test overall.

There are no hard-and-fast rules regarding the number of items to include for measuring a KSAPC. A developer can have few or many test items for any "testable KSAPC" (those that meet the criteria above); however, some rational or empirical process for internally weighting the written test is helpful and usually makes the test more effective. Here are some guidelines to consider:

- Some KSAPCs are more complex or broad than others, and thus may require more test items for adequate measurement. For example, finding out how much an applicant knows about advanced physics may require more items than assessing their simple multiplication skills, which can be assessed with fewer items.

- If several discrete KSAPCs will be measured on the same written test, be sure that they are not *divergent*. If they are, put them on separate tests (or on the same test as a subscale that is scored separately). If the test will be scored and used as one, overall assessment (i.e., with one final score for each applicant), the various KSAPCs on the test will need to be *homogeneous* (i.e., having similar types of variance because they are based on similar or inter-related content and items of similar difficulty levels). If one KSAPC is substantially different from others on the same test, the test items will be working against each other and will decrease the overall reliability (making the interpretation of a single score for the test inaccurate).

- As a general rule, do not measure a discrete KSAPC with fewer than 20 items, and be sure that the overall test includes at least 60 items if measuring more than one KSAPC. This will help insure that the test will have sufficiently high reliability.

One of the factors for choosing the number of items to include on the test (and from which KSAPCs) is to internally weight the test in a way that is relevant to the requirements of the job. One effective system for developing internal weights for a test is to have Job Experts assign point values to the various sections of the test. For example, if there are five different KSAPCs measured by the test, the Job Expert panel can be asked to assign 100 points among the five KSAPCs to come up with a final weighting scheme for the test.

The drawback to using this approach is that the items will now require *polytomous weighting* (e.g., 0.8 points for the items measuring KSAPC A, 1.2 points for each item measuring KSAPC B, etc.). This can be avoided by simply adding or removing the number of items to each section as necessary to match the test weighting provided by Job Experts, being careful not to have too few items on any given section.

CHOOSING THE TYPE OF TEST ITEMS

What type of test items should be included on the test to measure the KSAPCs? Complex? Easy? Difficult? When measuring job knowledge domains, should items be included that measure the difficult, complex, evaluative aspects of the knowledge, or just the simple facts and definitions? The key consideration regarding selecting the type of items for a test is making sure that the KSAPCs are measured in a *relevant* way using items that are appropriately geared to the level of the KSAPC that is required on the job.

One helpful tool for making item type considerations is Bloom's Taxonomy (1956), which can be adopted as a model for developing written test items that measure the intended KSAPC at various levels.

Table 3.1 Bloom's Taxonomy for item writing

Level	Skill demonstrated	Test item stem
1 – Knowledge	Recall of factual information	List the three major ...
	Knowledge of dates, events, places	Define the four parts of ...
	Terminology	What is the definition of ...
	Basic knowledge of major ideas	Which author ...
	Major classifications and categories	Who was responsible for ...
2 – Comprehension	Grasp key meanings	What is the difference between...
	Apply knowledge to a different context	Which of the following would occur...
	Infer causation	Summarize the major ...
	Compare/contrast	Use the following to estimate ...
	Determine sequences	How are these two similar ...
3 – Application	Use information to solve problems	Apply the concept of X to solve for Y ...
	Apply methods, theories, or calculations	What are the steps for completing ...
	Diagnose to possible outcomes	Calculate the X of Y ...
	Reduce to most plausible best answer	Complete the following by using ...
	Analyze within a concrete framework	Which of the following best describes ...
4 – Analysis	Detect patterns	Analyze and determine ...
	Comprehend in-depth meanings	Which of the following would not ...
	Evaluate organization of multiple parts	What are the key differences between ...
	Break down complex system into parts	Explain the difference between ...
	Diagnose complete systems	What are the key similarities between ...
5 – Synthesis	Make abstractions	Which of the following would occur ...
	Make generalizations from a set of facts	What would be the necessary steps to ...
	Make likely predictions	What would need to be substituted ...
	Draw conclusions based on ideas	Order the following by importance ...
	Make logical inferences	How could X be rebuilt if Y ...
6 – Evaluation	Discriminate between theories or ideas	Which of the following is the best ...
	Argue to a conclusion	Rank order the proposed solutions ...
	Detect biases or faulty conclusions	Which of the following would ...
	Make critical judgments using inferences	Assess and select the best ...
	Diagnose the most effective solutions	What would likely happen if ...

Test developers can use Bloom's Taxonomy (or an abbreviated version) to provide guidance for developing items that are at an appropriate level for the job (considering how the KSAPC is applied on the job – e.g., factual recall, application, analysis, etc.).

Another factor to consider regarding the item type is the format of the item. Common formats include multiple choice, true/false, open-ended, or essay. Multiple choice is perhaps the most common format used for fixed-response items (items with only a limited number of alternatives), and for a good reason. Applicants have a 50% likelihood of guessing the correct answer for true/false items, and only 25% likelihood for multiple choice items with four alternatives (or 20% likelihood for items with five alternatives).

Open-ended and essay formats require subjective scoring, which can be timely and costly. Another drawback with these formats is that another type of unreliability enters into the equation when the tests are scored: inter-scorer reliability. Inter-scorer reliability relates to the consistency between scorers who subjectively grade the tests. While there is nothing wrong with these types of item formats (in fact they are the best item formats to use for the higher level of Bloom's Taxonomy), they will not be discussed further in this text for the reasons stated above.

STEP 3: DEVELOP THE TEST CONTENT

Test items can be developed by personnel professionals and/or Job Experts. If Job Experts are used, begin at Step 1; if experienced test developers are used, begin at Step 6:

1. Select a panel of four to ten Job Experts who are truly experts in the content area and are diverse in terms of ethnicity, gender, geography, seniority (use a minimum of one year of experience), and "functional areas" of the target position. Supervisors and trainers can also be included.

2. Review the selection plan (see Chapter 2), test plan (see above), and Validation Surveys (discussed below) that will be used to validate the test. This step is critical because the Job Experts should be very well informed regarding the KSAPCs measured by the test (and their affiliated job duties), and the number and types of items to be included on the test.

3. Have each Job Expert review and sign a confidentiality agreement. Along with this agreement, create an atmosphere of confidentiality and request that no documents or notes are taken out of the workshop room. Lock the doors when taking breaks.

4. Conduct a training session on item writing (various guidelines are available for this, including one provided in the TVAP User Manual included on the Evaluation CD).

5. The training should conclude with an opportunity for Job Experts to write sample test items and then exchange and critique the items using the techniques learned in the training.

6. Write test items following the selection plan and test plan. Be sure that item writers reference the Validation Survey that will be used by the validation panel to be sure that the items will address the criteria used by this panel for validating the items. When determining the number of items, to write according to the test plan, double the number of items that are slated for measuring each KSAPC. This is necessary because the validation process will screen out some of the items and extra items that survive the validation process may be necessary for future selection processes to replace items that show poor item statistics. A Test Item Form should be used by item writers to record the KSAPC measured, correct answer, textual reference including distractor references (for job knowledge items), and other useful information for each draft item.

7. Have the item writers exchange and critique items, paying careful attention to:

    *   grammar, style, and consistency

    *   selection plan and test plan requirements

    *   criteria on the Validation Survey.

8. Never be afraid to delete a poor item early in the development/validation process! It is better to keep only the best items at this phase in the process.

9. Create a final version of the draft test that is ready for review by the validation panel. This version of the test should include the item, KSAPC measured, correct answer, and textual reference with distractor references (for job knowledge items).

STEP 4: VALIDATE THE TEST

Validating a written test requires convening a group of qualified Job Experts (see criteria above for selecting these individuals) and having them review and rate the written test using several factors. Some of these factors include the quality of the test items, fairness, relationship to the job, and proficiency level required. A suggested list of rating questions that can be used is provided below (see the TVAP software on the Evaluation CD for a Validation Survey that includes these survey questions):

1. Regarding the quality of the test item, does the item:

    a. Read well? Is it clear and understandable?

b.   Provide sufficient information to answer correctly?

c.   Contain distractors that are similar in difficulty? Distinct? Incorrect, yet plausible? Similar in length? Correctly matching to the stem?

d.   Have an answer key that is correct in all circumstances?2

e.   Provide clues to other items on the test?

f.   Ask the question in a way that is free from unnecessary complexities?

g.   Ask the question in a way that is fair to all groups?

2.   Regarding the job relatedness of the item, is the item:

a.   Linked to an important or critical KSAPC that is needed the first day of the job?

b.   Linked to an important or critical job duty (Job Experts should identify this using job duty numbers from the job analysis). (Note: if the KSAPCs measured by the test have been linked to essential job duties, this step is not required, but can be helpful).

3.   Regarding the proficiency level required for the KSAPC measured by the item, what percent of minimally qualified applicants would Job Experts expect to answer this item correctly? (This data can be used for setting validated cutoff scores – see Chapter 6).

4.   For job knowledge tests:

a.   Is the item based on current information?

b.   Does it measure an aspect of job knowledge that must be memorized?

c.   How serious are the consequences if the applicant does not possess the knowledge required to answer this item correctly?

See the Appendix for a complete discussion on developing and validating job knowledge written tests.

VALIDATION CRITERIA FOR TEST ITEMS

There are no firm minimum criteria that specifically apply to any of the key validation factors offered in the Uniform Guidelines or in the professional standards. In fact, it is quite possible to have a written test that could be considered as an "overall valid" selection procedure, but include several items that would be rated negatively on the ratings proposed above. However, the goal is to have every item address these criteria.

There are a few seminal court cases that can provide guidance on some of these key validation criteria. Two of these high-level court cases are Contreras v. City of Los Angeles (1981) and US v. South Carolina (1978). Because of the transportable concepts regarding written test validation that have been argued and decided in these cases, they have also been frequently referenced in other cases involving written tests. Because the judges in each of these cases ended up supporting the development and validation work surrounding the tests involved, they are worth discussing briefly here.

In the Contreras case, a three-phase process was used to develop and validate an examination for an auditor position. In the final validation phase, where the Job Experts were asked to identify a knowledge, skill, or ability that was measured by the test item, a "5 out of 7" rule (71%) was used to screen items for inclusion on the final test. After extensive litigation, the Ninth Circuit approved the validation process of constructing a written test using this process.

In the South Carolina case, Job Experts were convened into ten-member panels and asked to provide certain judgments to evaluate whether each item on the tests (which included 19 subtests on a National Teacher Exam used in the state) involved subject matter that was a part of the curriculum at their teacher training institution, and therefore appropriate for testing. These review panels determined that between 63% and 98% of the items on the various tests were content valid and relevant for use in South Carolina. The US Supreme Court endorsed this process as "sufficiently valid."

These two cases provide useful guidance for establishing the minimum thresholds (71% and 63% respectively) necessary for Job Expert endorsement necessary (at least on the job relatedness questions) for screening test items for inclusion on a final test. It is important to note that in both of these cases at least an "obvious majority" of the Job Experts was required to justify that the items were sufficiently related to the job to be selected for the final test. The TVAP Software and User Manual in the Evaluation CD include specific criteria that are proposed for each validation standard above, along with rating scales to be used for gathering Job Expert ratings.

STEP 5: SCORE AND ANALYZE THE TEST

Several years ago, I attended a two-day seminar on advanced statistical analyses for tests. There were at least 50 attendees – many with advanced degrees in statistics and testing. Almost no one understood the seminar content. For two days, the trainer spouted formulas and concepts that were supposedly useful for investigating the little nuances about tests and item analyses, but most people were just plain "missing it." To make matters even worse, the concepts and techniques they were proposing, while useful to the very advanced practitioner, would provide little practical benefit over the classical test analysis tools that practitioners have been using for decades! Have we progressed? Maybe some, but the important part of progression is breaking down the theoretical into something that the average practitioner can actually use in everyday work.

It is the intention of this section to achieve this goal. While there is no escaping the fact that test analysis requires the use of advanced statistical tools, some of this can be automated by software tools. Many analyses can be completed in common spreadsheet programs. The purpose of this section is to equip the reader with a basic knowledge regarding some of the fundamental, essential components of test analysis, and (most importantly) *interpretation rules* than can be applied to look for problem areas. Most of the test analysis concepts and functions discussed below are included in the TVAP Software included on the Evaluation CD.

Classical test analysis[3] (conducted after a test has been administered) can be broken down into two primary categories: item-level analyses and test-level analyses. Item-level analyses investigate the statistical properties of each item as they relate to other items and to the overall test. Test-level analyses focus on how the test is working at an overall level. Because the trees make up the forest, the item-level analyses will be reviewed first.

ITEM-LEVEL ANALYSES

While there are numerous item analysis techniques available, only three of the most essential are reviewed here: item–test correlations (called "point biserial" correlations), item difficulty, and Differential Item Functioning (DIF). Item *discrimination indices* are also useful for conducting item-level analyses, but are not discussed in this text.

Point biserials

Point biserial calculations result in values between -1.0 and +1.0 that reveal the correlation between the item and the overall test score. Items that have negative values are typically either poor items (with respect to what they are measuring or how they are worded, or both) or are good items that are simply mis-keyed. Values between 0.0 and +0.2 indicate that the item is functioning somewhat effectively, but is not contributing to the overall reliability of the test in a meaningful way. Values of +0.2 and higher indicate that the item is functioning in an effective way, and is contributing to the overall reliability of the test. For this reason, the single best way to increase the reliability of the overall test is to remove items with low (or negative) point biserials.

The point biserial of a test item can be calculated by simply correlating the applicant scores on the test item (coded 0 for incorrect, 1 for correct) to the total scores for each applicant on the overall test using the =PEARSON formula in Microsoft Excel. When the total number of items on the test is fewer than 30, a corrected version of this calculation can be done by removing the score of each item from the total score calculation (e.g., when calculating a point biserial for item 1, correlate item 1 to the total score on the test using items 2–30; for item 2, include only items 1 and 3–30 for the total score).

Item difficulty

Item difficulties show the percentage of applicants who answered the item correctly. Items that are excessively difficult or easy (where a very high proportion of test takers are either missing the item or answering it correctly) are typically the items that do not contribute significantly to the overall reliability of the test, and should be considered for removal. Typically, items that provide the highest contribution to the overall reliability of the test are in the mid-range of difficulty (e.g., 40% to 60%).

Differential Item Functioning

Differential Item Functioning (DIF) analyzes detected items that are not functioning in similar ways between the focal and reference groups. The Standards (1999), explain that DIF "...occurs when different groups of applicants with similar overall ability, or similar status on an appropriate criterion, have, on average, systematically different responses to a particular item" (p. 13). In some instances, DIF analyses can reveal items that are biased against certain groups (test bias can be defined as any quality of the test item, or the test, that offends or unnecessarily penalizes the applicants on the basis of personal characteristics such as ethnicity, gender, etc.).

It should be noted that there is a very significant difference between simply reviewing the *average item score differences* between groups (e.g., men and women) and DIF analyses. One might be tempted to just simply evaluate the proportion of men who answered the item correctly (say 80%) versus the proportion of women (say 60%) and then note the size of this difference (20%) when compared relative to other items on the test with less or more spread between groups.

What is wrong with this approach? There is one major flaw: it fails to take group ability levels into account. What if men simply have a 20% higher ability level than women on the KSAPC measured by the test? Does this make the test, or the items with this level of difference "unfair" or "biased"? Certainly not. In fact, this "simple difference" approach was used in one court case, but received an outcry of disagreement from the professional testing community.

The case was Golden Rule Life Insurance Company v. Mathias (1980) and involved the Educational Testing Service (ETS) and the Illinois Insurance

Licensure Examination. In a consent decree related to this case, the parties agreed that test items could be divided into categories (and some items removed) based only on black–white average item score differences on individual items. This practice did not consider or statistically control for the overall ability differences between groups on the test, and was subsequently abandoned after the president of ETS renounced the practice, stating:

> ... the practice was a mistake ... it has been used to justify legislative proposals that go far beyond the very limited terms of the original agreement . . . We recognized that the settlement compromise was not based on an appropriate "bias prevention" methodology for tests generally. What was to become known as the "Golden Rule" procedure is based on the premise – which ETS did not and does not share – that group differences in performance on test questions primarily are caused by "bias." The procedure ignores the possibility that differences in performance may validly reflect real differences in knowledge or skill (Anrig, 1987).

The criteria used in the Golden Rule case also sparked dissent in the professional testing community:

> The final settlement of the case was based on a comparison of group differences in sheer percentage of persons passing an item, with no effort to equate groups in any measure of the ability the test was designed to assess, nor any consideration of the validity of items for the intended purpose of the test. The decision was clearly in complete violation of the concept of differential item functioning and would be likely to eliminate the very items that were the best predictors of job performance (Anastasi & Urbana, 1997).

So, it is safe to say that the professional testing community sufficiently rebuked the idea of just simply comparing group differences on items or tests overall. This is precisely where DIF analyses provide a significant contribution to test analyses. Because DIF analyses are different than simple average item score differences between groups and take *overall group ability* into consideration when detecting potentially bias items, some courts have specifically approved of using DIF analyses for the review and refinement of personnel tests.[4]

Because DIF analyses function in this way, it is possible that even if 20% of minority group members answered a particular item correctly and 50% of the whites answered the item correctly (a large, 30% score gap between the two groups), the item might still escape a "DIF" designation. A DIF designation, however, would occur if the minority group and whites scored very close on the test overall (for example, 55% and 60% respectively), but scored so divergently on the test item.

Consider a 50-item word problem test that measured basic math skills. Assume it was administered to 100 men and 100 women, and men and women scored about equally overall on the test (i.e., their overall averages were about the same). Forty-nine (49) of the 50 items measure math skills using common, everyday situations encountered by men and women alike. One of the items, however, measures math skills using a football example:

> You are the quarterback on a football team. It is 4th down with 11 yards to go and you are on your own 41-yard line. You were about to throw a 30-yard pass to a receiver who would have been tackled immediately, but instead you were sacked on the 32-yard line. What is the difference between the yardage that you could have gained (had your pass been caught) versus how much you actually lost?

Does this test item measure some level of basic math? Yes, however, to arrive at the correct answer (39 yards), a test taker needs to use *both* math skills and football knowledge. Unless football knowledge is related to the job for which this test is being used, this item could possibly show bias (via the DIF analysis) against women.

There are numerous methodologies available for conducting DIF analyses. These methods vary in statistical power (i.e., the ability to detect a DIF item should it exist), calculation complexity, and sample size requirements. Perhaps the most widely used method is known as the Mantel-Haenszel method, which is known as one of the more robust and classical methods for evaluating DIF[5], which can be calculated after breaking scores into similar ability levels using the Standard Error of Difference.

DIF analyses, because they rely heavily on inferential statistics, are very dependent on sample size. As such, items flagged as DIF based on large sample sizes (e.g., more than 500 applicants) are more reliable than those based on small sample sizes (e.g., less than 100 or so). While the testing literature provides various suggestions and guidelines for sample size requirements for these types of analyses,[6] a good baseline number of test takers for conducting DIF analyses is more than 200 applicants in the reference group (whites or men) and at least 30 in the focal group (i.e., the minority group of interest).

DIF analyses provide the most accurate results on tests that measure the *same* or *highly related* KSAPCs (i.e., tests with high reliability). For example, if a 50-item test contains 25 items measuring math skills and 25 items measuring interpersonal abilities and, because these two test areas might not be highly inter-related, the test has low reliability, DIF analyses on such a test would be unreliable and possibly inaccurate. In these circumstances, it would be best to separate the two test areas and conduct separate DIF analyses.

Most DIF analyses (including the analysis used in the TVAP Software on the Evaluation CD), output standardized statistical values that can be used to assess varying degrees of DIF (sometimes called Z values). For example, a test item with a Z value of 1.5 would constitute a lesser degree of DIF than a Z value of 3.0, etc.

When should test items be removed based on DIF analyses? There is no firm set of rules for removing items based on DIF analyses, so this practice should be approached with caution. Before removing any item from the test based on DIF analyses, the following considerations should be made:

- The level of DIF: The minimum level of DIF that should be considered "meaningful" is a Z value of 1.645 (such values are statistically significant at the .10 level). Values exceeding 2.58 (significant at the .01 level) are even more substantial. Items that have DIF levels that exceed this value should be more closely scrutinized than items with lower levels of DIF. Items that have only marginal levels of DIF should be carefully evaluated in subsequent test administrations.

- The point biserial of the item: If the item has a very high point biserial (e.g., .30 or higher), but is flagged as DIF, one should be cautious before removing the item. Items with high point biserials contribute to the overall reliability of the test and, if removing the item based on a DIF analysis, significantly lowers the reliability of the test, the psychometric quality of the test will be decreased.

- The item–criterion correlation (if available): If the validity of the test is based on a criterion-related validity study (where test scores have been statistically related to job performance), evaluate the correlation between the particular item and the measure of job performance. For example, assume a test consisting of 30 items that has an overall correlation to job performance of .30. Then consider that one of these items is flagged as DIF when administered to an applicant pool of several hundred applicants, and this specific item has a 0 (or perhaps even a negative) correlation with job performance when evaluated based on the original validation study. Such an item may be a candidate for removal (when considered along with the other guidelines herein).[7]

- Qualitative reasons why the item could be flagged as DIF: Items that are sometimes flagged as DIF contain certain words, phrases, or comparisons that require culturally or group-loaded content or knowledge (which is unrelated to the KSAPC of interest) to provide an adequate response (see the football-based math test item example above). It is sometimes useful to evaluate the item alternative that the DIF group selected over the majority group (e.g., if one group selected option A with high frequency and the other option C).

- The Job Expert validation ratings for the item: Is the specific aspect of the KSAPC measured by the item (not just the general KSAPC to which the item is linked) necessary for the job? Did this item receive clear, positive validation ratings from the Job Expert panel? If the item had an unusual number of red flags when compared to the other items that were included on the test, it may be a candidate for removal.

- The DIF values "for" or "against" other groups: If an item shows high levels of DIF against one group, but "reverse DIF" for another group, caution should be used before removing the item. However, if the group showing the high levels of DIF is based on a much larger sample size than the group with reverse DIF, a greater weight should be given to the group with the larger sample size.

- How groups scored on the subscales of the test: DIF analyses assume that the test is measuring a single attribute or dimension (or multiple dimensions that are highly correlated). However, sometimes groups score differently on various subscales on a test, and these differences can be the reason that items are flagged DIF (i.e., rather than the item itself being DIF against the group, it may only be flagged as DIF because it is part of a subscale on which subgroups significantly differ). For example, consider a test with the following characteristics: high overall internal consistency (reliability of .90), and two subscales: Scale A and Scale B. Assume that the average score for men is 65% on Scale A, 75% on Scale B, and 70% overall. The average score for women is 70% overall, but they have opposite scale scores compared to men (75% on Scale A and 65% on Scale B). Then assume that a DIF analysis with all items included showed that one item on Scale B was DIF against women. In this case, it would be useful to remove all items from Scale A and re-run the DIF analysis with only Scale B items included to determine if the item was still DIF against women. This process effectively controls for the advantage that women had on the overall test because of their higher score on Scale A.

TEST-LEVEL ANALYSES

There are essentially two types of overall, test-level analyses: descriptive and psychometric. Descriptive analyses pertain to the overall statistical characteristics of the test, such as the average (mean), dispersion of scores (standard deviation), and others. The psychometric analyses evaluate whether the test is working effectively (e.g., tests reliability). Each of these is discussed below.

Descriptive test analyses

The two primary descriptive types of test analysis are the mean (mathematical average) and standard deviation (average dispersion – or spread – of the test scores around the mean). Only a very brief mention of these two concepts will be provided here.

The test mean shows the average score level of the applicants who took the test. Note that this does not have any bearing whatsoever on whether the applicant pool is qualified (at least the mean by itself does not). While the mean can be a useful statistic for evaluating the overall test results, it should be given less consideration when evaluating mastery-based or certification/licensing tests (because certain score levels are needed for passing the test, irrespective of the fluctuation in score averages based on various applicant groups).

The standard deviation of the test is a statistical unit showing the average score dispersion of the overall test scores, and is also useful for understanding the characteristics of the applicant pool. Typically, 68% of applicant scores will be contained within one standard deviation above and below the test mean, 95% will be contained within two, and 99% within three. The standard deviation can be used to evaluate whether the applicants, as a whole, are scoring too high or low on the test (hence the test is losing out on valuable information about test takers because they are magnetized to one extreme of the distribution).

The mean and standard deviation are sometimes inappropriately used for setting cutoff scores.[8] Test developers are encouraged to use these two statistics for mostly informative, rather than instructive, purposes.

Psychometric analyses

Like item-level analyses, numerous analyses can be done to evaluate the quality of the overall test. This discussion will be limited to the most frequently used, essential analyses for written tests, which include common forms of test reliability and the Standard Error of Measurement (SEM). Two other advanced psychometric concepts that pertain mostly to mastery-based tests (tests used with a pass/fail cutoff based on a pre-set level of proficiency required for the

Table 3.2   Guidelines for interpreting test reliability

Reliability value	Interpretation
.90 and up	Excellent
.80 - .89	Good
.70 - .79	Adequate
Below .70	May have limited applicability

job) will also be discussed at the end of this section: Decision Consistency Reliability (DCR) and Kappa Coefficients.

TEST RELIABILITY

Test reliability pertains to the consistency of applicant scores. A highly reliable test is one that measures a one-dimensional or inter-related KSAPCs in a consistent way. There are several factors that can have a significant impact on the reliability of a written test, however, the most important factor is whether the items on the test "hang together" statistically. The items on a test need to be highly inter-correlated for a test to have high overall reliability. The Uniform Guidelines and professional standards provide no minimum thresholds for what constitutes acceptable levels of reliability. The US Department of Labor (2000, p. 3-3), has provided some general guidelines.

Perhaps the most common type of reliability analysis used for written tests is Cronbach's Alpha. This method is widely used by statistical and psychometric software because it provides a highly accurate measure regarding the *consistency* of applicant scores. The Kuder-Richardson 20 (KR-20) formula is very similar to Cronbach's Alpha, but can be used for dichotomously scored items only (i.e., items that have only two possible outcomes: correct or incorrect). Cronbach's Alpha, however, can be used for polytomous items (i.e., items that have more than one point value).

The Kuder-Richardson 21 (KR-21) formula is another method for evaluating the overall consistency of the test. It is typically more conservative than Cronbach's Alpha, and is calculated by considering only each applicant's total score (whereas the Cronbach's Alpha method takes item-level data into consideration).

STANDARD ERRORS OF MEASUREMENT

To a certain extent, test reliability exists so that the SEM can be calculated. The two go hand-in-hand. The (traditional) SEM can be easily calculated by multiplying the standard deviation of the test by the square root of one minus the reliability of the test. This can be calculated in Microsoft Excel as: =SD *

(SQRT(1 − Reliability)), where SD is the standard deviation of applicant overall test scores and Reliability is the test reliability (using Cronbach's Alpha, KR-20, or the KR-21 formula, etc.).

The SEM provides a *confidence interval* of an applicant's "true score" around their "obtained score." An applicant's true score represents their true, actual ability level on the overall test, whereas an applicant's obtained score represents the score that they "just happened to obtain on the day the test was given." SEMs help testing professionals understand that if the applicant *as much as sneezes* during a hypothetical second test administration of an equally difficult test, their score could be lower than obtained on the first administration. Likewise, if the applicant had a better night's sleep for the second administration, their score would possibly be higher than the first administration.

How this concept translates into testing is relatively straightforward. After the SEM has been calculated, it can be used to *install boundaries for where each applicant's true abilities lie on the test*. Assume the SEM for a written test is 3.0. This means that an applicant who scores 50 on the test most likely (with 68% confidence) has a "true score" on the test ranging between 47 and 53 (one SEM, or 3.0 points, above and below their obtained score). Using two SEMs (or 6 points above and below their obtained score) provides a 95% likelihood of including a score that represents their true ability level. Using three SEMs provides 99% confidence.

There is one small limitation with the traditional SEM discussed above (the one calculated using the formula above). This limitation is due to the fact that a test's reliability typically changes throughout the distribution. In other words, the reliability of the highest scorers on the test is sometimes different than the average, and from the lowest scorers. This is where the *Conditional SEM* comes in.

CONDITIONAL SEM

The Standards (1999) require the consideration of the Conditional SEM when setting cutoff scores (as opposed to the traditional SEM) (see pp. 27, 29, 30 and Standard 2.2, 2.14, and 2.15 of the Standards, 1999).

The traditional SEM represents the standard deviation of an applicant's true score (the score that represents the applicant's actual ability level) around their obtained (or actual) score. The traditional SEM considers the *entire range of test scores* when calculated. Because the traditional SEM considers the entire range of scores, its accuracy and relevance is limited when evaluating the reliability and consistency of test scores within a certain range of the score distribution.

Most test score distributions have scores bunched in the middle and spread out through the low and high range of the distribution. Those applicants who score in the lowest range of the distribution lower the overall test reliability (hence affecting the size of the SEM) by adding chance variance caused by guessing and not by possessing levels of the measured KSAPC that are high enough to contribute to the true score variance of the test. High scorers can also lower the overall reliability (and similarly affect the size of the SEM) because high-scoring applicants possess exceedingly high levels of the KSAPC being measured, which can also reduce the true variance included in the test score range. Figure 3.1 shows how the SEM is not constant throughout a score distribution (this figure is derived from data provided in Lord, 1984).

Because the SEM considers the *average reliability* of scores throughout the *entire range* of scores, it is less precise when considering the scores of a particular section of the score distribution. When tests are used for human resource decisions, the entire score range is almost never the central concern. Typically in human resource settings, only a certain range of scores are considered (i.e., those scores at or near the cutoff score, or the scores that will be included in a banding or ranking procedure).

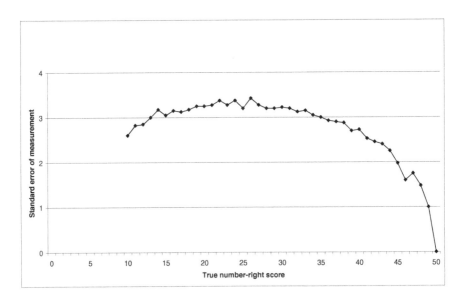

Figure 3.1   SEM by score level

The Conditional SEM attempts to avoid the limitations of the SEM by considering only the score range of interest when calculating its value. By only considering the scores around the critical score value, the Conditional SEM is the most accurate estimate of the reliability dynamics of the test that exist around the critical score.

Several methods are available for calculating the Conditional SEM. The Thorndike (1951) method[9] is a recommended procedure because it can be readily calculated using spreadsheet programs and because it provides results comparable to more sophisticated methods.[10] It is further recommended because the procedure considers true score and error variance throughout the entire score distribution, which allows its application on tests that measure different KSAPCs.

While the procedure may be conducted with less than 30 applicants, it is likely that the results may be more stable if 30 or more applicants are included (Feldt et al. 1985, p. 354) The test may have any number of items, but more meaningful results will be obtained from tests with ten or more items (Kolen et al., 1992, p. 293). The Thorndike method can be calculated by following these steps:

1. Select a group of test scores within a close range of the cutoff score (remaining as close as possible to the cutoff score value and only widening to gather an acceptable sample size of 30 or more applicants[11]).

2. For each applicant selected, divide their test score into two sections: one *representing their score for all odd items on the test and one for all even items*. If there is not an equal number of items for each of these sections (the odd score and even score), remove one item from the section with the extra item (e.g., the last item on the test).

3. Calculate a "difference" score for each applicant by subtracting the two test scores (total odd score minus even score).

4. Calculate the standard deviation of the difference scores. The resulting value is the Conditional SEM, or the standard error of measurement that is related to the set of scores within close range of the critical (or "minimum qualification" score).

Practitioners will observe that the Conditional SEM typically varies throughout the distribution as it accurately reflects the changing levels of reliability and variance throughout the score range.

PSYCHOMETRIC ANALYSES FOR MASTERY-BASED TESTS

Tests that require pre-determined levels of proficiency that are based on some job-related requirements are mastery-based tests. Mastery-based tests are used to classify applicants as "masters" or "non-masters," or those who "have enough competency" or "do not have enough competency" with respect to the KSAPCs being measured by the test (see Chapter 2 and Standard 14.15 of the Standards, 1999). Two helpful statistics for mastery-based tests are DCR and Kappa Coefficients.

Decision Consistency Reliability

Decision Consistency Reliability (DCR) is perhaps the most important type of reliability to consider when interpreting reliability and cutoff score effectiveness for mastery-based tests. DCR attempts to answer the following question regarding a mastery-level cutoff on a test: If the test was hypothetically administered to the same group of applicants a second time, how *consistently* would the test pass the applicants (i.e., classify them as "masters") who passed the first administration again on a second administration? Similarly, DCR attempts to answer: "How consistently would applicants who were classified by the test in the first administration as 'non-masters' fail the test the second time?" This type of reliability is different than internal consistency reliability (e.g., Cronbach's Alpha, KR-21), which considers the consistency of the test internally, without respect to the consistency with which the cutoff classifies applicants as masters and non-masters.

One very important characteristic about DCR reliability is that it is inherently different than the other forms of reliability discussed above (i.e., Cronbach's Alpha, KR-20, KR-21). Because DCR pertains to the consistency of classification of the test, which is an *action* of the test (rather than an *internal characteristic* of the test which is what the other reliability types reveal), its value cannot be used in the classical SEM formula.

Calculating DCR is beyond the built-in commands available in most spreadsheet programs, but can be calculated using the methods described in Subkoviak (1988) and Peng & Subkoviak (1980) (the TVAP Software in the Evaluation CD includes these calculations built into Microsoft Excel using calculations and embedded programming). DCR values between .75 and .84 can be considered "limited"; values between .85 and .90 considered "good"; and values higher than .90 considered "excellent" (Subkoviak, 1988).

Kappa Coefficients

A Kappa Coefficient explains how consistently the test classifies "masters" and "non-masters" beyond what could be expected by chance. This is essentially a measure of utility for the test. Calculating Kappa Coefficients also requires advanced statistical software or programming. For mastery-based tests, Kappa Coefficients exceeding .31 indicate adequate levels of effectiveness, and levels of .42 and higher are good (Subkoviak, 1988).

NOTES

1. If the test will be used to rank applicants, or a pass/fail cutoff that is above minimum competency levels will be used, the "Best Worker" rating should also be used as a minimum criteria, with a minimum level set for selecting KSAPCs for the test (see Chapter 6).

2. The developer may prefer to not allow Job Experts to review the test answer key because in some situations doing so can have an impact on their "minimum passing" ratings. Nonetheless, the answer key should always be verified by at least two people.

3. Classical test analysis refers to the test analysis techniques that use conventional analysis concepts and methods. More modern test theories exist (e.g., Item Response Theory), but are not discussed in this text.

4. See, for example: Edwards v. City of Houston, 78 F.3d 983, 995 (5th Cir., 1996) and Houston Chapter of the International Association of Black Professional Firefighters v. City of Houston, No. H 86 3553, U.S. Dist. Ct. S.D. Texas (May 3, 1991).

5. Narayanan, P. & Swaminathan, H. (1995), Performance of the Mantel-Haenszel and simultaneous item bias procedures for detecting differential item functioning. *Applied Psychological Measurement*, **18**, 315–328.

6. See: Mazor, K. M., Clauser, B. E., & Hambleton, R. K. (1992), The effect of sample size on the functioning of the Mantel-Haenszel statistic. *Educational and Psychological Measurement*, **52**, 443–451; Narayanan, P. & Swaminathan, H. (1995), Performance of the Mantel-Haenszel and simultaneous item bias procedures for detecting differential item functioning. *Applied Psychological Measurement*, **18**, 315–328; and Swaminathan, H. & Rogers, H. J. (1990), Detecting differential item functioning using logistic regression procedures. *Journal of Educational Measurement*, **27**, 361–370.

7. In any given criterion-related validity study, it is not likely that all items on the test will be statistically related to job performance (this is not the requirement for tests based on criterion-related validity, but rather that only the overall test is sufficiently correlated). However, if there is no *specific evidence* that the test item is related to job performance, while simultaneously there is *specific evidence* that the item could possibly be unfair against a certain group, it is justifiable to consider the item for removal (the other factors listed should also be considered).

8. See for example Evans v. City of Evanston (881 F.2d 382, 7th Cir., 1989).

9. Thorndike, R. L. (1951). Reliability. In E. F. Lindquist (Ed.), *Educational Measurement* (pp. 560–620). Washington DC: American Council on Education.

10. The Qualls-Payne (1992) study showed that the average Conditional SEM produced by the Thorndike method (across 13 different score levels) produced Conditional SEM values that were very close to five other methods (the average Conditional SEM value produced by the Thorndike method was 2.57, while the other five methods produced values of 2.81, 2.60, 2.58, 2.55, and 2.58). Further, a study conducted by Feldt et al. (1985, December), 'A comparison of five methods for estimating the standard error of measurement at specific score levels', *Applied Psychological Measurement*, **9**(4), 351–361) shows that, while the Thorndike method is less complicated than some other methods (i.e., those based on ANOVA, IRT, or binomial methods), it is "integrally related" and generally produces very similar results.

11. Fredrick Lord suggests selecting the scores of applicants "at (or near) a given observed score" (1984, p. 240); Feldt et al. (1985, p. 352) suggest grouping applicants into "short intervals of total score"; Feldt also suggested a procedure to "break the entire applicant sample into subgroups according to total score, using intervals of 3 or 5 points for the sub grouping" (personal communication, April 7, 2000), which allows the calculation of the Conditional SEM for each interval, with each Conditional SEM being a direct estimate of the Conditional SEM for the total score equal to the mid-point of the interval; R. K. Hambleton suggests including scores "within a point or two of the passing score" (personal communication, May 23, 2000).

CHAPTER 4

Developing, Validating, and Analyzing Structured Interviews

The purpose of any selection interview is to provide an applicant with a fair opportunity to demonstrate the KSAPCs and experiences that qualify them for the position. While the interview is the most commonly used component of selection systems, it can also be the most abused. Handled poorly, an interview can not only be ineffective, but may also have unintended adverse impact. Otherwise qualified applicants may be eliminated if the many variables contributing to a successful interview are not implemented properly.

Because an interview, by nature, will not measure characteristics of the entire applicant, it should be used in conjunction with the other selection procedures. A structured interview can serve as a useful supplement to the other selection procedures to allow the employer to gain valuable insight regarding certain aspects of an applicant's KSAPCs. It is different from unstructured interviews in that the same questions are asked of every applicant in the same way to ensure that all applicants are assessed using the same criteria.

METHODS FOR IMPROVING THE INTERVIEW PROCESS

There are ways of improving a typical interview that can improve the process and help insure that the interview is as job related as possible. The following observations are based upon research into past characteristics of typical interviews, and include some suggestions to improve the validity of the process:

- How valid and reliable the interview is may be highly specific to both the *situation* and to the *rater*.

- The interview should be used to evaluate factors that are not typically better measured by other means.

- The use of the interview is best accomplished if a standardized, or structured, approach is followed. In an unstructured interview, material is not consistently covered.

- The rater should be skilled (i.e., trained) in eliciting full and complete responses from the applicant and synthesizing all of the information obtained.

- Even when a panel of raters obtains the same information, each panel member can interpret or weigh the information differently. It is best to use mechanically combined scoring systems that consider several dimensions (rather than broad sweeping holistic judgments or ratings).

- The form of the question(s) affects the answer(s) obtained.

- The raters' attitudes affect their interpretations of what the applicant says.

- Raters appear to be influenced more by unfavorable than by favorable information.

- Rapport, or the lack thereof, between rater and the applicant is a situational variable that can unduly influence the interview's effectiveness.

- Structured or patterned interviews show stronger inter-rater reliabilities, meaning that there is generally a greater agreement across different raters when a standardized interview is used.

- Raters typically develop stereotypes of a good/poor applicant and seek to match applicants with stereotypes.

- Biases are established by raters early in the interview and these tend to be followed by a bias-matching favorable or unfavorable decision.

- Raters seek data to support or deny their own personal hypotheses and, when satisfied, may turn their attention elsewhere and miss important information. This means raters tend to weigh heavily on a small amount of information that supports their preconceived notions about applicants. Sometimes this also means that raters tend to dismiss any disconfirming information that does not coincide with their preconceived notions.

While many of the characteristics about interviews are unfortunately beyond the control of the practitioner, two variables within control are: the amount of *structure* provided for the interview and the *content* of the interview. A structured interview is controlled by three factors:

1.   the interview questions asked (content);

2.   the way the rater controls the actual interview situation (structure); and

3.   the standardized scoring of the interviews.

The remainder of this chapter will explain the various question types that can be included in an interview, and give a detailed, step-by-step process for developing and administering effective, valid, structured interviews.

TYPES OF QUESTIONS TO INCLUDE IN STRUCTURED INTERVIEWS

There is an entire landscape of question types that can be asked legally and effectively during an interview process. Some are more effective than others; and as a general rule, the more time and preparation work invested in developing the question set, the better the questions. This chapter covers three basic question types: situational, behavioral, and competency-based.

SITUATIONAL QUESTIONS

Situational questions ask applicants: "What would you do if ...?" These questions are based on events that have previously occurred on the job (or would be likely to occur) and ask the applicant to explain how they would handle the situation (limited of course by not having job experience in the position for which they are applying). Situational types of questions typically have good validity coefficients when correlated to measures of job performance (typically .30 to .46) and solid reliability (inter-rater reliability estimates are typically between .76 and .87) (Gatewood & Feild, 1994 [1986], p. 537; see also Cascio, 1998, p. 198). These questions can be powerful selection tools because they immediately place the applicant in a tough job situation and demand that they adequately address the situation. Consider the following example from an electrical trade position:

> *Workers at XYZ company have a practice of checking tools for proper operation prior to leaving the shop to go to a job site. This allows workers to be assured that tools will work properly at the job site. Your supervisor asks you to work with three helpers to collect and test the tools that will be brought to the next job site. After the helpers work with you to gather and test the tools, the tools are loaded in the truck and brought to the work site. After starting work at the site, your supervisor finds that one of the tools that you and the three helpers loaded is not working*

properly, and he then gets mad at you and requires you to drive all the
way back to the shop to obtain a new tool. You know which one of the
helpers gave you the faulty tool. What would you do in this situation?
What would you expect to accomplish by taking these steps?

Typically for situational questions of this type, scoring guidelines and anchors are developed that provide raters with benchmarks for high, acceptable, and low levels of applicant responses.

BEHAVIORAL QUESTIONS

Behavioral questions ask applicants: "What have you done when …?" These questions are based on the (reasonable) assumption that the best predictor of future behavior is past behavior. As such, these questions ask applicants to explain how they have handled difficult or complex situations in previous settings. Generally speaking, these questions are the most limited type of interview questions since they can sometimes be "faked" with information the interviewer has no way of confirming. Below is an example of a behavioral question:

It is sometimes necessary to work as part of a team to accomplish a
project. Can you tell me about a time during a job or school project
where you were part of a team and one or more of the members were
difficult to work with? Please explain how you handled this situation.
What was the outcome? What would you have done differently?

COMPETENCY-BASED QUESTIONS

Competency-based questions ask applicants: "Explain how you would …" These questions drill deep into the applicant's knowledge and skill set in a way that leaves little room for impression management or faking. When properly developed, administered, and scored, these questions are one of the most powerful selection tools for complex jobs that require high levels of knowledge and skill upon entry. A well-designed, competency-based question is one that simply cannot be faked by the applicant.

Consider an Information Technology (IT) manager position. IT managers need to possess good interpersonal and project management skills, but most importantly, they need to possess solid, mastery-level knowledge and skills relevant to the computer systems they will be managing. Only asking situational and behavioral types questions when interviewing IT managers is an almost certain recipe for disaster (unless the situational questions include competency-based characteristics). It is entirely possible during an interview that asks only situational and behavioral questions to *completely miss* whether the IT manager applicant possesses the mastery-level knowledge and skill necessary to *actually perform* their job.

While the situational and behavioral questions can help evaluate how the applicant will likely work with people and handle projects, such questions may completely overlook the depth and breadth of an applicant's true computer-related knowledge and skill. Including some solid competency-based questions into the mix of other questions quickly addresses this problem.

The best competency-based question is one that the applicant *cannot possibly answer* without possessing the desired level of knowledge and skill. For example, a competency-based question for the IT manager position might be:

> *Our company has 35 employees and we use Microsoft Mail Server version 4.0 for our e-mail services. If Microsoft released a new version of the Mail Server program next month, what steps would you take to migrate our company to the new version? Please be specific and be sure to describe each step you would take and why. Feel free to take your time to prepare your response before answering.*

After the applicant has provided their complete response, follow-up questions for this question (to be asked of every applicant) might include:

- How would you notify staff of the change?

- What backup plans would you have in place before starting the work?

- When would you start the project?

- What problems have you had with Mail Server Version 4.0?

- What strengths do you like about Mail Server Version 4.0?

- What steps would you follow to set up a new employee's mail account?

- What books or reference sources would you consult before or during the migration process?

Because these questions require applicants to apply very specific knowledge and skill sets, it makes a very difficult barrier for unqualified applicants to overcome (especially when coupled with follow-up questions and when scored by IT staff who are at least generally familiar with the topics covered in the interview). Competency-based questions and follow-ups can be even more specific than the example above (generally speaking, more specific questions are better, provided that the question does not measure knowledge that will be trained on the job). The best competency-based question is one that absolutely requires the applicant to respond with mastery-level competencies that demonstrate that they currently possess the levels of the KSAPCs needed on the first day of the job.

STEPS FOR DEVELOPING SITUATIONAL QUESTIONS

The following is a detailed description of the steps necessary for developing validated situational questions for a structured interview:

1. Complete a job analysis for the target position. Be sure that the job analysis includes (at a minimum) duties, KSAPCs, linkages between the duties and KSAPCs (required to address Section 14C4 of the Uniform Guidelines), and Best Worker ratings (see the job analysis ratings discussed in Chapter 2). These key ingredients are necessary before proceeding further in the development process.

2. Select the KSAPCs to measure on the interview by following the steps for completing a selection plan outlined in Chapter 2. Be sure that the KSAPCs that are selected for the interview can be appropriately measured in an interview format (for example, KSAPCs such as reading ability, math, and "hands-on" type of skills cannot usually be properly assessed by an interview and are typically better assessed using other methods). Also be sure that the KSAPCs selected for the interview are those that are rated highest on the Best Worker rating scale (i.e., are performance differentiating). This is helpful, especially if the interview will be used as the final, ranked, or banded selection procedure.

3. Prepare for a one-day workshop with Job Experts by compiling a final list of the selected KSAPCs and create a Situational Interview Question Form that provides space for the Job Experts to record a *critical incident* (see below) that has occurred on the job (or is very likely to occur), the KSAPC that is related to the incident, and least effective, acceptable, and most effective responses to the situation.

4. Convene seven to ten Job Experts for the one-day workshop to generate draft situational questions for the interview. Start the workshop by explaining the work completed so far (e.g., the job analysis, selecting KSAPCs for the interview), the benefits of using a job-related interview process (it helps to specifically mention that the end goal of the process is to effectively select new employees for the job who will be excellent co-workers!), and the final product (a valid structured interview).

5.   Break the Job Experts into two to three teams (each having at least two individuals) with each team having relatively the same number of KSAPCs (e.g., if there are 12 KSAPCs that survived the selection plan screening process (above), divide the Job Experts into four teams with each having three KSAPCs). Have each team review their set of KSAPCs and the duties to which they are linked. This will re-familiarize the Job Experts with the KSAPCs and how they are specifically applied on the job.

6.   Define and review the concept of *critical incidents* with the Job Experts. Spend some time with the concept, asking for group input and examples of critical incidents that have recently occurred on the job (this can be a fun process as the group recalls blunders and/ or successes of their co-workers!). When discussing the concept of critical incidents, define them as:

> An event or set of circumstances on the job that presented an *opportunity* for job incumbents to "rise to the occasion" by demonstrating stellar performance, or "fall down" by making ineffective choices.

The critical incidents should not include common, everyday events or circumstances that merely provide an opportunity for incumbents to make "average" or "just enough" reactions to sufficiently address the situation. The best critical incident is one where the words and actions of the incumbent directly translated to a positive or negative outcome on an important aspect of the job.

7.   Prepare the panel for developing situational questions based on these critical incidents by reviewing the criteria presented below. The situational questions should:

a.   Not measure KSAPCs that an employee will be expected to learn on the job, or can be trained in a brief orientation (i.e., avoid "tricks of the trade").

b.   Provide sufficient content and complexity to stimulate a response from the applicant that would allow raters to provide an adequate assessment of the applicant. Situations that have simple solutions or present only absolute alternatives should be avoided.

c.   Be job-related (i.e., it should represent an incident that has occurred, or is very likely to occur on the job).

d. Not require job-specific knowledge to provide an adequate response. That is, the question should not penalize applicants who have a high level of KSAPC measured by the question, but are unable to respond with much information to the question because they do not have experience in the target position. The question should allow applicants to relate the situation to their past life experiences to provide a response.

e. Not be too easy or too difficult.

f. Be culturally and politically sensitive and appropriate. Further, it should present a situation that allows qualified applicants of various socio-ethnic backgrounds to provide an ample response relevant to the job.

8. Ask the individual team members to independently develop critical incidents that relate to their assigned KSAPCs. Remind them that critical incidents can include situations that have occurred on the job (to them or someone else) or would be very likely to occur. Ask the Job Experts to record these incidents on the Situational Interview Question Form. Be sure they complete all parts of the survey. It sometimes helps to do the first one as an example with the overall group. Allow ample time for this process. Ask each Job Expert to come up with at least four incidents.

9. Have the Job Experts exchange their completed forms and ask each team to refine the incidents within their team and select the best ones. So, if there are three team members and each Job Expert developed four incidents (12 total), the team might select a final set of eight of their "best incidents."

10. Have the Job Experts submit the incidents and read each one (anonymously without revealing the author of the incident) to the entire group. Have the group informally grade each one "A," "B," or "C."

11. Keep the incidents that were graded A or B by the group. Work with the entire team to *convert the incidents into final situational questions* by following three steps:

a. Convert the incidents into question form to be asked directly of the applicant (e.g., Assume you are a clerical worker at XYZ corporation and the following event occurs ...).

b. Refine the possible responses (least effective, acceptable, and most effective) to include typical responses that applicants are likely to provide during the interview. This step is important because these response guidelines will be used in the interview scoring process.

c.   Develop customized follow-up questions for each situational question. These follow-up questions are useful for escalating the situation (in a standardized format) for applicants who provide "pat answers" for how they would address the situation.

12. Develop a final interview package that includes the final situational questions along with standardized rating forms and scoring summary forms (to be used to compile scores from individual raters to the panel as whole). Because practical judgment, decision making, and verbal communication are measured inclusively along with each situational question, they can be scored for each situational question or in terms of the overall performance of the applicant (after answering all questions).

13. It is possible to conclude at this step with a set of situational questions that are highly job related and will effectively screen applicants for relevant KSAPCs. However, an additional step can be included in the process at this point that will have two benefits: (1) it will generate validation evidence and documentation should the interview ever be challenged; and (2) it can refine the final set of questions to be even better than the initial set. This step involves convening a Job Expert team of seven to ten members who have not yet seen the final set of situational questions and having them review and provide validation ratings on the situational questions. This step is sometimes beneficial just from a practical standpoint because it serves to have a "fresh perspective" on the situational questions as the final product is reviewed by Job Experts who have never seen them. This step can be completed by having the new Job Expert team evaluate the set of situational questions using the following ratings:

a.   Is the question clear and understandable?
b.   Is the question written at an appropriate difficulty level?
c.   Does the question measure a KSAPC that is needed the first day of the job?
d.   Is this question fair to all groups of people?
e.   Is the question job related? (Does it represent a situation that has occurred or is very likely to occur on the job?)
f.   What KSAPC is measured by this question?

g.   Will applicants be able to provide a sufficient response without possessing job-specific (or employer-specific) knowledge?

The court-endorsed rating guidelines presented in Chapter 3 for written tests can readily be adopted as criteria for selecting a valid set of situational questions.

ADMINISTERING AND SCORING AN INTERVIEW

The steps below can be followed to administer and score an interview in a fair and defensible manner:

1.   Select raters to serve on interview panels. Raters can be supervisors of the target position and/or human resource staff members. If high-level knowledge competency type questions will be used, knowledge of the subject matter is essential for raters (in many instances this will necessitate using only supervisors).

2.   Train the raters on the questions, scoring forms, and common rating errors. The following rating errors should be explained *and demonstrated* to raters:

   •   Halo: Halo refers to the tendency of the rater to rate an applicant in about the same way on all domains because of a general, overall impression – whether favorable or unfavorable. This error usually results because the rater becomes impressed, either favorably or unfavorably, with one or two of the qualification areas and tends to base ratings in all qualification areas according to this initial impression.

   •   Leniency: This error refers to the tendency of raters to place their ratings in the higher end of the scale for all applicants. A major reason for this error can be attributed to the fact that raters often feel that placing everyone in the top categories is helpful or kind. In actuality, it can render ratings useless.

   •   Severity: This error refers to the tendency for raters to put a greater proportion of their ratings in categories below the average than in those above.

   •   Central tendency: This error is very common in the rating situation. It refers to the tendency of the rater to place all ratings at the center of the scale. This may occur because the rater is not entirely clear as to the meaning of the ratings or perhaps wishes to "play it safe" by giving no extreme ratings in either direction. Of course, this results in little or no variability between applicants and thus detracts from the objectives of the interview. This can also render the ratings useless.

- Similar-to-me: This type of rating error occurs when certain characteristics about the applicant bias the scores high when they are similar to the rater and low when they are not.

It is typically a good practice to complete the rater training process by holding one or two mock interviews and having the raters complete and pass a brief rater training test. The critical factor regarding rater training is that raters should share a similar *frame of reference* for what constitutes a strong, mediocre, and low scoring applicant on each of the scales.

3. Assemble panels and randomly assign applicants to panels. Rating panels should consist of at least three members, and preferably no more than six. Two-member panels are also plausible, but detecting rater bias is limited when only two raters are used.[1] Insure that the panels are diverse with respect to ethnicity and gender.

4. Administer and score the interview. After the scores are compiled, they should be double-checked for accuracy.

5. If multiple rater panels are used and each panel rates more than 20 applicants (or so), *standard score* each panel before combining all applicant scores onto the final score list. Standard scoring can be accomplished by creating a *Z score* for each applicant by subtracting each applicant's score from the average (mean) score of all applicants rated by the panel and dividing this value by the panel's standard deviation (of all applicant total scores on that panel). Only after completing this step for each panel should the applicant scores be combined and ranked on a final score list. This process statistically equates applicant scores between panel (sometimes rater panels have higher or lower averages for applicant scores and this process places them on the same level).

NOTE

1. When only two raters are on a panel, there is no way to form a "consensus score" (where at least two raters agree) that can be compared against a third (potentially biased) rater. When only two raters are used, there are simply two different opinions on the applicant's ability level. With three raters, two can agree and one can possibly be detected as "biased" when they rate applicants of certain gender or ethnicity types higher or lower when compared to the other two.

CHAPTER 5

Developing, Validating, and Analyzing Training, Education, and Experience Requirements

How many years of on-the-job experience should a police officer have before being eligible for promotion to sergeant? How many years experience should a firefighter possess before becoming eligible for promotion to captain? What is the minimum number of years a person should be an apprentice in an industrial trade before becoming a licensed journey worker? How many years of flying experience should a pilot possess before being eligible to become a commercial airline pilot for a major airline? Should a person possess an undergraduate degree plus two years of experience before applying for a management position? A degree plus four years of experience? Five years?

Personnel and human resource professionals regularly struggle with these types of questions for both entry-level and promotional processes. When time-in-grade or other training, experience, and education (referred to hereafter as "TEE") requirements are used and generate adverse impact, they instantly become subject to validation scrutiny if challenged in arbitration or legal settings.

Because TEE requirements are frequently established using nothing other than "best judgment" by executive and management staff, employers often find themselves in litigation situations explaining to the judge why they thought a five-year minimum time-in-grade requirement was better than a four-year requirement, or three and one-half years – down an endless slippery slope of subjectivity.

But this does not need to be the case. There are several defensible methods for validating TEE requirements. Some of these are discussed later in this chapter. But first, a brief tour through the various government and professional standards and criteria surrounding TEE requirements will be provided.

The Uniform Guidelines and Principles (2003) provide very specific criteria for validating TEE requirements. Before reviewing these detailed requirements, first consider using the following questions as a checklist for insuring that a proposed TEE requirement rating or scoring system includes the necessary "basic elements."

Is the TEE requirement:

1. *Objective?* For example, rather than requiring that candidates possess a relevant degree from a "good or respectable school," simply require that they possess the degree from an accredited school or licensing program.

2. *Uniformly applied to all applicants?* Be sure that the rating structure and process used for the TEE requirement is standardized and applied consistently to all applicants.

3. *Likely to discriminate (distinguish between qualified and unqualified applicants)?* Be sure that the TEE requirement will actually screen out unqualified applicants while screening in the qualified ones. Employers sometimes spend needless time developing TEE requirements that are actually unnecessary, or ineffective, in the selection process.

4. *Clearly job related?* There should be a clear nexus between the TEE requirement and measurable KSAPCs from a job analysis (i.e., KSAPCs that are definitely needed on the first day of the job – Section 14C1 and 5F of the Uniform Guidelines prohibit measuring KSAPCs that applicants will learn on the job, or those that can be trained in a "brief orientation").

5. *Provided in such a way that all applicants will have an equal opportunity to demonstrate that they possess the desired KSAPC?* This is critical, because simply reviewing resumes to assess whether applicants meet the desired TEE requirements without specifically asking them to identify if they possess the TEE requirement so they are not screened out just because they failed to omit a qualification they were not asked about. Applicants should be directly asked whether they possess the TEE requirement.

6. *Scored using a system that is consistent and reliable?* It is best to use two raters to score the TEE requirements (if they are scored and not just pass/fail) so that inter-rater reliability can be evaluated.

Several of the TEE validation requirements will be addressed by following the six criteria presented above. However, in some cases, special steps and consideration should be taken.

One general limitation with TEE rating systems is that they depend on the applicant providing honest information about their background. Related to this, the accuracy of TEE rating systems depends on whether the employer chooses to verify the information provided. At the very least, employers should include a "lie warning" on TEE surveys that informs applicants that any information provided that turns out to be false will be immediate grounds for disqualification. Have the applicants acknowledge this warning by providing their signature on the survey.

UNIFORM GUIDELINES CRITERIA REGARDING TEE REQUIREMENTS

The Uniform Guidelines present a rather conservative set of criteria for validating TEE requirements:

> *Prior training or experience: A requirement for or evaluation of specific prior training or experience based on content validity, including a specification of level or amount of training or experience, should be justified on the basis of the relationship between the content of the training or experience and the content of the job for which the training or experience is to be required or evaluated. The critical consideration is the resemblance between the specific behaviors, products, knowledges, skills, or abilities in the experience or training and the specific behaviors, products, knowledges, skills, or abilities required on the job, whether or not there is close resemblance between the experience or training as a whole and the job as a whole. (Section 14C6; emphasis added)*

The subparts of this section require that at least two criteria be addressed when using a content validation strategy to support the use of TEE requirements (or ratings) in a selection process. These are: (1) specifying the *level* or *amount* of the TEE requirements (or rating systems); and (2) conducting some form of *linkage* to establish the resemblance between the content (and levels) of the TEE requirement and the content of the job itself.

Rather than using global, holistic Job Expert ratings to establish the "resemblance" between the TEE requirement and the job *in general*, the Uniform Guidelines require that the resemblance is evaluated at a *micro-level*, with specific attention to the behaviors (or duties, including their affiliated work products) and the KSAPCs of each.

While this section of the Uniform Guidelines requires that specific linkages are established between the TEE requirement and the job, the requirement is less stringent on the *inferential leap* (the level of inference being made between two areas, in this case the TEE requirement and the job) criteria of content validity that is required for other types of selection procedures.

This is because the last sentence in Section 14C6 ("… whether or not there is *close resemblance* between the experience or training as a whole and the job as a whole") and Question #73 of the Uniform Guidelines ("… users may justify a requirement for training, or for experience … on the basis of content validity, even though the prior training or experience *does not duplicate the job*).

Thus, these two sections leave some room for prior training, experience, or education to sufficiently meet the content validation requirements *even if they are not directly related to duties of the job*. For example, consider an employer in the food service industry who desires to use a TEE requirement of "at least two years' supervisory experience." Should applicants who possess two years' supervisory experience at a manufacturing plant be eligible to apply? Certainly, because the supervisory skills that are acquired at the manufacturing plant are likely to translate directly to the food services industry. Skills such as holding employees accountable, team work, meeting deadlines, and conducting performance evaluations are likely to be very similar and transportable between these two trades.

PROFESSIONAL STANDARDS REGARDING TEE REQUIREMENTS

The Principles (2003) present a set of criteria that almost exactly match the Uniform Guidelines:

> *A content-based selection procedure may also include evidence of specific prior training, experience, or achievement. This evidence is judged on the basis of the relationship between the content of the experience and the content of the work requiring that experience. To justify such relationships, more than a superficial resemblance between the content of the experience variables and the content of the work is required. For example, course titles and job titles may not give an adequate indication of the content of the course or the job or the level of proficiency an applicant has developed in some important area. What should be evaluated is the similarity between the behaviors, activities, processes performed, or the KSAOs [knowledges, skills, abilities, and other characteristics] required by the work. (p. 23; emphasis added)*

The contribution that the Principles provide beyond that of the Uniform Guidelines is the requirement of "more than a superficial resemblance" and the example of "course titles and job titles may not give an adequate indication of the content of the course or the job of proficiency an applicant has developed in some important area."

The criteria set forth in the Uniform Guidelines and Principles for validating TEE requirements will not typically be addressed when employers simply arbitrarily and subjectively determine TEE requirements. It is exactly this practice that brings employers to court to defend TEE requirements (which are often the most difficult types of selection procedures to defend). So how can employers develop validated TEE requirements in an efficient way? With so many detailed requirements surrounding the validation of TEE requirements, it would appear that validating them must be a challenging endeavor. Not necessarily.

The validation system described below provides steps and guidelines that will work for many types of TEE requirements. While these recommendations are designed to address the key validation criteria proposed in the Uniform Guidelines and Principles, practitioners are advised to reference these documents when specific questions arise.

USING TEE REQUIREMENTS IN OPEN SELECTION/ PROMOTIONAL PROCESSES

Described below is a validation system for scoring and rating TEE requirements that is used in selection or promotion processes where applicants from *outside the employer* are allowed to apply (i.e., "open systems"). This system is based on the presumption that applicants can bring any combination of training, experience, and education to the job and a "wide net" needs to be cast to capture those that are specifically related to the requirements of the job.

Sometimes employers use simple "fixed checkbox" surveys for essential TEE requirements where applicants simply check a box indicating whether they possess the specified level of the KSAPC. Such surveys are simple to develop and require almost no scoring (only sorting into qualified and unqualified stacks). There are some serious drawbacks to using this strategy. Because applicants can obtain relevant training, experience, and education qualifications in *so many different ways*, it is almost impossible to build a one-size-fits-all checklist where applicants individually assess whether they meet certain specific requirements and then check the box indicating "yes" or "no."

There are endless ways in which applicants can acquire competency in the KSAPCs required for the job. Training and experience can be acquired through on-the-job training, military training, rehabilitation programs, apprenticeship programs, or self-employment. In fact, the Uniform Guidelines allow *volunteer experience* to be counted toward meeting training and experience requirements for a job (see Questions & Answers #73). This presents a serious challenge for a one-size-fits-all checkbox system.

Another limitation to these types of surveys is that they typically ignore the "level" of the KSAPC that is required (a requirement of Section 14C6 of the Uniform Guidelines). Just how much of the KSAPC training or experience is *enough*? Six months? Two years? How can this be predefined without knowing how frequently each applicant applied the relevant KSAPC during the two years of experience they claim to possess?

The only clear way of addressing these limitations is to conduct a scored TEE rating system, which is described below. Many employers, however, will not be able to setup such scored TEE rating systems because of the operational limitations of running an efficient selection process (i.e., they just don't have time to score TEE requirements for all applicants). Employers in this situation are advised to consult Chapter 8 for guidelines for establishing the unscored "checkbox" types of TEE requirements.

STEPS FOR DEVELOPING A VALID TEE RATING SYSTEM FOR OPEN SELECTION/PROMOTION PROCESSES

1.   Conduct a job analysis that addresses the requirements of the Uniform Guidelines (see Chapter 2). It is especially important for this TEE requirement validation system that job knowledges are *operationally defined* as "that body of learned information which is used in, and is a necessary prerequisite for, observable aspects of work behavior of the job" and skills and abilities are operationally defined in terms of "observable aspects of work behavior of the job" (Section 14C4 of the Uniform Guidelines).

2.   Identify KSAPCs that can be appropriately and effectively measured in a TEE rating process. Make sure to include at least eight KSAPCs if inter-scorer reliability will be calculated (see below).[1] Completing a selection plan is perhaps the best way of doing this. If a selection plan has not been completed, be sure to at least use the criteria described in Chapter 2 for selecting KSAPCs that can be measured using a content validity process (e.g., necessary the first day of the job, important or critical, and rated high on the Best Worker rating if the TEE system will be used to rank applicants or used with a cutoff above minimum competency levels). The following are examples of KSAPCs that *should not* be measured using a TEE rating system:

      • math skills

      • reasoning or problem solving

      • verbal communication

      • reading ability

      • physical abilities

      • personality characteristics

      • interpersonal skills.

      These KSAPCs should not be measured in a TEE rating system for obvious reasons. Be careful about including KSAPCs that, while critical for the job, might be better measured using other methods.

3.   Develop a TEE survey that provides applicants with the necessary fields (with plenty of space) to describe their relevant training, experience, and education for each KSAPC selected. A sample TEE survey is provided in Figure 5.1.

Knowledge, Skill, Ability, or Personal Characteristic	Training (including professional, military, or other)	Experience (professional or volunteer)	Education (list by course title)
(Provide KSAPC from job analysis here)	(Applicant completes)	(Applicant completes)	(Applicant completes)
Did you receive any grades, awards, credentials, certificates, performance ratings, or commendations? If so, describe each.			
How long was the training, experience, or educational course?			
If applicable, what levels were attained? Entry-level? Advanced levels?			
When was it completed?			
Where was it completed (name of employer or institution)?			
Name and contact information of a person or institution that can verify this information.			

Figure 5.1   Sample TEE survey

(This sample survey has been compressed for printing purposes. The survey should be printed using landscape format and should provide applicants with plenty of space to handwrite their responses.)

4.   Develop a scoring system for the TEE survey. Each KSAPC on the survey can be unit weighted (with each counting equally) or weighted based on the relative importance of each TEE requirement to the job. Weights for each KSAPC on the survey can be developed by asking a panel of Job Experts to assign 100 points among the KSAPCs, and then averaging the results. The job analysis data should be considered by the Job Experts when assigning point values; however, it is not necessary that the point ratings be agreement with the job analysis data.[2]

5.   After the TEE surveys have been completed and submitted by applicants, two raters score the TEE surveys (e.g., using a 1–5 rating system for each scored item). The raters should review the job analysis for the position before providing ratings, and should use a consistent scoring taxonomy for providing scores. See the sample TEE rating guidelines provided in Figure 5.2.

TEE Rating Guidelines	
Criteria	**Explanation**
R Relevancy	How relevant is the TEE description? How well is it linked to the target KSAPCs? How well does the TEE resemble the job requirements? If not, how transportable is it?
A Achievement	What level of achievement or proficiency is indicated (if any)? Were any credentials or awards attained?
T Time	How much time did the applicant spend completing the training, experience, or education? Months? Years? How frequently was the training or experience repeated?
E Extent	To what extent was the TEE acquired? To what level? At only a baseline level? Mastery? Expert?
D Date	When was the TEE acquired? How recently? Was it acquired recently enough to still be relevant?

Figure 5.2 Sample TEE rating guidelines

The ratings for each KSAPC should be a holistic judgment based on the collection of training, experience, and education described by the applicant, with specific attention being given to each of the RATED factors.

6.   The final score for each applicant should be calculated and placed on a final score list and used on a pass/fail, banding, or rank-ordered fashion based on the reliability of the two raters, adverse impact, and the other factors discussed in Chapter 6.

USING TEE REQUIREMENTS IN CLOSED SELECTION/ PROMOTIONAL PROCESSES

In some employment situations, promotional opportunities are closed to outside applicants and only applicants from inside the employer who meet certain seniority or work experience requirements are eligible to apply. While using work seniority in closed promotional systems has relaxed validation requirements under Title VII,[3] they should still be evaluated for objectivity, fairness, and validity. Provided that the seniority system is bona fide and is the result of a negotiated labor contract, a straight-line seniority can be used in close promotional processes with little liability exposure for the employer.

DEVELOPING MINIMUM TIME-IN-GRADE REQUIREMENTS FOR A CLOSED PROMOTIONAL PROCESS

In some situations, there is only one "feeder" job that can promote into the target position and the employer desires to set a predefined "time-in-grade" experience requirement for promotion into the target job (e.g., a police officer promoting to a police sergeant). Under these circumstances, a minimum time-in-grade requirement can be established by surveying Job Experts in the target position and their supervisor regarding the minimum amount of experience that is needed for being eligible to promote into the target position (i.e., eligible to apply for the position and then compete on the remaining selection procedures).[4]

Using "number of hours" in this rating (rather than months or years of experience) can address the fact that there may be part-time workers in the feeder positions. Calculate the average of the minimum hours ratings from Job Experts and supervisors and reduce this value by one SEM (Standard Error of the Mean) to help compensate for sampling error in the ratings (e.g., average rating of 3500 hours minus 1 SEM of 500 hours = 3000 hours minimum required to apply for the promotional position). The SEM can be calculated by dividing the standard deviation of the Job Expert ratings by the square root of the number of Job Experts minus 1.

DEVELOPING A VALID WORK HISTORY EVALUATION FOR A CLOSED PROMOTIONAL PROCESS

Now consider a target promotional position that has several feeder jobs, or only one feeder position that includes numerous "functional areas" (subclassifications of the same position based on work area or specialization) and the target position supervises any or all of these areas. An example of this is a police sergeant who supervises police officers who work in several different various functional roles such as investigation, patrol, training, or booking. Another example is a foreman for a stevedoring industry who supervises various longshore (dock) workers who work in different functional areas such as crane operator, loader, lasher, transport driver, and others.

In these circumstances, a promotional process can be developed that assigns weights to the various feeder positions and/or functional areas based on their value in preparing incumbents for the target position. Developing such a scoring system requires calculating a *relative importance* weight for each of the feeder positions/functional areas and a *minimum and maximum number of hours* in each to be used in a selection procedure for promotion called a Work History Evaluation (WHE). A WHE can be used with a pass/fail cutoff or weighted and combined with other selection procedures in the promotional process. The steps for developing a WHE are provided below.

1. Create a WHE development survey that includes two sections, described below:

    a. The first section should include a description of each of the feeder positions or functional areas (if there is only one feeder position) that promote into the target position. Next to each should be a field for Job Experts to write the relative weight of the feeder position or functional area considering how well experience in the position prepares incumbents to perform in the target position (Job Experts will distribute 100 points to each according to its relevant value).

    b. The second section should include a field for Job Experts to write a minimum and maximum number of hours next to each feeder position or functional area. These ratings will be used for determining a minimum amount of time that incumbents must possess in each before accruing points, and a maximum limit where excessive experience in an area is capped in the scoring system. The minimum hours is necessary because incumbents who work only a very limited time in some feeder positions or functional areas are not likely to develop sufficient levels of the KSAPCs that are related to the target position. In positions where low levels of training are required, a very low minimum will be expected. A maximum number of hours is necessary because incumbents who choose to remain in one feeder position or functional area for extended periods will not likely continue to accrue valuable levels of the KSAPC for the target position beyond a certain level (i.e., there is a diminishing value for remaining in some positions for extended periods).

2. Convene a panel of Job Experts and supervisors of the target position. The number of panel members required for this step depends on the sampling confidence desired (see Figure 2.1). In many situations a panel of seven to ten qualified and experienced panel members is sufficient.

3. Provide the panel members with the job analysis (including a description of the various feeder positions/functional areas that

will be weighted in this process). Describe the purpose of the workshop (developing a validated WHE for promotion into the target position) and discuss how the WHE will be used.

4.   Have Job Experts complete both sections of the survey and input, and double-check the data.

5.   Calculate the average and standard deviation for each feeder position or functional area for each section of the survey. Discard Job Expert ratings that are 1.645 standard deviations above or below the average rating for each (this process helps remove outliers, or extreme data points, from the data set and helps insure that the majority opinions are used for making the final weighting values)[5].

6.   Calculate a final weight and minimum/maximum value for each feeder position or functional area and use these values for calculating points for applicants using the weight of each multiplied by the percentage of the minimum/maximum values. For example, assume position A is worth 10% of the overall weight (based on Section 1 of the survey) and Section 2 of the survey revealed a "minimum hours" value of 250 and a maximum of 1500 for this position. If an applicant worked 1500 hours in this position, they would have worked 100% of the target range. If they worked only 249 hours, they would have worked 0% of the target range. Assume an applicant has worked 1250 hours in this position. This is 80% of the target range – which is the total number of hours the applicant worked within the target range divided by the number of hours above the minimum, but below the maximum. So their points for this position would be calculated as: 10% [the position's relative weight from Section One] * (1000 / 1250), or 10% * 80% = 8%. Note that the numerator (1000) hours was determined by summing the number of hours this applicant had *above the minimum* (e.g., 1250 – 250). The denominator (1250) was determined by subtracting the maximum hours from the minimum (1500 – 250). When combined with their scores on the other positions, a final score can be obtained for each applicant.

7.   If applicants can possibly have work experience hours in a feeder position or functional area that has substantially changed over the years, a minimum recency factor can also be included into this process.

NOTES

1. TEE rating systems can also be applied to job duties. The KSAPC rating method is proposed here because having the applicants provide descriptions of their training, experience, or education as it relates to job duties can sometimes present problems with the TEE raters giving credit for areas that will be trained on the job and are not necessarily required upon job entry (which can be problematic according to Section 14C1 of the Uniform Guidelines). The proposed KSAPC rating method should avoid this problem if the KSAPCs selected for the TEE rating process are screened using the selection plan process described in Chapter 2.

2. This is because Job Experts will view the importance level of KSAPCs differently *based on which ones are available to be weighted* on the selection device, or in a selection process overall. In addition, KSAPCs can receive more or less weight based simply on how broadly or specifically they are described on the job analysis. For example, if a major KSAPC is simply worded in an over-encompassing way on the job analysis, it may receive less weight during a weighting process than a KSAPC that is divided into two aspects and written twice on the job analysis, which provides it with twice the opportunity to be evaluated and weighted by Job Experts.

3. Section 703(h) of Title VII states: "Notwithstanding any other provision of this Title, it shall not be an unlawful employment practice for an employer to apply different standards of compensation, or different terms, conditions, or privileges of employment pursuant to a bona fide seniority or merit system, or a system which measures earnings by quantity or quality of production or to employees who work in different locations, provided that such differences care not the result of an intention to discriminate because of race, color, religion, sex, or national origin …" Therefore, absent a showing of a deliberate intent to use a seniority system for discriminatory purposes, they are less susceptible to Title VII lawsuits than other types of selection procedures.

4. Employers should use caution when establishing these requirements because many occupations have only recently received influx from women and minority incumbents.

5. If there are 3–5 raters or less than 20 ratings provided by each rater, it is recommended to eliminate individual ratings (and not entire raters) that have been identified as outliers using a 1.645 standard deviation rule (all ratings that are 1.645 standrad deviations above or below the mean are deleted). If there are more than five raters or the raters are providing more than 20 ratings each, consider removing entire raters from the data set if they are identified as outliers using this same rule. Using this criteria will serve to "trim" the average ratings that are in the upper or lower 5% of the distribution.

CHAPTER 6

Using Selection Procedures: Cutoff Scores, Banding, Ranking, and Weighting

A perfectly valid selection procedure can be *invalidated* through improper use. Validation has to do with the *interpretation of scores*. A valid selection procedure produces scores that can be informative in both absolute and relative terms. A person who scores 90% on a written test absolutely answered about 9 out of each set of 10 questions correctly. In an absolute sense, they answered just about every test item correctly. But what if they scored in the lowest 10% of all test takers (i.e., about 90% of the applicants scored higher)? This paints a completely different picture. Relative to the other applicants, they scored very low (i.e., the test may have been easy, or perhaps the rest of the applicants just had exceptional abilities).

Scores on a selection procedure should be used in such a fashion that the validation evidence supports the way the selection procedure is interpreted. If classifying applicants into two groups – qualified and unqualified – is the end goal, the test should be used on a pass/fail basis (i.e., an absolute classification based on achieving a certain level on the selection procedure). If the objective is to make relative distinctions between substantially equally qualified applicants, then banding is the approach that should be used. Ranking should be used if the goal is making decisions on an applicant-by-applicant basis (making sure that the requirements for ranking discussed in this chapter are addressed). If an overall picture of each applicant's combined mix of KSAPCs is desired, then a weighted and combined selection process should be used.

For each of these procedures, different types of validation evidence should be gathered to justify the corresponding manner in which the scores will be interpreted. This chapter will explain steps that can be taken to develop and justify each procedure.

DEVELOPING VALID CUTOFF SCORES

Few things can be as frustrating as being the applicant who scored 69.9% on a test with a cutoff of 70%! Actually, there *is* one thing worse: finding out that the employer elected to use 70% as a cutoff for no good reason whatsoever. It was chosen as a cutoff on the basis that 70% *seemed* like a good, fair place to set the cutoff. After all, isn't 70% a grade of C in school? And doesn't a grade of C mean "satisfactory"?

How about being on an operating table where the chief surgeon missed 30% of the qualifying test items on their written board exams? You would certainly hope that the 30% of the items they missed had nothing to do with your type of surgery!

Arbitrary cutoffs simply do not make sense, either academically or practically. Further, they can incense applicants who might come to realize that a meaningless standard in the selection process has been used to make very *meaningful decisions* about their lives and careers.

For these reasons, and because the US courts have so frequently rejected arbitrary cutoffs that have adverse impact, it is essential that practitioners use *best practices* when developing cutoffs. And, when it comes to best practices for developing cutoffs, there is perhaps none better than the modified Angoff method.[1]

The Angoff (1971) method is solid because it makes good practical sense, Job Experts can readily understand it, applicants can be convinced of its validity, the courts have regularly endorsed it,[2] and it stands up to academic scrutiny. Here is a quick overview of how it works. Job Experts review each item on a written test and provide their "best estimate" on the percentage of minimally qualified applicants they believe would answer the item correctly (i.e., each item is assigned a percentage value). These ratings are averaged and a valid cutoff for the test can be developed. The *modified* Angoff method adds a slight variation: After the test has been administered, the cutoff level set using the method above is lowered by 1, 2, or 3 Conditional SEMs to adjust for the unreliability of the test (see Chapter 3 for a discussion related to the SEM).

The modified Angoff method can be used for several types of selection procedure, but is perhaps most widely used for written tests. The complete process for developing a cutoff using this method is described below.

STEPS FOR DEVELOPING AND USING THE MODIFIED ANGOFF CUTOFF

The following steps can be used to develop and use a cutoff for a written test using the modified Angoff method. (It is critical that all test items have been validated before completing this step – see Chapter 3 for the steps required for validating written test items).

1. Select a panel of four to twelve[3] Job Experts who are truly experts in the content area and are diverse in terms of ethnicity, gender, geography, seniority (use a minimum of one year experience), and "functional areas" of the target position. Supervisors and trainers can also be included.

2. Provide a copy of the job analysis for each Job Expert. Be sure that the job analysis itemizes the various job duties and KSAPCs that are important or critical to the job.

3. Make a copy of the test for each Job Expert and stamp all tests and keys with a numbered control stamp (so that each Job Expert is assigned a numbered test and key). The answer key may also be provided to Job Experts, however, they should be urged to assess the difficulty level of the item without readily referencing the key.

4. Explain the confidential nature of the workshop, the overall goals and outcomes, and ask the Job Experts to sign confidentiality agreements. Also explain the overall test development and validation steps, including the steps that have been completed so far and which still remain to be completed.

5. Review the mechanics of a test item with the Job Expert panel, including the item "stem" (the part of the item that asks the question), alternates (all choices including the key), distractors (incorrect alternatives), and answer key. Also review any source linkage documentation for the items (i.e., for job knowledge tests where the correct answers are located in a book or manual).

6. Facilitate a discussion with the Job Expert panel to clarify and define the concept of a "minimally qualified applicant." This is perhaps the most important part of this process, because it will set the stage for the remaining steps that will ultimately "calibrate" the test. The definition should be limited to *an applicant who possesses the necessary, baseline levels of the KSAPC measured by the test item to successfully perform the first day (before training) on the job*. It is sometimes useful to ask the Job Experts to imagine 100 minimally qualified applicants in the room (in the various states that an applicant can be) and ask, "How many of the 100 minimally qualified applicants do you believe will answer this item correctly?"

7. Ask the Job Experts to provide their ratings regarding percentage of minimally qualified applicants they believe will answer the test item correctly. Warn the Job Experts against providing ratings below a "chance score" (50% for true/false items; 25% for multiple choice items with four alternatives; 20% for items with five). In addition, Job Experts should not assign ratings of 100% because this rating assumes that *every* minimally qualified applicant was having a "perfect day" on the testing day, and allows no room for error.

8. Allow the Job Experts to continue rating the first five test items and then stop. Select one of the first five test items as a "group discussion" item. Ask each of the Job Experts to share their percentage ratings for the item. Allow the Job Experts to debate over their ratings. This will help centralize the panel and "rein in" any extreme outliers before they rate the remaining items. It is acceptable to stimulate the Job Experts by discussing and contrasting their ratings, though the facilitator should not require nor coerce any Job Expert to make any changes. The facilitator and the Job Experts can prod, argue, discuss, and gently challenge any individual Job Expert rating during group discussion. However, each Job Expert should be encouraged to "cast their own vote" after discussion.

9. Collect all rating surveys and remind Job Experts of the confidential nature of their workshop participation.

10. Input and double-check all Job Expert ratings.

11. Detect and remove outlier Job Experts from the data set. Experience shows that one or more outliers exist in almost every Job Expert panel. Outliers are raters who purposefully rated items too low (i.e., were interested in lowering the standard), too high (wanted to raise the standard), or just plain randomly. Statistical control processes should be used to detect each of these potential rating biases and the identified Job Expert removed from the data set before the final cutoff level is set. While a variety of techniques are available to accomplish this goal, two that can be readily computed using spreadsheet programs are described below:

    a. To detect Job Experts who are providing random responses, or just responses that were not congruent (to an extent) with the ratings of the other Job Experts, create an inter-correlation matrix (using the =PEARSON command in Microsoft Excel) for all Job Experts on the panel. Look for Job Experts who were not correlated with their peers (or less correlated than most other raters) and remove them from the data set (judgment will need to be used at this step to make considerations for the number of Job Experts, number of items rated, statistical power, etc.).

    b. To check for a Job Expert who is rating items systematically too low or too high compared to the rest of the panel, calculate the average and standard deviation of the Job Expert averages for all items on the test (yes, an average of their averages).

Then remove any Job Expert whose average ratings are 1.645[4] standard deviation above or below the average of all Job Experts.

Because removing Job Experts using step (a) or (b) above will change the data set (possibly creating new problems with the remaining data), it is recommended to only complete this iteration once, and to be sure to complete the steps in order (a) first, then (b)).

12. Calculate a *pre-administration cutoff percentage* (also called an "unmodified Angoff score" because it has not yet been reduced using the Conditional SEM) with the remaining data. The pre-administration cutoff percentage score is the *average of the Job Expert panels' average ratings for each item* on the final test. Each item's average percentage rating receives equal weight in the calculation of this score – if only two Job Experts rated an item, the item's average is only based on two values but the item is given equal weight to the item rated by the entire panel.

13. Administer the test and remove any items if necessary based on item- or test-level analyses. If items are removed from the test, also remove that item's average percentage rating from the calculation of the pre-administration cutoff percentage.

14. Calculate the three *post-administration cutoff raw score options* by multiplying the pre-administration cutoff percentage by the number of items in the test (e.g., 76.7% * 90 items = 69.03 of the 90 items answered correctly) and reducing this value by 1, 2, or 3 Conditional SEMs (see Chapter 3). This process provides three viable cutoff score options for the test. In the US Supreme Court decision made in US v. South Carolina (1978), five statistical and human factors were considered when deciding whether to use 1, 2, or 3 SEMs when setting the final cutoff score:

   • Size of the SEM: As discussed in Chapter 3, using the Conditional SEM is recommended over the traditional SEM because it considers the error variance (unreliability) only for test takers around the cutoff score, which is the area of decision-making interest. Large SEMs indicate low test reliability and/or high levels of variance in the applicant pool.

   • Possibility of sampling error in the study (this relates to the number of Job Experts who served on the cutoff development panel): Panels with only a few Job Experts raise concern based on this factor (especially if there are a large number of incumbents in the workforce – see the Job Expert sample size discussion in Chapter 2).

- Consistency of the results (internal comparisons of the panel results): Panels that included biased Job Experts raise concern here (only if they were not removed using the proposed steps above).

- Supply and demand for teachers in each specialty field (this pertains to the demand for workers needed in the work force).

- Racial composition of the teacher force (the levels of adverse impact on each of the three cutoff options should be considered).

While these factors were based upon the specific needs and circumstances in US v. South Carolina, they provide some useful considerations for employers when setting cutoff scores.

The Uniform Guidelines require that pass/fail cutoffs should be "… set so as to be reasonable and consistent with the normal expectations of acceptable proficiency in the workforce" (Section 5H). The modified Angoff method addresses this requirement on an item-by-item basis.

SETTING CUTOFFS THAT ARE HIGHER THAN THE "MINIMUM LEVEL" ESTABLISHED BY THE MODIFIED ANGOFF METHOD

What should be done if the employer cannot feasibly process all applicants who pass the validated cutoff score? Theoretically speaking, all applicants who pass the modified Angoff cutoff are qualified; however, if the employer simply cannot process the number of applicants who pass the given cutoff, two options are available.

The first option is to use a cutoff that is *higher* than the three cutoff options calculated above. If this option is used, the Uniform Guidelines are clear that the degree of adverse impact should be considered (see Section 3B and 5H). One method for setting a higher cutoff is to subtract one Standard Error of Difference (SED) (see the Banding section below for a discussion of the SED) from the highest score in the distribution, and passing all applicants in this score band. Using the SED in this process helps insure that all applicants within the band are substantially equally qualified. Additional bands can be created by subtracting one SED from the score immediately below the band for the next group, and repeating this process until the first cutoff score option is reached (i.e., one Conditional SEM below the cutoff score).

While this option may be useful for obtaining a smaller group of applicants who pass the cutoff score and are substantially equally qualified, a second option is strict rank ordering. Strict rank ordering is not typically advised on written tests because of the high levels of adverse impact that are likely to result. To hire or promote applicants in strict rank order on a score list, the employer should be careful to insure that the criteria in the Ranking section below are sufficiently addressed.

BANDING

In some circumstances applicants are rank-ordered on a selection procedure and hiring decisions between applicants are based upon score differences at the one-hundredth or one-thousandth decimal place (e.g., applicant A who scored 89.189 is hired before applicant B who scored 89.188, etc.). The troubling issue with this practice is that, if the selection procedure was hypothetically administered a second time, applicants A and B could very likely change places! In fact, if the reliability of the selection procedure was low and the standard deviation was large, these two applicants could be separated by several whole points!

Banding addresses this issue by using the SED (which is calculated by multiplying the SEM[5] by the square root of 2) to group applicants into "substantially equally qualified" score bands. The SED is a tool that can be used by practitioners for setting a confidence interval around scores that are substantially equal. Viewed another way, it can be used for determining scores in a distribution that represent *meaningfully different* levels of the KSAPCs measured by the selection procedure.

For example, assume a selection procedure with a score range of 0 to 100 and an SED of four. If the highest scoring applicant obtained a score of 99, subtracting 1 SED from this score (99 − 4) arrives at a score of 95, which can be considered the *first* meaningful stopping place in the distribution of scores. That is, the applicant who scored 99 and the applicant who scored 94 have different ability levels, but the applicant who scored 99 and the applicant who scored 95 *do not*.

Using one SED to set these markers in the score distribution provides a 68% level of confidence that the "true ability levels" of the applicants in the outermost scores of the band do not significantly differ in true ability level. Using two SEDs provides about 95% confidence. Practitioners can use either one to two SEDs to set these confidence boundaries in a score distribution in a way that allows for groups of substantially equally qualified applicants to move through the hiring process with administrative ease.

Banding has been a hotly debated issue in the personnel field, especially over the last 15 years.[6] Proponents of strict rank ordering argue that making hiring decisions in rank-order preserves meritocracy and ultimately insures a slightly more qualified workforce. Supporters of banding argue that, because tests cannot adequately distinguish between small score differences, practitioners should remain blind to miniscule score differences between applicants who are within the same band. They also argue that the practice of banding will almost always produce less adverse impact than strict rank ordering.[7] The good news is that various types of score banding procedures have been successfully litigated and supported in court[8] and banding remains as an effective tool that can be used in most personnel situations.

RANKING

The idea of hiring applicants in strict order from the top of the list to the last applicant above the cutoff score is a practice that has roots back to the origins of the merit-based civil service system. The limitation with ranking, as discussed above, is that the practice treats applicants who have almost tied scores as if their scores are meaningfully different *when we know that they are not*. The SEM shows the degree to which scores would likely shuffle if the selection procedure was hypothetically administered a second time.

Because of these limitations, the Uniform Guidelines and the courts have presented rather strict requirements surrounding the practice of strict rank ordering. These requirements are provided below, along with some specific recommendations on the criteria to consider before using a selection procedure to rank order applicants.

Section 14C9 of the Uniform Guidelines states:

> *If a user can show, by a job analysis or otherwise, that a higher score on a content valid selection procedure is likely to result in better job performance, the results may be used to rank persons who score above minimum levels. Where a selection procedure supported solely or primarily by content validity is used to rank job candidates, the selection procedure should measure those aspects of performance which differentiate among levels of job performance.*

Performance differentiating KSAPCs distinguish between acceptable and above-acceptable performance on the job. Differentiating KSAPCs can be identified either absolutely or relatively using the Best Worker rating discussed in Chapter 2. A strict rank-ordering process should not be used on a selection procedure that measures KSAPCs that are only needed *at minimum levels* on the job and do not distinguish between acceptable and above-acceptable job performance (see Uniform Guidelines, Questions & Answers #62).

Content validity evidence to support ranking can be established by linking the parts of a selection procedure to job duties and/or KSAPCs that are performance differentiating.[9] So, if a selection procedure is linked to a job duty and/or KSAPC that is "performance differentiating" either *absolutely* or *relatively* (e.g., with an average Job Expert Best Worker rating that is 1.0 standard deviation above the average Best Worker rating or higher when compared to all other duties and/or KSAPCs), some support is provided for using the selection procedure as a ranking device.

While the Best Worker rating provides some support for using a selection procedure as a ranking device, some additional factors should be considered before making a decision to use a selection procedure in a strict rank-ordered fashion:

1. Is there adequate score dispersion in the distribution (or a "wide variance of scores")? Rank ordering is usually not preferred if the applicant scores are "tightly bunched together"[10] because such scores are "tied" to even a greater extent than if they were more evenly distributed. One way to evaluate the dispersion of scores is to use the Conditional SEM (see Chapter 3). Using the Conditional SEM, the employer can evaluate if the score dispersion is adequately spread out within the relevant range of scores when compared to other parts of the score distribution. For example, if the Conditional SEM is very small (e.g., 2.0) in the range of scores where the strict rank ordering will occur (e.g., 95–100), but is very broad throughout the other parts of the score distribution (e.g., double or triple the size), the score dispersion in the relevant range of interest (e.g., 95–100) may not be sufficiently high to justify this criteria.

2. Does the selection procedure have high reliability? Typically, reliability coefficients should be .85 to .90 or higher for using the results in strict rank order.[11] If a selection procedure is not reliable (or "consistent") enough to "split apart" candidates based upon very small score differences, it should not be used in such a way that considers small differences between candidates as meaningful.

3. What KSAPC is being measured by the selection procedure? If the selection procedure measures cognitive ability, the Principles (2003, p. 47) provide some latitude for rank ordering the scores (compared to selection procedures that measure other KSAPCs):

> Given the unitary concept of validity and the underlying premise ... that inferences regarding predictors of a cognitive nature and performance criteria are linear ... cognitively based selection techniques developed by content-oriented procedures and differentiating adequately within the range of interest can usually be assumed to have a linear relationship to job behavior. Such content-oriented procedures support rank ordering and setting the cutoff score as high or as low as necessary. Research has not yet established whether this same set of premises holds true for other types of predictors (e.g., personality inventories, interest inventories, indices of values).

While the guidelines above should be considered when choosing a rank ordering or pass/fail strategy for a selection procedure, the extent to which the test measures KSAPCs and/or job duties[12] that are performance differentiating should be the *primary consideration*.

Employers using a selection procedure that is based on criterion-related validity evidence have more flexibility to use ranking than with selection procedures based on content validity. This is because criterion-related validity demonstrates scientifically what content validity can only speculate is occurring between the selection procedure and job performance. Criterion-related validity (see Chapter 3 for a more detailed discussion) provides a correlation coefficient that represents the strength or degree of correlation relationship between some aspects of job performance and the selection procedure.

While the courts have regularly endorsed criterion-related validity studies, they have placed some minimum thresholds for the correlation value necessary (about .30 or higher) for strict rank ordering on a selection procedure based on criterion-related validity:

- Brunet v. City of Columbus (1993): This case involved an entry-level firefighter Physical Capacities Test (PCT) that had adverse impact against women. The court stated, "The correlation coefficient for the overall PCT is .29. Other courts have found such correlation coefficients to be predictive of job performance, thus indicating the appropriateness of ranking where the correlation coefficient value is .30 or better."

- Boston Chapter, NAACP Inc. v. Beecher (1974): This case involved an entry-level written test for firefighters. Regarding the correlation values, the court stated: "The objective portion of the study produced several correlations that were statistically significant (likely to occur by chance in fewer than five of one hundred similar cases) and practically significant (correlation of +.3 or higher, thus explaining more than 9% or more of the observed variation)."

- Clady v. County of Los Angeles (1985): This case involved an entry-level written test for firefighters. The court stated: "In conclusion, the County's validation studies demonstrate legally sufficient correlation to success at the Academy and performance on the job. Courts generally accept correlation coefficients above +.30 as reliable ... As a general principle, the greater the test's adverse impact, the higher the correlation which will be required."

- Zamlen v. City of Cleveland (1988). This case involved several different entry-level firefighter physical ability tests that had various correlation coefficients with job performance. The judge noted that, "Correlation coefficients of .30 or greater are considered high by industrial psychologists" and set a criteria of .30 to endorse the City's option of using the physical ability test as a ranking device.

WEIGHTING SELECTION PROCEDURES INTO COMBINED SCORES

Selection procedures can be weighted and combined into a composite score for each applicant. Typically, each selection procedure that is used to make the combined score is also used as a screening device (i.e., with a pass/fail cutoff) before including scores from applicants into the composite score. Before using a selection procedure as a pass/fail device and as part of a weighted composite, the developer should evaluate whether the KSAPCs measured by the selection procedures are performance differentiating – especially if the weighted composite will be used for ranking applicants.

There are two critical factors to consider when weighting selection procedures into composite scores: determining the weights and standardizing the scores. Developing a reliability coefficient for the final list of composite scores is also a critical final step if the final scores will be banded into groups of substantially equally qualified applicants. These steps are discussed below.

Determining a set of job-related weights to use when combining selection procedures can be a sophisticated and socially sensitive issue. Not only are the statistical mechanics often complicated, choosing one set of weights versus another can sometimes have a very significant impact on the gender and ethnic composition of those who are hired from the final list. For these reasons, this topic should be approached with caution and developers should make decisions using informed judgment.

Generally speaking, weighting the selection procedures that will be combined into composite scores for each applicant can be accomplished using one of three methods: *unit weighting*, weighting based on *criterion-related validity* studies, and using *content validity* weighting methods.

Unit weighting is accomplished by simply allowing each selection procedure to share an equal weight in the combined score list. Surprisingly, sometimes unit weighting produces highly effective and valid results (see the Principles, 2003, p. 20). This is probably because each selection procedure is equally allowed to contribute to the composite score, and no selection procedure is hampered by only contributing a small part to the final score. Using unit weighting, if there are two selection procedures, they are each weighted 50%. If there are five, each is allowed 20% weight.

If the employer is using selection procedures that are based on one or more criterion-related validity studies, the data from these studies can be used to calculate the weights for each. The steps for this method are outside the scope of this text and will not be discussed here.[13]

Using content validity methods to weight selection procedures is probably the most common practice. Sometimes practitioners get caught up in developing complicated and computationally intensive methods for weighting selection procedures using job analysis data. Sometimes these procedures involve using complicated formulas that consider frequency and importance ratings for job duties and/or KSAPCs, and job duty/KSAPC linkages.

While this helps some practitioners feel at ease, these methods can produce misleading results. There are easier methods available (proposed below). For example, consider two KSAPCs that are equally important to the job. Now assume that one is more complex than the other, so it is divided into two KSAPCs on the job analysis and the other (equally important) KSAPC remains in a single slot on the job analysis. When it comes time to use multiplication formulas to determine weights for the selection procedures that are linked to these KSAPCs, one is likely to receive more weight *just because it was written twice on the job analysis*. The same problem exists if selection procedures are mechanically linked using job duties that have this issue.

What about just providing the list of KSAPCs to a panel of Job Experts and having them distribute 100 points to indicate the relative to the importance of each? This method is fine, but can also present some limitations. Assume there are 20 KSAPCs and Job Experts assign importance points to each. Now assume that only 12 of these KSAPCs are actually tested by the set of selection procedures chosen for the weighted composite. Would the weight values turn out differently if the Job Experts were allowed to review the 12 remaining KSAPCs and were asked re-assign their weighting values? Most likely, yes.

Ask a friend to list their top ten favorite cars in no certain order. Then ask them to distribute 100 points among the ten, indicating the relative importance of each. Then take away five cars and have them distribute 100 points to the remaining five (not considering their original weighting). The weights they assign the second time to the five remaining cars will likely be different than the weights that would be calculated by taking their original list of ten (along with the corresponding weights of each), removing the same five cars, then recalculating the weights by dividing the original weight of each by the new total based on only the remaining five.

Another limitation with weighting selection procedures by evaluating their relative weight from job analysis data is that sometimes different selection procedures are linked to the same KSAPC (this can be because the weights for each selection procedure are no longer unique and become convoluted with other selection procedures). One final limitation is that sometimes selection procedures are linked to a KSAPC for collecting the weight determination, but they are weak measures of the KSAPC (while others are strong, relevant linkages). For these reasons, there is a "better way."

STEPS FOR WEIGHTING SELECTION PROCEDURES USING CONTENT VALIDITY METHODS

The following steps can be taken to develop content valid weights for selection procedures that are combined into single composite scores for each applicant:

1. Select a panel of four to twelve Job Experts who are truly experts in the content area and are diverse in terms of ethnicity, gender, geography, seniority (use a minimum of one year experience), and "functional areas" of the target position. Supervisors and trainers can also be included.

2. Provide a copy of the job analysis for each Job Expert. Be sure that the job analysis itemizes the various job duties and KSAPCs that are important or critical to the job.

3. Provide each Job Expert with a copy of each selection procedure (or a highly detailed description of the content of the selection procedure if confidentiality issues prohibit Job Experts from viewing actual copies). Make a copy of the selection procedure and key for each Job Expert and stamp with a numbered control stamp (so that each Job Expert is assigned a numbered set).

4. Explain the confidential nature of the workshop, the overall goals and outcomes, and ask the Job Experts to sign confidentiality agreements.

5. Discuss and review with Job Experts the content of each selection procedure and the KSAPCs measured by each. A selection plan is helpful for this step (see Chapter 2). Also discuss the extent to which certain selection procedures may be better measures of certain KSAPCs than others. Factors such as the vulnerability of certain selection procedures to fraud, reliability issues, and others should be discussed.

6. Provide a survey to Job Experts that asks them to distribute 100 points among the selection procedures that will be combined. Be sure that they consider the importance levels of the KSAPCs measured by the selection procedures, and the job duties to which they are linked, when completing this step.

7. Detect and remove outlier Job Experts from the data set (see this same step under the section titled, "Steps for developing and using the modified Angoff cutoff" above, for details on how to complete this step).

8. Calculate the average weight for each selection procedure. These averages are the weights to use when combining the selection procedure into a composite score.

STANDARDIZING SCORES

Before individual selection procedures can be weighted and combined, they must be *standard scored*. This step is crucial! Standard scoring is a statistical process of *normalizing* scores and is a necessary step to place different selection procedures on a level playing field.

Assume a developer has two selection procedures: one with a score range of 0–10 and the other with a range of 0–50. What happens when these two selection procedures are combined? The one with a high score range will greatly overshadow the one with the smaller range. Even if two selection procedures have the same score range, they should still be standard scored. This is because if the selection procedures have different means and standard deviations, they will produce inaccurate results when combined unless they are first standard scored.

Standard scoring selection procedures is a relatively simple practice. Converting raw scores into Z *scores* (a widely used form of standard scoring) can be done by simply subtracting each applicant's total score from the average (mean) score of all applicants and dividing this value by the standard deviation (of all applicant total scores).   After the scores for each selection procedure are standard scored, they can be multiplied by their respective weights and a final score for each applicant calculated. After this final score list has been compiled, the reliability of the new combined list can be calculated.[14]

NOTES

1. When tests are based on criterion-related validity studies, cutoffs can be calibrated and set based on empirical data and statistical projections that can also be very effective.

2. For example US v. South Carolina (434 US 1026, 1978) and Bouman v. Block (940 F.2d 1211, C.A.9 Cal., 1991) and related consent decree.

3. Various Job Expert sample sizes are suggested throughout this text. A minimum of four Job Experts is proposed in this section (rather than the minimum of seven used elsewhere) because the exposure of confidential test information may be of high concern to the employer for completing this step.

4. If there are 3–5 raters or less than 20 ratings provided by each rater, it is recommended to eliminate individual ratings (and not entire raters) that have been identified as outliers using a 1.645 standard deviation rule (all ratings that are 1.645 standard deviations above or below the mean are deleted). If there are more than five raters or the raters are providing more than 20 ratings each, consider removing entire raters from the data set if they are identified as outliers using this same rule. using this criteria will serve to "trim" the average ratings that are in the upper or lower 5% of the distribution.

5. The SEM is extensively discussed conceptually and practically in Chapter 3.

6. For example, Schmidt, F. L. (1991), Why all banding procedures in personnel selection are logically flawed. *Human Performance*, **4**, 265–278; Zedeck, S., Outtz, J., Cascio, W. F., and Goldstein, I. L. (1991), Why do "testing experts" have such limited vision? *Human Performance*, **4**, 297–308.

7. One clear support for using banding as a means of reducing adverse impact can be found in Section 3B of the Uniform Guidelines, which states: "Where two or more selection procedures are available which serve the user's legitimate interest in efficient and trustworthy workmanship, and which are *substantially equally valid* for a given purpose, the user should use the procedure which has been demonstrated to have the lesser adverse impact." Banding is one way of evaluating an alternate use of a selection procedure (i.e., one band over another) that is "substantially equally valid."

8. Officers for Justice v. Civil Service Commission (CA9, 1992, 979 F.2d 721, cert. denied, 61 U.S.L.W. 3667, 113 S. Ct. 1645, March 29, 1993). See also Henle, C. A. (2004), Case review of the legal status of banding, *Human Performance*, **17**(4), 415–432.

9. See Section 14C9 of the Uniform Guidelines.

10. Guardians v. CSC of New York (630 F.2d 79). One of the court's reasons for scrutinizing the use of rank ordering on a test was because 8928 candidates (two-thirds of the entire testing population) was bunched between scores of 94 and 97 on the written test.

11. Gatewood, R. D. & Feild, H. S. (1994 [1986]), *Human Resource Selection* (3rd ed.; p. 184). Fort Worth, TX: The Dryden Press; Aiken, L. R. (1988), *Psychological Testing and Assessment* (2nd ed.; p. 100). Boston: Allyn & Bacon (p. 69); Weiner, E. A. & Stewart, B. J. (1984), *Assessing Individuals* (p. 69). Boston: Little, Brown.

12. For selection procedures that are designed to directly mirror job duties (called "work sample tests"), only test-duty (and not test-KSAPC) linkages are required for a content validity study (see Section 14C4 of the Uniform Guidelines). In this case, the Best Worker ratings on the duties linked to the work sample test should be the primary consideration for evaluating its use (i.e., ranking or pass/fail). For tests measuring KSAPCs (and not claiming to be direct "work sample tests"), the extent to which the selection procedure measures KSAPCs that are differentiating should be the primary consideration.

13. See Uniform Guidelines Questions & Answers #47, the Principles (2003, pp. 20, 47), and Cascio, W. (1998), *Applied Psychology in Human Resource Management*, Upper Saddle River, NJ: Prentice-Hall, for more information on this approach.

14. See Feldt, L. S., & Brennan, R. L. (1989), Reliability. In R. L. Linn (Ed.), *Educational Measurement* (3rd ed.; pp. 105–146). New York, Macmillan.

CHAPTER 7

Using Multiple Regression Analysis to Examine Compensation Practices

Jim Higgins

This chapter presents an overview of an exceptionally powerful statistical technique that can be applied to determine whether significant differences exist among applicant or employee groups. Specifically, Multiple Regression (MR) will be reviewed; how it can be used to evaluate employee compensation to determine whether males or whites are compensated higher than females or minorities for reasons that are not legitimately job related.

To fully appreciate the power and usefulness of MR it is helpful to first review more basic statistical tools. The traditional, and most straightforward, approach that has been used to determine whether specific groups of employees (i.e., whites or males) are differentially compensated when compared to other groups (e.g., specific minority groups or females) is to conduct a simple comparison of average compensation rates using t-tests from independent samples. T-tests are statistical tools that compare average scores between two groups (e.g., test scores, compensation, job performance, etc.) to determine whether the differences between the groups are statistically significant. If a difference is statistically significant, it is said to be "real" and "reliable" rather than a "fluke" or chance event.

The advantage of using this approach was its simplicity. For example, if males receive an average compensation that is significantly statistically higher than females, one might conclude that potential compensation bias exists in the way a company is paying these two groups.

The most significant problem with a simple comparison of average salaries, is that there could be legitimate reasons for the two groups being compensated differently. For example, if a job has been traditionally staffed by males and only recently have females begun to account for a significant proportion of the workforce, then it is likely that the males will have had more time to work their way up the pay scale. If this is the case, then at least some portion of the difference between the salaries is due to a factor other than gender—time in job.

Clearly, the practice of making simple comparisons between the average salary of males and females or whites and minority groups is inadequate for developing a complete understanding of whether or not evidence exists for discrimination. What is needed is a statistical tool that allows a researcher to compare the average salaries of various groups of employees incorporating the legitimate job-related factors that are influencing employee pay. MR is a statistical tool that allows practitioners to do exactly that. Because MR is such a powerful tool, it is the method of choice that has been used by the courts for decades, and has more recently been endorsed by the OFCCP[1].

This chapter provides an overview of a methodology that may be used to perform an MR analysis to determine whether reliable differences in compensation rates exist between males and females or whites and members of minority groups. A description of how to compute the analysis using both the SPSS® software package as well as Microsoft Excel® will be presented.

It is important to note that there are many features and reports in both SPSS and Excel that will not be discussed in this Chapter. This is not because they are not important. On the contrary, both of these programs offer MR tools and reports that are highly useful and important. However, to explain MR in this level of detail would require an entire book. Rather, this Chapter is devoted to running basic MR analyses and interpreting some of the key analysis outputs.

HOW DOES MULTIPLE REGRESSION (MR) WORK?

In the realm of compensation analyses, MR compares two types of variables. A variable is any factor that can be used to differentiate people; time in job, compensation, and gender, for example.

VARIABLES

As far as MR is concerned, there are only two types of variables: independent and dependent. There is only one dependent variable that is always used in compensation-equity MR analyses—compensation[2] because the goal is to determine whether compensation is based on fair and valid criteria. Compensation is what one is trying to *predict* with the other variables—which are *independent* variables. Sometimes independent variables are called "predictors" because they are used to predict the dependent variable—pay or other compensation factors.

Because the ultimate goal of using MR in compensation analyses is to find out whether gender or minority status are significant independent variables, these variables should be added to the MR model after other job-related variables. In this way, we are setting up the analysis to first allow the job relevant factors to explain pay, before gender/minority status is allowed into the equation. This process essentially mirrors the philosophy behind Title VII because it first assumes that job factors account for pay before looking for discrimination.

CORRELATIONS OF VARIABLES

MR analyses result in a series of statistical outputs that explain how well the independent variables predict compensation. The most basic and fundamental concept in MR analysis is the correlation coefficient. This is simply a measure of relationship or association between two variables. Correlation coefficients can range between 0 and 1.0 (where two variables are directly related and increased values of one variable tend to correspond with increased values in the other —e.g., height and weight) and -1.0 to 0 (where two variables are inversely related—e.g., engine horsepower and fuel consumption). Correlations close to 0 are trivial; correlations closer to 1 (either positive or negative) indicate stronger relationships.

KEY OUTPUTS

One of the key outputs is called the "Multiple R Squared" (R^2). This value is important because it indicates the significance of given variables within the model. For example, an R^2 of .30 shows that 30% of the overall differences among employees' pay rates can be explained by the independent variables in the MR analyses.

Another key output is called the "R^2 Change." This output is useful because it shows how the MR model is improved by the addition of each new variable included in the model. For example, you might include four relevant job factors such as time in job, performance evaluation scores, outside experience, and educational level as independent variables in the model, and then add gender in a new layer to the MR model. This will enable you to establish whether the addition of gender significantly improves the model. For example, if the model has 30% power when only the four job factors are included, but then increases by 4% to 34% after the gender variable is included, we would want to know if this *increase* was statistically significant.

Correlations between independent variables, the R^2 value, and the R^2 Change all have corresponding probability values (called "p-values") that allow the researcher to determine if they are "statistically significant," which occurs when they have p-values less than .05 (or 5%). This applies to p-values for correlations between variables and for the overall MR model (i.e., the p-value of the R^2 or R^2 Change values). It is not necessary that each job factor used as an independent variable in the MR model will be statistically significant when used to predict compensation. However, when the gender or minority status variable is statistically significant (even after accounting for all other variables), a "red flag" occurs.

Let's assume a researcher builds an MR model that includes the following four independent variables which have the p-values: time in job (.03), performance evaluation scores (.10), outside experience (.14), and educational level (.01). Note that only time in job and education are statistically significant because they fall below the .05 "statistical significance" threshold. Performance evaluation scores and outside experience, however, are *approaching* the .05 threshold (with p-values of .10 and .14 respectively), but are not quite low enough (remember that greater correlation values correspond with *lower* p-values). These two factors, however, may nonetheless be *practically significant* (even though they are not statistically significant) to this employer's pay system (as may be evidenced by the employer's pay policies or practices, and to some extent by the p-values that are "leaning" toward significance).

When considering which factors to include in the MR model, researchers need to be selective because it is not advisable to include independent variables into a MR analysis that are neither statistically nor pratically relevant to an employer's pay system. Including excessive and/or irrelevant factors in a MR model may leave no room for gender or minority status to show up as statistically significant even if it really is. One must be careful to not overshadow such possible relationships with a cloud of irrelevant independent variables. The philosophy is to create the most "parsimonious" model (i.e., one that best predicts compensation with the least number of variables).

STEPS FOR CONDUCTING MULTIPLE REGRESSION (MR) ANALYSIS

The steps below describe a general process for conducting MR analyses. However, because MR analyses can be highly complicated and technical, these steps should be regarded as guidelines only. Also, many of these steps can turn from a linear to a circular process due to the dynamic nature of MR analyses.

These steps can also vary based on why the employer is conducting the study. For example, MR analyses that are completed on a proactive basis (i.e., without any pressure from a government agency or pending litigation) can utilize employee grouping variables that are readily available (e.g., job title). However, employers that are under scrutiny will need to carefully create analysis groupings (see "SSEGs" below) before conducting MR analyses because the results of the MR analyses will be more impacted by how the employees are grouped than by any other factor in the analysis process.

STEP 1 – IDENTIFY AND REVIEW AVAILABLE DATA

The first step that must be completed prior to attempting any statistical analysis is to review the contents of the dataset (i.e., spreadsheet). In so doing, one should develop a solid understanding of every relevant variable and verify that it is formatted in a manner that facilitates analysis in SPSS, Microsoft Excel, or other statistical software packages. Typical variables that are useful for conducting an MR analysis to investigate pay differences include:

- Employee ID;

- Job grouping variables such as job title, job group, and Similarly Situated Employee Groups (SSEGs);

- Race/Ethnicity (White, Black, Hispanic, Asian/Pacific Islander, American Indian/Alaskan Native);

- Gender;

- Date of last degree earned;

- Highest degree earned (and type and degree area);

- Date of birth (this information is sometimes used as a substitute, or proxy, for overall work experience)[3];

- Time with company or date of hire;

- Time in current position or date of last change in grade/title;

- Current annual salary or hourly wage;

- Part-time vs. full-time status;

- Exempt vs. non-exempt status;

- Employee location (if not housed at the facility);

- Prior experience data (can take a variety of forms);

- Job performance ratings.

When considering which of these variables to use and how to use them, try to fit them into the MR model in a manner that mirrors the way in which compensation decisions are actually made on the job (this is difficult, but sometimes produces very accurate MR results). For example, if education is treated on the job as simply an "either/or" factor when directly or indirectly determining pay (where those with Bachelors degrees receive more pay, but higher degrees don't necessarily matter), then consider "dummy coding" education using 1s and 0s (see dummy coding discussion below). If, however, education is (directly or indirectly) a continuous factor for compensation decisions (where increasingly higher levels of education may factor into increasingly higher levels of pay), then treat education as a continuous variable in the MR model (e.g., using "12" for high school education, "14" for Associates degree, "16" for Bachelors, "18" for Masters, and "20" for doctorate level degrees). We now turn to how to mechanically include these variables into the MR analysis.

Excel typically creates variables using what it calls a "General" format. While Excel is able to handle these variables appropriately in an MR analysis, other software packages (e.g., SPSS) may or may not import these data correctly. This is especially true with "date" variables. SPSS may also tend to import numbers as "text" if they are in Excel's "general" format. To prevent complications surrounding these issues in Excel, right click on the column label (e.g., "A", "B", etc.), click on "Format Cells" and verify column format. If the column contains:

- Any values that are text, select the "text" format;

- Date values, select the format that uses "3/14/2001";

- Number values, select the "number" format and adjust the number of decimals appropriately;

- Currency values (e.g., Total Compensation), select the "Currency format" and make sure that the specific currency format is set to "$1,234.10."

STEP 2 – CREATE AND VERIFY VARIABLE CODING

It is critical that variables are coded correctly when running any statistical analysis. MR may only be used on numeric variables and therefore it is necessary to confirm that each variable to be included in a MR-based compensation analysis be coded appropriately. Each of the following steps should be completed prior to attempting any actual analyses.

Recode the independent variables, as necessary. This is especially important for the variables of Gender and Ethnicity. For the purposes of clarity and consistency, it is recommended that the variables of gender and ethnicity be coded as follows:

Gender: Recode gender so that males = 0 and females = 1

Ethnicity: Recode ethnicity into a "minority/non-minority" variable with whites = 0 and the minorities = 1. If the compensation of a specific minority group (e.g., African Americans) is of primary concern, whites should be coded as "0" and African Americans would be coded with a "1."

The process of converting categorical data (like gender and minority status) into 1s and 0s is called "dummy coding." The dummy coding protocols above have been provided as suggestions only—it really makes no difference which group is coded 1s or 0s—it only changes the direction in which the correlations will be interpreted (i.e., either positively or negatively). By following the coding procedures recommended above, the researcher will need to look for negative correlations on the gender/minority status variable—indicating that the effect of being a woman or minority is negatively, or inversely, correlated with compensation.

STEP 3 – CONDUCT PRELIMINARY DATA ANALYSIS

Prior to conducting an MR analysis, it is important to begin with a preliminary exploration of the data set. The primary goal of this process is to confirm that the data are valid and to examine the interactions or relationships between variables—particularly the independent variables that will be used to model compensation practices.

By generating a correlation matrix, it is possible to determine the extent to which each of the independent variables is related to compensation. Large and significant correlations mean strong relationships exist between the variables and that each significantly correlating variable by itself has a strong ability to explain or account for why employees receive the compensation they do. Statistical programs like SPSS have menu-driven programs for calculating correlation matrices to evaluate the relationships between the variables in the MR model. To calculate a correlation matrix in Microsoft Excel, follow these steps:

1. Click on the "Tools" menu option;

2. Click on "Data Analysis";

3. Select "Correlation" from the list of available statistical procedures;

4. Click "OK";

5. Select the data to be included in the analysis (including column names if any are being used). However, if column names are included, make sure the Column Labels checkbox is checked;

6. Click on "OK"

Review the correlation matrix and consider the following questions:

- Is there a statistically significant correlation (either positive or negative) between gender or minority status and compensation? While these results by no means represent definitive tests, they do reveal where the employer stands before taking job factors into account.

- What other variables are correlated with compensation?

- Are there any very large correlations that are statistically significant between any of the predictor variables (e.g., age and time in job)? If there are any very large correlations between predictors, this could result in a problem with multicolinearity which may lead to errors in the model (see later in this chapter for a complete discussion on multicolinearity).

Note that because this exploratory analysis was conducted before splitting the employees into their relevant job grouping variable (e.g., job title or SSEG), the results are useful only for informative purposes. As such, this step is helpful for gaining an understanding of which variables are showing correlation tendencies with other variables, including pay.

STEP 4 – CREATE GROUPS OF EMPLOYEES FOR ANALYSES

The process (and related outcomes) used for dividing the employees into analysis groups is the most contentious issue in the realm of MR analyses when compensation is the target of the study. This is because, at least in litigation settings, MR analyses will almost always show fewer "hot spots" (jobs where the gender or minority status variable is statistically significant, even after taking job factors into account) where employees are divided into smaller groups. Plaintiff groups, on the other hand, generally desire to group employees into the largest groups possible because this maximizes their chances of unveiling "hot spots."

With these two opposite extremes at odds, how does a researcher divide employees into analysis groups? Proponents of both extremes will have heated debates about exactly how to divide employees for analysis. We attempt to "split the middle" by offering some guidelines.

The first and primary consideration is to create employee groups that are similarly situated with respect to four primary factors:

1. similarity of the work they perform;

2. levels of responsibility required in their position(s);

3.   skills needed to perform their jobs; and

4.   qualifications needed to perform their jobs.

Employers that have thousands of employees may find this task daunting. In actuality, however, creating SSEGs is a manageable project when knowledgeable professionals are involved. Seasoned veterans who work in the employer's compensation or HR department are usually well-equipped to complete the (sometime tedious) project of grouping the thousands of employees into SSEGs based on these four factors. Usually, grouping the first 30-50% of an employer's workforce goes quickly when professionals who are intimately familiar with the jobs are involved. The remaining portions of the workforce take more time as the odd jobs are combined together (or removed) for analysis purposes.

Job analysis and/or job descriptions are almost always the most informative resources that can be consulted for grouping employees based on these criteria. For many employers, content-specific job titles can provide very clean classification groups with respect to these factors. Combining employee groups across locations can also be done, provided that the pay systems are similar and geographical pay differentials are taken into consideration.

The second consideration surrounds the issue of statistical power[4]. Put simply, statistical power is the ability of a statistical test (i.e., MR) to detect a statistically significant finding if it exists to be found in the dataset. Larger sample sizes will always yield higher statistical power; while smaller sample sizes have lower statistical power. For example, when conducting an MR analysis with three variables (if a researcher is looking for what's called a "medium effect size," or a modest R^2 value of about .13), the researcher can be 80% confident of finding a statistically significant correlation if it exists to be found when a sample of about 80 employees is included in a single analysis group (e.g., a SSEG).

While this value is based on a calculated power analysis that takes the number of variables (3), the desired effect size (.13), and the desired power level (80% confidence) into consideration, there are other "rules of thumb" that can be considered. One such general guideline is to have no less than 50 employees for an MR analysis[5], with the number increasing with larger numbers of independent variables by multiplying the number of independent variables by 8. For example, if the study includes three independent variables, calculate the minimum number of employees needed by adding 50 to 8 x 3 = 24, or 74 employees.

Two additional rules of thumb are available. Where five or fewer independent variables are included in the MR analyses, just exceed the number of independent variables by at least 50 employees (i.e., the total number of subjects equals the number of independent variables plus 50)[6]. Another rule of thumb for MR analyses (that include six or more independent variables), is to simply include a minimum of 10 employees per independent variable.

However, when discussing the minimum overall sample size, one important factor should also be considered: the minimum number of men/women and whites/minorities in the analysis sample (e.g., SSEG). Some have recommended using five as a minimum sample for women or minority groups.[1] This certainly seems to be a reasonable threshold.

These guidelines should be regarded as minimums for statistical power. In practice, however, researchers must deal with the realistic constraints of grouping employees that are similarly situated, and this sometimes dictates conducting MR analyses on smaller groups than what might be ideal under statistical power considerations. It is never recommended to combine dissimilar employees simply in the quest for statistical power.

Here is why statistical power is so important for MR analyses: If a researcher has a large sample in an MR analysis (e.g., a SSEG with 300 employees and three independent "job factor" variables) and the analysis results show that gender or minority status is not statistically significant, the researcher can rest assured that the employer has no evidence of pay discrimination for this SSEG. This is because the analysis had high levels of statistical power, yet it did not find statistical evidence attributed to gender or minority status.

Now consider an MR analysis that includes a SSEG that has only 15 employees with the same three independent variables, and it results in the same finding (i.e., with no statistical evidence of pay discrimination). Under these circumstances one cannot be confident that the analyses resulted in meaningful statistical findings—because the sample size was too small to yield a highly reliable evaluation of the pay differences between groups. On the flipside, if one *does* find statistically significant results with such a small sample size, it cannot be regarded as a highly stable finding because it was based on such a small sample. This is because, in small datasets, just 1-2 employees in the extreme high or low pay range can sometimes have weighty impact in the results.

There is another important consideration that should be made about statistical power and MR analysis. Consider a situation where men earn $45,000/year and women earn $44,500 ($500 less than men). This $500 difference may not be statistically significant in an analysis group where 100 employees (50 men and 50 women) are being compared. However, when the sample size is increased to say 400 employees, with 200 men and 200 women, the same $500 gap may become statistically significant—and this being just a function of statistical power.

Somewhere between the two competing goals of grouping employees based on the similarity of the work they perform, their responsibility level, and the skills and qualifications involved in their positions—yet still taking statistical power into consideration, lays the marriage between the art and science of MR analyses.

STEP 5A1 – CONDUCT THE MULTIPLE REGRESSION (MR) ANALYSIS USING SPSS

Step 5 is broken into two parallel sections that describe how to use SPSS and Excel for conducting MR analyses. Steps 5A1 and 5A2 explain how to conduct MR analyses using SPSS, and this section includes interpretation guidelines that pertain to the output provided exclusively by SPSS. Steps 5B1 and 5B2 explain how to conduct (limited) MR analyses using Excel, followed by a section that describes how to calculate and interpret interaction terms in MR analyses (a process that can be completed using either SPSS or Excel).

To complete an MR analysis using SPSS, follow these steps:

1. Access the regression menu by clicking "Analyze" then "Regression" and then "Linear."

2. Select the Dependent Variable for analysis. This will be the variable that contains compensation information for all employees (e.g., "Total Compensation" or "Base Annual Salary"). Be sure that the variable selected includes the same metric for all employees (e.g., annual salary for all employees—not annual salary for some and the hourly equivalent for others). Also, be sure to remove any bonuses or commissions that are not part of the "typical" pay package from the total compensation amount, unless the reason that bonuses or commissions fluctuate is included as an independent variable in the MR model. For example, if a commission is based on the amount of product a sales person sells each year, then the amount of product sold by the sales person should be included as an independent variable in the MR model.

3. Select the Independent Variables for analysis. This is the heart of MR model development. Selecting these variables should be done using three steps:

    a. Enter the practical factors related to pay as independent variables. These are the variables for which there are policy and/or business practice reasons to include in the analysis because they are used to make compensation decisions, such as tenure on the job or performance ratings.

    b. Click on the "Next" button and enter the "gender" variable into Block 2 of the model. (Note: Gender and race/ethnicity analyses should be conducted separately. With that in mind, this step will be repeating using the minority/non-minority variable when developing a model to examine potential compensation disparities by minority status.)

c.   Make sure that the "Method" drop down menu is set to "Enter."

Regression diagnostics and supplemental statistical procedures

SPSS will generate a range of additional statistics that will help evaluate the model developed as a result of the analyses. Follow these steps to obtain these supplemental reports:

1.   Click on the "Statistics" button at the bottom of the linear regression menu/interface and select the following options:

a.   Click on the "Confidence Intervals" check box.

b.   Click on the "R Square Change" check box.

c.   Click on the "Descriptives" check box.

d.   Click on the "Colinearity Diagnostics" check box.

e.   Click the "Continue" button.

Note: Advanced researchers will want to explore the "Casewise Diagnostics" option, which provides reports showing employees that are outside of their predicted pay levels. This feature is useful for identifying possible data entry errors, or employees that are significantly under- or over-paid based on the factors accounted for in the MR model.

2.   Run the MR analysis and develop an initial model by clicking on the "OK" button.

STEP 5A2–INTERPRET INITIAL RESULTS

After the MR analysis has been run, the next step is to interpret the output. The steps below provide interpretive comments and guidelines for each part of the SPSS output.

Review the model summary

Several parts of the SPSS results shown in Table 7.1 are of major interest. First, notice that the first column is called "Model," and that there are two models (i.e., Model 1 and Model 2). Model 1 contains all of the predictors except the gender or minority/non-minority variable, which is entered in Block 2. Model

Model Summary[c]

Model	R	R Square	Adjusted R Square	Std. Error of the Estimate	R Square Change	F Change	df1	df2	Sig. F Change
					Change Statistics				
1	.659[a]	.435	.343	$11,055.43949	.435	4.764	5	31	.002
2	.754[b]	.569	.483	$9,812.28210	.134	9.353	1	30	.005

a. Predictors: (Constant), HighestDegree, YrsInGrade, Age, PerfCode, YrsOfService

b. Predictors: (Constant), HighestDegree, YrsInGrade, Age, PerfCode, YrsOfService, Gender

c. Dependent Variable: BaseSalary

2 includes all of the independent variables found in Model 1, but also includes the gender or minority/non-minority variable.

Table 7.1   SPSS Model Summary Report

The essential components of this report are explained below:

- The values under the "R" column represent the correlation between all of the predictors taken together and the dependent variable (pay). Higher values of "R" indicate stronger combined relationships and therefore the more explanatory the model.

- The "R Square" (or R^2) column shows the percent of variation in the dependent variable (i.e., compensation) that is accounted for by the information provided by the entire set of independent variables. In the example in Table 7.1, the R^2 in Model 1 is .435 before taking gender into account, and .569 after gender is accounted for (see Model 2).

- The "R Square Change" values show the increase in R^2 over Model 1 (i.e., the percentage of additional variance that is explained by the inclusion of the gender or minority status variable). Notice in Table 7.1 that the R^2 increases from .435 to .569 after taking gender into account, and this increase (.134, or a "13.4% change") is statistically significant (see the Significant F Change discussed below). This implies that the addition of the gender variable significantly enhanced the explanatory power of the model (indicating possible pay discrimination). Small values that are not statistically significant contribute little to the explanatory power of the model.

- The "Significance of F Change" statistic for Model 2 shows the statistical significance of the change between Model 1 and Model 2. If the value is less than .05 in the Model 2 row, the change in R^2 was statistically significant. This suggests that even after accounting for the predictors in Model 1, gender/minority status still explains some of the remaining differences in compensation (in this case, gender accounts for 13.4% more than the job factors alone). If the change in R^2 was not statistically significant, the increase in R Square, if there was any, may have simply been due to chance.

Review the ANOVA Report

The ANOVA Report provides the results of the Analysis of Variance test, which

ANOVA[c]

Model		Sum of Squares	df	Mean Square	F	Sig.
1	Regression	2911334329.63	5	582266865.9	4.764	.002[a]
	Residual	3788905011.55	31	122222742.3		
	Total	6700239341.18	36			
2	Regression	3811812942.53	6	635302157.1	6.598	.000[b]
	Residual	2888426398.65	30	96280879.96		
	Total	6700239341.18	36			

a. Predictors: (Constant), HighestDegree, YrsInGrade, Age, PerfCode, YrsOfService

b. Predictors: (Constant), HighestDegree, YrsInGrade, Age, PerfCode, YrsOfService, Gender

c. Dependent Variable: BaseSalary

essentially reveals if the overall MR model was a "good fit." In other words, this test helps show the researcher if the set of independent variables provide a solid statistical model for predicting pay for the employees included in the study.

Table 7.2 SPSS ANOVA Report

The essential components of this report are explained below:

- The "Regression Sum of Squares" indicates the amount of variation that is explained by the model.

- The "Residual Sum of Squares" is a measure of how much variation is not explained by the model. Therefore, if the Regression Sum of Squares is large compared to the Residual Sum of Squares, this means that the model explains a large portion of the variance in compensation.

- This table is useful for comparing the Regression and Residual Sum of Squares in Model 1 and Model 2 to see whether each of the models has a significant ANOVA value (meaning that the model is effective at explaining a statistically significant portion of the variance).

Coefficients[a]

Model		Unstandardized Coefficients B	Std. Error	Standardized Coefficients Beta	t	Sig.	Collinearity Statistics Tolerance	VIF
1	(Constant)	31038.561	18694.132		1.660	.107		
	Age	371.211	240.275	.220	1.545	.133	.902	1.109
	PerfCode	-370.996	4297.297	-.012	-.086	.932	.875	1.143
	YrsOfService	2079.554	654.699	.460	3.176	.003	.871	1.148
	YrsInGrade	341.916	1059.453	.047	.323	.749	.848	1.179
	HighestDegree	9036.374	2472.815	.508	3.654	.001	.943	1.060
2	(Constant)	40645.955	16886.809		2.407	.022		
	Age	201.791	220.335	.119	.916	.367	.845	1.184
	PerfCode	52.133	3816.585	.002	.014	.989	.873	1.145
	YrsOfService	1575.253	604.024	.348	2.608	.014	.806	1.241
	YrsInGrade	144.362	942.536	.020	.153	.879	.844	1.185
	HighestDegree	6715.482	2322.258	.378	2.892	.007	.843	1.187
	Gender	12165.496	3977.985	.413	3.058	.005	.787	1.270

a. Dependent Variable: BaseSalary

Review the Coefficients Report

The Coefficients Report provides the heart of the analysis results because it shows how well each independent variable predicted compensation. Note that the report includes the independent variables for each model that was included in the analysis.

Table 7.3   SPSS Coefficients Report

The essential components of this report are explained below:

- The values in the "B" column under the "Unstandardized Coefficients" section show how much the dependent variable (i.e., compensation) increases for each 1 unit increase in that particular independent variable while holding all of the other predictors constant. For example, each additional year of service translates to $2,079.55 in compensation (before gender is added in Model 2). Also notice the impact of being female (see Model 2) is about $12,165.50 (even after job relevant factors are accounted for in the model).

- The "Standardized Regression Coefficients" (called "beta-weights") show the predictive power of each independent variable in a uniform way so they can be compared to each other. The values in this column are useful for two reasons: they show the strength of the correlation relationship of each independent variable with the dependent variable, and the direction of the correlation relationship (either positive or negative). Higher absolute values have a stronger impact on the dependent variable (i.e., pay). For example, the "Years of Service" and "Highest Degree" variables have the highest values in Model 1 (.46 and .508 respectively), and are therefore the strongest predictors in that model.

- The "t" and the "Sig." columns contain important data. The "t" shows the direction of the relationship with compensation (using positive and negative values). The "Sig." column reveals the p-value (values less than .05 are statistically significant). A basic rule is that when "t" values exceed 2.0, they become statistically significant at the .05 level (i.e., higher "t" values are associated with lower p-values). Notice that the p-value associated with gender is 0.005—revealing that gender is statistically significant even after controlling for legitimate job-related factors.

- The values in the Tolerance and Variance Inflation Factor (VIF) columns are useful for investigating whether multicollinearity is an issue (see discussion on this topic below). These two values are mathematically related (VIF is inversely related to the Tolerance value). Tolerance has a range from zero to one, and the closer the value is to zero the higher the level of multicollinearity caused by that variable. VIF shows how much the standard error variance of each of the independent variables coefficients increased as a result of multicollinearity. Thus, it is a measure of the cost of multicollinearity in loss of precision, and is directly relevant when performing statistical tests and calculating confidence intervals (which show the range of accuracy for the MR model). High VIF values (a usual threshold is 10.0, which corresponds to a Tolerance value of .10) indicate that the associated variable is a cause of multicollinearity in the model.

While the Regression Coefficients Report (in Figure 7-3) places emphasis on statistical significance (whether the independent variables are significantly correlated with compensation—indicated when the "Sig." column is less than .05 for that variable), what about considering the practical significance of a pay difference? For example, an annual pay difference between groups of $5,000 that is statistically significant represents a greater concern than a pay difference of $2,000 that is also statistically significant. Even pay differences that are large, but are not statistically significant are still a concern to those being underpaid!

On the other hand, what about pay differences between groups that are very small (e.g., $300 per year where average compensation is in the $80,000 per year range) that are statistically significant? Certainly these situations make it easier for employers to make corrections that remove the statistical significance findings. Certainly practical considerations like these should also be considered when interpreting MR analysis results.

Multicollinearity

If two of the variables that are being used to explain compensation are highly correlated, they are referred to as "collinear." When more than two variables are collinear, multicollinearity exists, which may limit the usability of the model. At a minimum, it is not advisable to include independent variables in the same model if they are correlated higher than .80 with each other. If this occurs, consider dropping one of them from the analysis.

Collinearity Diagnostics[a]

Model	Dimension	Eigenvalue	Condition Index	(Constant)	Age	PerfCode	YrsOfService	YrsInGrade	Highest Degree	Gender
1	1	5.560	1.000	.00	.00	.00	.00	.01	.00	
	2	.216	5.077	.00	.00	.02	.04	.61	.01	
	3	.131	6.523	.00	.00	.00	.83	.25	.02	
	4	.050	10.574	.00	.45	.20	.01	.06	.04	
	5	.037	12.237	.00	.02	.37	.08	.05	.65	
	6	.007	27.671	1.00	.52	.40	.03	.02	.27	
2	1	6.324	1.000	.00	.00	.00	.00	.00	.00	.00
	2	.243	5.100	.00	.00	.02	.00	.01	.00	.73
	3	.213	5.455	.00	.00	.01	.04	.65	.01	.10
	4	.130	6.981	.00	.00	.00	.79	.22	.02	.01
	5	.049	11.377	.00	.45	.15	.01	.04	.08	.02
	6	.034	13.589	.00	.00	.46	.11	.05	.57	.09
	7	.007	30.226	.99	.54	.36	.06	.02	.32	.05

a. Dependent Variable: BaseSalary

Many more advanced statistical techniques exist for assessing multicollinearity. SPSS provides two sets of tools that can be used for evaluating this potential limitation. The first set of tools is the Tolerance and Variance Inflation Factor (VIF) noted above. Independent variables that have Tolerance values less than .10 or corresponding Variance Inflation Factor (VIF) values higher than 10.0 indicate multicollinearity. Another set of tools is provided by the Collinearity Diagnostics Report shown in Table 7-4.

Table 7.4   SPSS Collinearity Diagnostics Report

The Condition Index in the third column is the key in this report. The Condition Index measures the "dependency" of the independent variables, and values in this column will increase as additional related variables are added to the MR model (it's cumulative). Various guidelines are available for interpreting the results in this report. For example, SPSS provides conservative guidelines that Condition Index values over 15 indicate possible problems with collinearity and higher than 30 suggests a serious problem with collinearity.

Evaluating the Condition Index values can be done in conjunction with an evaluation of the "Variance Proportions" data also in this report, which are shown for each of the independent variables. For example, some advise that multicollinearity exists if (first) the Condition Index exceeds a threshold of 30 and (second) two or more Variance Proportions in those rows exceed .50[7]. Others advise using the same process, but with a .90 threshold (again for at least two independent variables) for the Variance Proportions in those rows where the Condition Index exceeds 15 or 30 (with 30 being the typical criteria of choice)[8].

If the goal of the MR analysis is simply to predict pay using a collection of independent variables that are statistically or practically relevant to compensation, then multicollinearity may only be a minor limitation (i.e., the predictions may still be accurate). However, if the goal of the MR analyses is to understand exactly how the various independent variables impact compensation, multicollinearity can be a significant issue. This is because the individual p-values for the independent variables can be misleading and the "confidence intervals" (which shows the range of accuracy) may be very wide.

What can be done about multicollinearity? Perhaps the best solution is to find out why it is occurring and remove the variables that are creating the problem. This is especially true if the variables creating the problem are either redundant to other variables or are not practically relevant to predicting pay. Another way to address multicollinearity is to combine the co-linear variables. This can be done by first standardizing[9] each variable then simply adding them together to create a new variable. Multicollinearity can also be reduced by "centering" the variables, which can be done by computing the mean of each independent variable and replacing each value with the difference between it and the mean.

The key to the interpretation

While reviewing the Coefficients Report in Table 7.3, the particular area of interest is whether the gender or minority status variable is statistically significant in Model 2. If it is not, it means that gender (or minority status) did not appear to be related to differences in compensation after the effects of the other variables are accounted for and therefore there is no statistical evidence of possible pay discrimination. It is important to note that the two-model process that has been used in this example has been provided for clarity purposes only. Assessing whether the R^2 Change in Model 2 is statistically significant is effectively the same as simply placing all independent variables in the same "model" or block and then assessing whether the gender/minority status variable is statistically significant. This is exactly the process followed for the MR analysis using Excel described later. In other words, the p-value of the R^2 Change between the two MR models (where gender/minority status is the only variable in the second model) will be exactly the same as the p-value of the gender/minority status variable that is simply included in the first model with the other variables.

STEP 5B1 – CONDUCTING MULTIPLE REGRESSION (MR) USING MICROSOFT EXCEL

There are two ways to use Excel to perform statistical analyses. One way is to program formulas from scratch into the spreadsheet. This process, however, can be complex and is certainly time consuming. Thankfully, there is an alternative that is easy to use, relatively straightforward, and which presents the relevant statistical results in a way that is easy to understand. Before this can be done, however, the Excel "Analysis ToolPak" needs to be installed (this tool is included on the Microsoft Excel installation CD but it needs to be intentionally installed when Excel is first loaded onto a computer or added later using the instructions below).

Installing the Analysis ToolPak

The following is a step-by-step process for installing the Analysis ToolPak:

1. Have the original Microsoft Office installation CD available in case the installation process requests the CD during the process (do not place it in the drive at this time unless prompted).

2. Start Microsoft Excel and click on the "Tools" menu located at the top of the screen.

3. Click on the "Add-Ins" option that is located inside the "Tools" menu.

4. After clicking on the "Add-Ins" menu option, a window will open. Make sure that the check box located next to "Analysis ToolPak" has a checkmark. If there is already a checkmark in this box, it means that the Analysis ToolPak is already installed.

5. Click on "OK." Excel will now begin installing the Analysis ToolPak (if it was not already installed).

6. At this point, the installation process may request inserting the Microsoft Office installation CD. If this occurs, follow the instructions, and after this process is complete, the Analysis ToolPak will be ready for use. Now, when accessing the "Tools" menu in Excel, a new menu option called "Data Analysis" will be available.

Conducting step-by-step MR analyses using Excel

This section provides a step-by-step guide to using Microsoft Excel to perform a basic MR analysis. A copy of the Excel file used in the examples in this section is included on the Evaluation CD included with this book. Readers are encouraged to follow along and actually run the analysis while reading.

1. Create an Excel worksheet that contains the variables relevant for

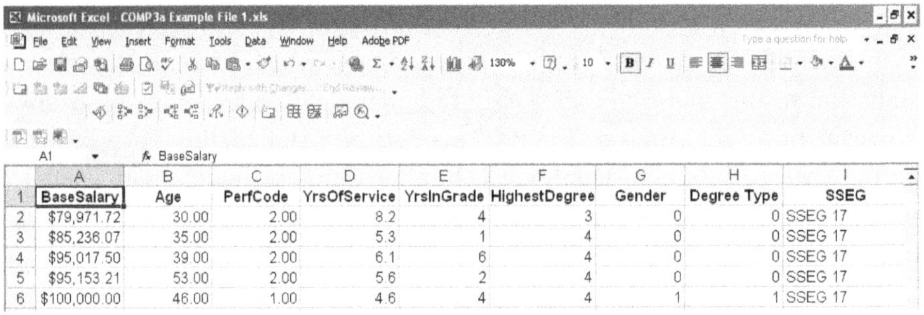

Figure 7.1 Setting up an Excel file for use in multiple regression

the MR analysis. Place the dependent variable (pay) in Column A. Place the independent variables (e.g., age, time with company, time in job, years of education, starting salary, performance appraisal score) starting in column B and continuing across columns (with one variable per column). It is important to make sure that all independent variables are next to each other without any separations (columns cannot be skipped when selecting variables to include in the MR analysis—see Figure 7.1).

2. Click on the "Tools" menu, then on the "Data Analysis" menu option. The Data Analysis window shown in Figure 7.2 will appear.

3. Using the scroll bar, scroll down to access the "Regression" option and select it. The window shown in Figure 7.3 will appear. Pay

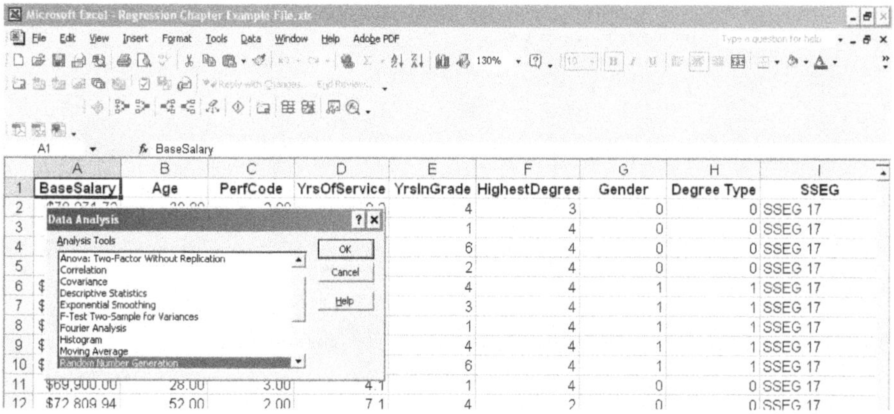

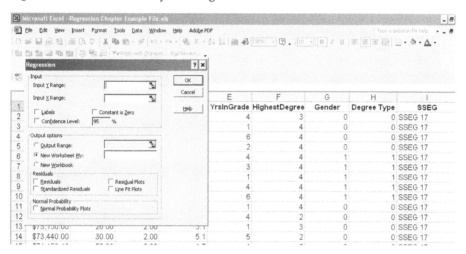

Figure 7.2   Excel Data Analysis dialogue box

Figure 7.3   Excel Regression window

particular attention to the following parts of this window. First, there is a text box titled "Input Y Range" which is where the compensation variable will be identified (which in this case is BaseSalary). Next, there is a text box titled "Input X Range" where the independent variables will be identified (i.e., the variables that will be used to model, or explain, why employees receive the compensation they do). At the far right side of each of these text boxes is a button that, when selected, allows use of the mouse to select the relevant data.

4.   Click on the button located at the right end of the "Input Y Range" text box. The computer screen will look like Figure 7.4.

5.   Place the mouse pointer over the BaseSalary column label that is located in cell A1. Holding down the right mouse button, highlight

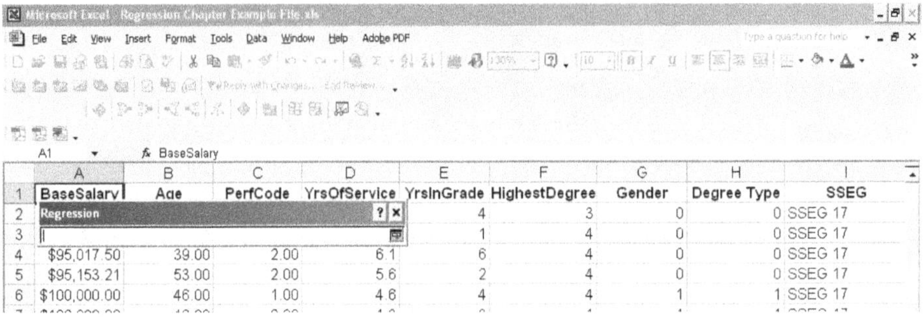

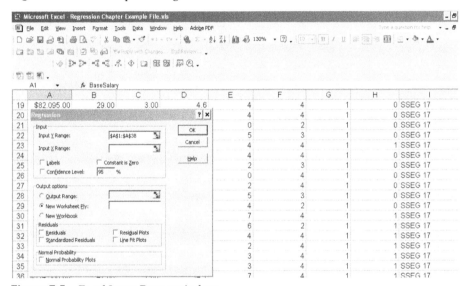

Figure 7.4   Excel Input Y range window

Figure 7.5   Excel Input Range window

the BaseSalary title and all of the data included in column A under BaseSalary. After highlighting the data in column A and releasing the mouse button, click on the button that is located at the right edge of the Regression dialogue box. The computer screen will look like Figure 7.5.

6. Click on the button located at the right end of the "Input X Range" text box.

7. Place the mouse pointer over the Age column label that is located the cell B1. Holding the right mouse button down, highlight the Age title, drag the mouse to the right until column G and then all of the data included in columns B through G underneath the column labels. Note that Column G identifies the employee's gender and so this analysis will seek to determine whether reliable differences

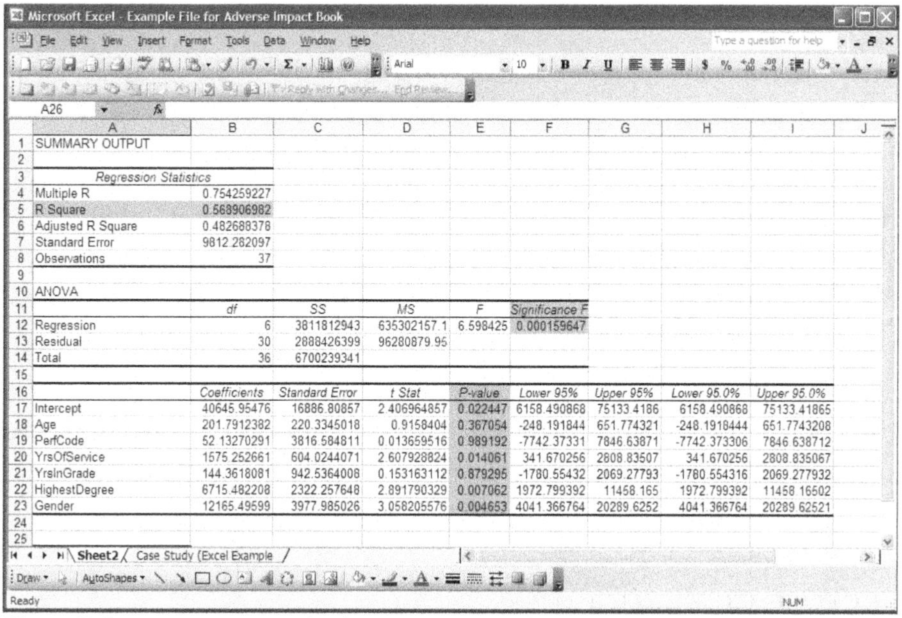

SUMMARY OUTPUT

Regression Statistics	
Multiple R	0.754259227
R Square	0.568906982
Adjusted R Square	0.482688378
Standard Error	9812.282097
Observations	37

ANOVA

	df	SS	MS	F	Significance F
Regression	6	3811812943	635302157.1	6.598425	0.000159647
Residual	30	2888426399	96280879.95		
Total	36	6700239341			

	Coefficients	Standard Error	t Stat	P-value	Lower 95%	Upper 95%	Lower 95.0%	Upper 95.0%
Intercept	40645.95476	16886.80857	2.406964857	0.022447	6158.490868	75133.4186	6158.490868	75133.41865
Age	201.7912382	220.3345018	0.9158404	0.367054	-248.191844	651.774321	-248.1918444	651.7743208
PerfCode	52.13270291	3816.584811	0.013659516	0.989192	-7742.37331	7846.63871	-7742.373306	7846.638712
YrsOfService	1575.252661	604.0244071	2.607928824	0.014061	341.670256	2808.83507	341.670256	2808.835067
YrsInGrade	144.3618081	942.5364008	0.153163112	0.879295	-1780.55432	2069.27793	-1780.554316	2069.277932
HighestDegree	6715.482208	2322.257648	2.891790329	0.007062	1972.799392	11458.165	1972.799392	11458.16502
Gender	12165.49599	3977.985026	3.058205576	0.004653	4041.366764	20289.6252	4041.366764	20289.62521

Figure 7.6 Interpreting Multiple Regression Analysis Output

in compensation exist between males and females. For conducting an MR analysis comparing whites and minorities, the variable in column G would need to indicate the employee's white/minority status (0 = white; 1 = minority). In general, do not include both gender and minority status variables in the same analysis because the results will be difficult to interpret. After highlighting the data in columns B through G and releasing the mouse button, click on the button that is located at the right edge of the query box (similar to the step completed while selecting data for pay using the BaseSalary variable).

8. Note that in this example file each column has a descriptive label in row 1. Because these labels are included (which is always a good idea because it will make the results of the analysis much easier to understand), a check mark must be placed in the "Label" checkbox located just below "Input X Range." This tells Excel to ignore the first row and only use that information to label specific output information. Click on "OK" and Excel will compute the requested regression analysis. The computer screen will look like Figure 7.6.

STEP 5B2 – INTERPRET INITIAL RESULTS

After calculating the appropriate statistical analyses, Excel automatically opens a new worksheet and pastes the information presented in Figure 7.6. To draw the reader's attention to the important components of this analysis, various areas have been shaded (Excel does not automatically provide this shading). However, these shaded areas will be referred to in the following step-by-step guide to interpreting these results:

1. Under "Regression Statistics," view the shaded row titled "R Square." Notice that the number presented is 0.568906982 (rounded to 0.57). Earlier in this chapter, it was pointed out that when a correlation is squared, it indicates the percent of variation in compensation that is accounted for or explained by the variable (or variables) with which it is being correlated. The R Square simply shows the percentage of variation across employees in their compensation that is explained by the combination of all the variables included in the model. In this case, the R Square of .57 shows that a total of 57% of an employee's compensation appears to be explained by a combination of a) age, b) performance appraisal score, c) years of service, d) years in grade, e) highest degree earned, and f) gender.

2. In the section titled ANOVA (which stands for Analysis of Variance), notice that a cell titled "Significance F" is shaded. This is a very important part of the report. Remember that MR is designed to be used to study data where the relationships between variables is "linear." This ANOVA table is a statistical test that measures whether the relationships between the independent variables and compensation is linear and therefore appropriate for use in MR analyses[10]. Specifically, if the number listed under Significance F is less than .05, it indicates that the relationships are characterized by a linear relationship. If the number is .05 or greater, it means that something about the data makes it inappropriate for use with MR. There are strategies for dealing with these kinds of data problems called "non-linear transformations" but they are beyond the scope of this book. Simply be aware that if the Significance F is .05 or greater, the results of the analysis will be questionable and may not be reliable. In this case, the number shown under Significance F is 0.000159647—which is definitely less than 0.05! In this case, it is safe to assume that the relationship between compensation and the set of independent variables is linear and significant.

3.   Evaluate the p-values for each of the independent variables. This information is highlighted to make it easier to evaluate. Notice that each independent variable is identified in a row and a variety of numbers is listed to the right of the independent variable. Each of these numbers provides important information. However, to simply answer the question of whether there is a statistically significant difference in compensation for males and females exist (after taking into account legitimate job related factors that could explain these differences), the only number that needs to be reviewed is the p-value associated with gender. Note that the p-value associated with gender is 0.004653 (which can be rounded to 0.005). If the p-value shown is less than 0.05 (which is true in this case), it reveals that even after controlling for legitimate job-related factors there were statistically significant differences in the compensation of males and females. There are at least two possible explanations for this:

- First, it is very possible that important and legitimate job-related factors that could explain the differences in compensation were not included in the analysis. Available data should be more carefully reviewed to determine if there are other variables that should be included in the MR analysis.

- Another possibility is that the decision process used to establish the compensation of males and females was based on something other than legitimate job-related factors.

Interaction terms: When two variables create a third

Interactions occur in MR analyses when two independent variables interact in a way that creates a third "phantom" variable or phenomenon. For example, habitual smoking has a negative correlation with life expectancy. Being obese also has a negative correlation with life expectancy. But when these two variables are combined together (i.e., a person habitually smokes *and* is obese), a third, synergistic effect emerges—that of the *combined* effect of smoking and being obese.

Standard MR models that include only the "main effects" (or the natural variables like those discussed above) are forced to assume that these variables impact all the employees in the group in the same way. From a purely statistical perspective, this means that the employees grouped together should exhibit similar relationships to these pay-related variables for the model to work properly. However, when significant interactions are occurring between the variables, it is incorrect to interpret the MR model that includes only the natural variables. For this reason, it is useful for the researcher to determine whether interactions exist between the variables being used in the MR analysis. In this way, the researcher can determine the extent to which the effects of one predictor variable depends upon levels of another predictor variable.

The interaction between two independent variables is obtained by multiplying the two variables to create a new variable (called an "interaction term"). For example, multiplying the gender variable (coded 0 for male; 1 for females) by the "time in job" variable will create a Gender/Tenure interaction variable. By using interactions in the MR analyses, the combined dynamic of being a female and one's level of job tenure would be allowed to statistically interact with one another in their influence on the dependent variable (pay).

Interactions are typically included in the MR model by first entering each of the two variables that were used to make the interaction (e.g., Gender and Tenure), and then including the interaction term in the second block (e.g., if using SPSS) of the model. By using this process, the statistical significance of the interaction effect (shown by the significance of the R^2 Change) can be attributed to the interaction of the two independent variables, beyond what they contributed to the regression model independently.

STEP 6 – CONDUCT A COHORT ANALYSIS

The last step in the compensation analysis is to conduct a Cohort Analysis for the employee groups (e.g., SSEGs) where statistically significant differences exist for gender or minority status. This process can be completed by examining the highest paid males/whites and the lowest paid females/minorities (based on whether the statistically significant finding is based on gender or minority status in the at-issue SSEG) to determine if there are other factors that seem to explain why these differences exist. These can be soft factors or qualitative factors that may not be statistical in nature, or can be variables that are statistical in nature but for some reason were not captured in the MR analysis. For example, it is common practice for many employers to base starting salary on an applicant's previous salary and/or experience, but it is but it is rare that employers will have this information included in their HRIS databases. While MR is a powerful tool for evaluating differences in compensation, it can only take the researcher so far. If, after careful consideration of relevant factors and analysis groupings, gender/minority status continues to be significant predictors of pay, nothing can replace the importance of a thorough review of personnel files, applicant vitae/resume, and interview notes. And for those significant differences that remain unexplainable by such factors, corrective actions should be made.

When it comes to making overall conclusions about a particular employer's pay practices and whether they have been "fair" or "discriminatory," careful attention should be given to the trend of the findings. For example, it is not uncommon in practice to identify a similar number of SSEGs with significant pay disparities for men and women alike (e.g., five significant findings against men and five against women for the same employer, where a total of only 10 significant pay disparities were found).

NOTES

1   OFCCP Compensation Analysis Guidelines: Interpreting Nondiscrimination Requirements of Executive Order 11246 with respect to Compensation Discrimination (71 FR 35124-35141) and related voluntary self-analysis guidelines (71 FR 35114-35122); Federal Register, June 16, 2006.

2   There are multiple types of compensation metrics that can be used in MR analyses, such as "Total Compensation," "Base Annual Salary," "Pay per Hour," and bonuses, just to name a few. Only one type of compensation metric should be used for each analysis, unless it makes logical sense to combine several together. For example, it might make logical sense to combine "Base Annual Salary" with commissions when computing overall compensation for sales personnel. However, this should only be done if the factors used to pay employees based on commission were also factored into the MR analyses as independent variables. However, all analyzed employees should have equivalent metrics (i.e., if one person in the job class has their base annual salary and commissions combined for analysis purposes, all people in that same job class should have their base annual salary and commissions combined).

3   Because employee age is oftentimes a solid predictor of pay, but is sometimes compressed due to the diminishing relationship between age and compensation that typically occurs at various age levels, sometimes using transformations on the age variable is necessary (e.g., squaring).

4   Statistically speaking, power has to do with Type I and Type II errors. Type I errors occur when a researcher concludes "there is a statistically significant difference" when there really is not. In the realm of compensation analyses, this can be costly because an employer has essentially wrongfully concluded that their employer has potentially discriminatory pay practices. Type II errors occur when the researcher concludes "a statistically significant difference does not exist," but it actually does. This leads employers to miss a real difference in pay practices that could have possibly been identified if the study had higher levels of statistical power.

5   Green, S. B. (1991). How many subjects does it take to do a regression analysis? Multivariate Behavioral Research, 26, 499-510.

6   Harris, R. J. (1985). A primer of multivariate statistics (2nd ed.). New York: Academic Press.

7   Tabachnick, B. G., & Fidell, L.S. (2001). Using multivariate statistics (4th ed.). Needham Heights, MA: Allyn & Bacon.

8   Hair, J. F., Anderson, R. E., Tatham, R. L., & Black, W. (1998). Multivariate data analysis (5th ed.). New Jersey: Prentice Hall.

9   Standardizing variables can be done by converting them into Z-scores so they can be compared relevant to each other. This function can be readily completed using SPSS or other statistical programs.

10   The ANOVA table simply shows whether the R^2 for the model is statistically significant. If it is non-significant, then a nonlinear relationship is one of the many possible reasons for the non-significance. It could be restricted range in the variance of the independent variables, low statistical power, the fact that no relationship really exists at all, or a host of other possible reasons. Analysis of residual plots is needed to identify nonlinearity.

CHAPTER 8

Internet Applicant Regulations: Record-Keeping, Adverse Impact, and Basic Qualifications (BQs)

Patrick Nooren

INTRODUCTION

When the Uniform Guidelines were first published in 1978, it would have been impossible to envision a tool that would someday allow people to instantly apply for open positions across America, submit their resumes to "banks" of databases to be evaluated by hundreds or thousands of employers, or sift through and apply to multitudes of open positions from the comfort of their own homes. Remember, in 1978 personal computers weren't much more than elaborate calculators and word processors. That all changed as the popularity of the Internet exploded in the early 1990s. Websites such as Monster.com sprang to life and changed the way people applied for job vacancies. No longer were pencil-and-paper resumes the norm—they were now the exception—and it didn't stop there. Once employers realized the scope of the Internet as a recruitment tool they began to develop their own websites to allow people to view open positions, read job descriptions, and apply for specific jobs "online." The paradigm had shifted virtually overnight.

Unfortunately, rapid growth is often accompanied by growing pains, and there has been no exception in this case. As employers began to see the utility of the Internet and related technologies as a means for collecting information on greater volumes of prospective applicants, it became apparent that enforcement agencies were also going to have to change to reflect the need for enforcement of EEO within this new paradigm. The requirement that employers analyze their hiring processes for discrimination didn't change, but it did become much more complicated as a result of the technological advancements. Per the 1978 Uniform Guidelines, "[t]he precise definition of the term 'applicant' depends upon the user's recruitment and selection procedures. The concept of an applicant is that of a person who has *indicated an interest* in being considered for hiring, promotion, or other employment opportunities (emphasis added)." In other words, under the Uniform

Guidelines definition, *everyone* who indicated an *interest* in a position was considered an applicant and subject to analysis. In a world where applicants can use software to "spam" resumes to thousands of employers instantly or apply to hundreds of jobs at once using a "shopping-cart" mentality, how can employers properly analyze their hiring processes for discriminatory impact? It is because of these and other similar issues that on October 7, 2005, the OFCCP issued the Obligation to Solicit Race and Gender Data for Enforcement Purposes: Final Rule (hereafter referred to as the "Internet Applicant Regulations") and associated recordkeeping rules[1].

INTERNET APPLICANT REGULATIONS

Issued on October 7, 2005, the Internet Applicant Regulations and recordkeeping rules became effective 120 days later on February 6, 2006. The primary purpose of the rule was to clarify three important issues: 1) define "Internet applicants," 2) outline recordkeeping requirements relative to the hiring carried out through the Internet or related electronic data technologies, and 3) describe the information employers must solicit and submit to the OFCCP to evaluate impact within their selection processes.

The Internet Applicant Regulations require that employers analyze all expressions of interest meeting the following four criteria[2]:

1. The individual submits an expression of interest in employment through the Internet or related electronic data technologies;

2. The employer considers the individual for employment in a particular position;

3. The individual's expression of interest indicates the individual possesses the basic qualifications (BQs) for the position; and,

4. The individual at no point in the employer's selection process prior to receiving an offer of employment from the employer, removes himself or herself from further consideration or otherwise indicates that he or she is no longer interested in the position.

Each of these four criteria is discussed at length below.

CRITERIA 1: SUBMITS AN EXPRESSION OF INTEREST THROUGH THE INTERNET OR RELATED ELECTRONIC DATA TECHNOLOGIES[3]

Despite its advantages, the Internet and related technologies are still relatively new, not yet adopted by all employers and/or applicants, and not evenly distributed amongst all race/ethnic and socioeconomic groups. In fact, according to a study by the US Department of Commerce (2000)[4]:

- People with a college degree are eight times more likely to have a PC at home and 16 times more likely to have Internet access at home than those with an elementary school education.

- A high-income household in an urban area is 20 times more likely to have Internet access than a rural, low-income household.

- A child in a low-income white family is three times more likely to have Internet access than a child in a comparable black family, and four times more likely than a child in a comparable Hispanic family.

- A wealthy household of Asian descent is 34 times more likely to have Internet access than a poor black household.

- A child in a two-parent white household is twice as likely to have Internet access as a child in a single-parent household. If the child in a two-parent household is black, he or she is four times more likely to have Internet access than his single-parent counterpart.

- Disabled people are nearly three times less likely to have home access to the Internet than people without disabilities.

There will continue to be a need for traditional paper applications and resumes for the foreseeable future for the above reasons and several others. As a result, the Internet Applicant Regulations distinguish between "traditional applicants" and "Internet applicants," stating that if an employer considers expressions of interest from the Internet or related data technologies *and* more traditional paper submissions then the Internet definition will apply. However, if the employer does not allow individuals to apply electronically, then the traditional OFCCP recordkeeping rules apply[5]: "The precise definition of the term 'applicant' depends on the user's recruitment and selection procedures. The concept of an applicant is that of a person who has indicated an interested in being considered for hiring, promotion, or other employment opportunities. This interest might be expressed by completing an application form, or might be expressed orally, depending on the employer's practice."

Realizing that technologies would continue to advance and quickly make obsolete any current definition, the OFCCP avoided a precise definition of "Internet or related electronic data technologies." However, the preamble to the Uniform Guidelines "Additional" Questions and Answers do provide six examples of technologies that would meet the standard and are currently in use today[6]:

1. Electronic mail/email: To include emails either sent or received.

2. Resume databases: These are databases of personal profiles/resumes that can be searched by employers for individuals with certain BQs (e.g., Monster.com).

3. Job banks: The opposite of resume databases, these are databases of available job openings that applicants can search based upon certain criteria. Typically, job banks are created by third-party providers such as America's Job Bank or they can be maintained by companies through their own websites.

4. Electronic scanning technology: This technology scans hard-copy resumes and/or applications into a database to later be searched using relevant criteria.

5. Applicant tracking systems/Applicant service providers: Most applicant tracking systems allow individuals to apply online and then track the individual's progress, identifying where they are in the overall process, their scores in any tests/interviews, and where/why they fall out of the hiring process (if applicable). Some systems even compile applicants from both internal and external databases for combined searches.

6. Applicant screeners: Typically third-party vendors that focus on providing employers with applicants that meet certain skillset requirements.

CRITERIA 2: CONSIDERS THE INDIVIDUAL FOR EMPLOYMENT IN A PARTICULAR POSITION[7]

Identifying applicants who are considered for a particular position seems like a simple task. Unfortunately, more often than not it is the exact opposite. According to the Internet Applicant Regulations, a person does not become an applicant until that person is "considered," and an individual is not considered until "the employer assesses the substantive information provided with the expression of interest with respect to any qualifications involved with a particular position."

So, how do employers successfully navigate the complexities of documenting those they consider while concurrently meeting the legitimate business needs of a diverse and qualified, yet manageable, applicant pool? Fortunately, the

Internet Applicant Regulations provide for a number of ways to address these concerns. If employers receive a high volume of applications, the Internet Applicant Regulations permit the use of standardized protocols by which employers can refrain from considering applications that are not submitted in accordance with established procedures. Requiring applicants to apply for specific positions, in a specific manner, within a specific timeframe are just some of the strategies employers can use to refine and restrict applicant pools. Not accepting unsolicited resumes or requiring that all resumes be submitted to a centralized location can also be helpful.

When pools of applicants become excessive, the Internet Applicant Regulations also permit the use of "data management techniques" to further refine the pool of those who are being considered. These techniques include, but are not limited to, random sampling (e.g., selecting every 9th record) and absolute numerical limits (e.g., selecting the first 50 applicants resulting from a database search, etc.). When using data management techniques, it is important that they be objective and not just consider an applicant's qualifications. It is also important that, after using data management techniques, the resulting pool of applicants is similar in composition to the original pool of those submitting expressions of interest.

Although there are many different scenarios which may affect whether an applicant is "considered" by an employer, one typical example is worth mentioning in more detail. Does a contractor "consider" an individual merely by running a search of basic qualifications that brings up the individual's resume, if the contractor never opens the resume? The answer is no. If the contractor does not open the resume as a result of appropriate data management techniques that limit the number of resumes to review, then the contractor has not "considered" that individual. Keep in mind, however, that the resumes for all who met the basic qualifications must be retained.

CRITERIA 3: THE INDIVIDUAL MEETS THE BASIC QUALIFICATIONS (BQS)[8]

For the past several decades, employers have argued that for practical reasons it was necessary to consider for employment only those individuals possessing the requisite Basing Qualifications (BQs). Unfortunately, during that same timeframe, enforcement agencies have been required to adhere to the definition of applicant set forth in the Uniform Guidelines, which was silent on the topic of qualifications. Fortunately for employers, the ability to consider an individual's BQs is a cornerstone of the Internet Applicant Regulations.

According to the Internet Applicant Regulations, acceptable BQs must be *established in advance*, prior to considering any expressions of interest (regardless of whether they are advertised to potential applicants): "The final rule provides that if the contractor does not advertise for the position, the contractor may use 'an alternative device to find individuals for consideration (for example, through an external resume database),' and establish the qualification criteria by making and maintaining a record of such qualifications for the position prior to considering any expression of interest for that position. Contractors must retain records of these established qualifications in accordance with section 60–1.12(a)" (p. 58953). In addition, acceptable BQs must meet *all* of the following three conditions. BQs must be:

1.   Noncomparative (i.e., used as hurdles);

2.   Objective and not depend on subjective judgment; and

3.   Relevant to the performance of the particular position and enable the employer to accomplish business-related goals.

How can employers develop BQs that will survive scrutiny from government enforcement agencies (e.g., OFCCP)? What about challenges that are brought by private plaintiff groups? Employers that are challenged because of their BQs will generally not have a difficult time defending the first two criteria indicated above (unless of course they were clearly violated). This is because the first two requirements are very clear-cut and uncomplicated. Employers can address these by insuring that BQs operate as "hurdles" (i.e., are either met or not met) and are sufficiently objective that a third-party, with the contactor's technical knowledge, would be able to evaluate whether the job seeker possesses the BQs.

It is the third criteria that will, or will not, carry the day when an employer's BQs are challenged. The reason for this is straightforward, the "relevant to performance" criterion has *two levels*. The first level is exactly as it is written and applies to an employer's recordkeeping requirements. The second level however, is where employers should be most concerned. This "second level" exists whenever the employer's BQs *create adverse impact*. Once this happens, the full weight of federal anti-discrimination laws (Title VII of the 1991 Civil Rights Act) immediately applies, which is a much higher standard. Rather than the first level (showing that the BQ is simply "relevant" to job performance), now an employer will be required to prove—using the Uniform Guidelines and other relevant standards—that the BQ is "job related and consistent with business necessity."

This has been true of BQs that have adverse impact since the Griggs v. Duke Power Company (1971) case, where the BQ of having a high school diploma had adverse impact against blacks and was not justified on the basis of job relatedness. When outlined in 1978, the Uniform Guidelines adopted much of the Griggs standard for establishing the "job relatedness" threshold that selection procedures (including BQ screens) need to meet if they have adverse impact. And, this "job relatedness" standard has been essentially coined "validity" ever since.

So how can employers meet the *level two* standard (showing "job relatedness" or "validity" for their BQs when they have adverse impact)? Below are some guidelines for doing just this. Firstly, however, the reader is referred to Chapter 5 for a complete discussion on validating training, education, and experience requirements. This chapter provides guidelines for setting up rated and scored BQ requirements that are limited to training, education, and experience types of BQs. The reason for this is because BQ screening systems that are scored allow applicants to demonstrate their qualifications for the job by any combination of education or experience (even including volunteer experience). Thus, it is essentially a scored selection procedure, rather than "prescreening" BQs where applicants self-report whether they possess a pre-defined level of a certain BQ. Chapter 5 does not review steps for establishing BQs that are self-reported or self-rated by an applicant; this is provided here.

Steps for validating BQs that are self-reported by applicants

There are various methods that can be used to validate BQs. At the heart of all acceptable methods is a "linkage" or a clear connection that traces the BQ back to the essential requirements of the job. These are usually found in a job analysis that outlines the knowledges, skills, abilities, and personal characteristics (KSAPCs) of the target position (see Chapter 2 for a full discussion on conducting job analyses). Section 14C6 of the Uniform Guidelines also provides clear guidance on the type of evidence required for proving validity of BQs that are based on training or experience.

The five-step process outlined below provides steps that, when conducted in order and completely, should survive a full "job relatedness" review when employers need to justify BQs that have adverse impact. However, these steps are not provided to simply justify a BQ that has adverse impact. This is because a BQ that is valid is one that is truly anchored in the actual requirements of the job. Making sure that the actual requirements of the job are embedded in the BQ is the net goal of any thorough BQ validation process. The five steps suggested for validating BQs are:

1.   Develop a job analysis for the target position. A job analysis process results in a document that is more in-depth than most

"job description" or "job specification" documents. A Uniform Guidelines-style job analysis will include an analysis of duties, KSAPCs, physical requirements, and other requirements (e.g., licenses). Job analyses should always include input from qualified Job Experts, and it is typically recommended to include at least seven Job Experts in the process (more is helpful with positions that have more than 50 incumbents). The final job analysis should represent all KSAPCs with at least 70% agreement from Job Experts (e.g., "70% of Job Experts agree that KSAPC #4 is at least critically important").

2.　Isolate critical KSAPCs from the job analysis that are necessary on the first day on the job (i.e., before any training is provided). See the "Selection Plan" section in Chapter 2 for further details on setting apart KSAPCs that can be included in a selection process.

3.　Develop multiple levels (between 4 and 9) for each BQ requirement (to be reviewed and rated by Job Experts). This can be accomplished by working with 1-2 Job Experts, trainers, or supervisors to draft a set of BQ requirements for a similar area (i.e., education/experience, weight handling requirements, licenses, etc.) which range in qualification from the lowest to highest level that might possibly be required for entering the position. For example, consider the following four BQ levels for an HR Consultant position (the BQ in this example pertains to training, education, and experience—the same process can be used for other BQs, such as weight handling requirements).

- Level 1: Must possess BA/BS in statistics, business, psychology, or HR.

- Level 2: Must possess BA/BS in statistics, business, psychology, or HR and two years (FT/equiv.) experience in HR, personnel, or EEO field applying statistical and data analysis methods/concepts; or, Masters degree in same fields with no experience.

- Level 3: Must possess BA/BS in statistics, business, psychology, or HR and four years (FT/equiv.) experience in HR, personnel, or EEO field applying statistical and data analysis methods/ concepts; or, Masters degree in same fields with two years experience; or, Doctorate degree in same fields with no experience.

Basic Qualification (BQ) Development Survey											
Target Position: _____ Job Expert's Name: _____ Date: _____											
BQ Level	Description	What **KSAs** are linked to the BQ?	Is the BQ based on a clear resemblance between the specific behaviors, products, and KSAs required on the job?		Is the BQ based on **objective criteria related to actual job requirements**? Answer "Yes" if a third-party with your employer's technical knowledge would be able to evaluate whether the applicant possesses the qualification (without more information about your employer's judgment).		Is the BQ the **MINIMUM** level/amount needed on the **FIRST DAY** of the job (before training)?		Will the BQ be **easily understood** by applicants?		Is the BQ designed to differentiate whether an applicant is minimally qualified for the job (rather than being used to differentiate one applicant from another)?
		List #s from Job Analysis	Yes	No	Yes	No	Yes	No	Yes	No	Yes	No
Note: If the suggested BQs in this survey do not meet the requirements, please feel free to suggest new and/or revised BQs to management. Also, notify management if there are different Basic Qualifications that a person could possess prior to the first day on the job that that would be equally acceptable but that would exclude fewer job applicants than the Basic Qualification(s) offered here.											

Table 8.1   Basic Qualification (BQ) Development Survey

- Level 4: Must possess BA/BS in statistics, business, psychology, or HR and six years (FT/equiv.) experience in HR, personnel, or EEO field applying statistical and data analysis methods/concepts; or, Masters degree in same fields with two years experience; or, Doctorate degree in same fields with no experience.

4. Convene a panel of seven to ten Job Experts to review and rate each draft BQ level on several factors, including:

a. Is the BQ based on a clear resemblance between the specific behaviors, products, and KSAPCs required on the job?

b. Is the BQ based on objective criteria related to actual job requirements? Job Experts should be instructed to answer "Yes" if a third-party with their employer's technical knowledge would be able to correctly evaluate whether the applicant possesses the qualification (without more information about their employer's judgment).

c. Is the BQ the minimum level/amount needed on the first day of the job (before training)?

d. Will the BQ be easily understood by applicants?

e. Is the BQ designed to differentiate whether an applicant is minimally qualified for the job (rather than being used to differentiate one applicant from another)?

See Table 8.1 for a sample survey that includes these questions.

5.   Evaluate the survey results and set the BQ at the most stringent level with at least 70% Job Expert consensus. For example, assume 10 Job Experts rated the four BQ levels in the example above (with level 4 being the "BA plus six years" requirement), and their ratings supported the following levels: 4, 4, 3, 3, 3, 2, 2, 1, 1, and 1. Because seven Job Experts supported setting the BQ level at least at "level 2" (a BA plus two years or a Master's degree with no experience), the final BQ would be set at this level (assuming all other ratings on the suggested questions above came out with acceptable levels of agreement).

You may think, why not just develop definitive and final BQ statements and have them "blessed" by Job Experts? Developing BQs can be done this way, but only for some jobs where the requirements are very clear and highly specific. You must consider: would Job Experts have come up with something totally different had they not be "spoon fed" the single BQ they were asked to endorse? This is one reason why presenting multiple levels is useful.

Another process to use for validating BQs might be to have Job Experts "fill in the blank" with the education and experience requirements they believe are most appropriate—such as "Applicants must possess ___ degree in ___ fields and have ___ years experience in ___ areas." The limitation of this technique, however, is that the responses of Job Experts cannot be compared to each other because such ratings are compound and inter-related—one Job Expert's rating regarding a combination of education and experience cannot be compared to another, as they may have placed more value in one area and not the other.

It is important to note that BQs can be used in sequence to further refine applicant pools to manageable levels, so long as the search criteria are established in advance. For example, according to the Internet Applicant Recordkeeping Rule, Frequently Asked Questions[9]:

An employer initially searches an external job database with 50,000 job seekers for 3 basic qualifications for a bi-lingual emergency room nursing supervisor job (a 4-year nursing degree, state certification as an RN, and fluency in English and Spanish). The initial screen for the first three basic qualifications narrows the pool to 10,000. The employer then adds a fourth, pre-established basic qualification, 3 years of emergency room nursing experience, and narrows the pool to 1,000. Finally, the employer adds a fifth, pre-established, basic qualification, 2 years of supervisory experience which results in a pool of 75 job seekers. Under the Internet Applicant rule, only the 75 job seekers meeting all five BQ would be Internet Applicants, assuming the other three prongs of the "Internet Applicant" definition were met.

A strategy often utilized by enforcement agencies or plaintiff groups is to look for exceptions to supposedly objective, standardized protocols as a way of attacking the components of a selection process. Circumventing BQs to hire the nephew of the Executive Vice President can cause a chain reaction, ultimately resulting in the downfall of the BQ screening process, and subsequently the entire selection process. In short, ensuring BQs are noncomparative, objective, and relevant to the performance of the particular position is only one piece of the equation. Applying BQs in a uniform and consistent manner can be equally important.

Since employers are only required to solicit demographic information from applicants, and people only become applicants once they meet all four aspects of the Internet applicant definition, the OFCCP realizes that it is possible for employers to evade scrutiny of their BQs by not soliciting demographic information from those deemed unqualified. Realizing this, the OFCCP has reserved the right to evaluate the impact of BQs by comparing the demographic composition of those meeting the BQs to external labor force statistics and/ or census data. According to the Internet Applicant Recordkeeping Rule, Frequently Asked Questions[9]:

> *The Internet Applicant rule emphasizes that OFCCP will compare the proportion of women and minorities in the contractor's Internet Applicant pool with labor force statistics or other data on the percentage of women and minorities in the relevant labor force in order to evaluate the impact of BQ. If there is a significant difference between these figures, OFCCP will investigate further as to whether the contractor's recruitment and hiring practices conform with E.O. 11246 standards.*

CRITERIA 4: THE INDIVIDUAL DOES NOT REMOVE THEMSELVES FROM CONSIDERATION[10]

How often do recruitment personnel attempt to contact applicants only to find that they have already found another position and are no longer interested? Similarly, applicants are allowed to proceed through the entire selection process only to find that their salary requirements are too high for the position or that they are unwilling to relocate? Because of these and many similar issues, the Internet Applicant Regulations provide for the removal of applicants (from adverse impact analyses, not from record retention) if the employer concludes that an individual has removed themself from consideration, or has otherwise indicated that they are no longer interested in the position. According to the Internet Applicant Regulations, an applicant can either actively or passively remove themselves from consideration. An example of active removal would be an expressed statement of disinterest. Examples of passive removal from consideration may include:

- Declining an employer's invitation to interview;

- Declining a job offer;

- Repeatedly failing to respond to an employer's telephone and/or email inquiries asking about his/her interest in the job;

- No-show for an interview;

- No-show for a drug test.

An employer may also presume a lack of interest based upon a review of the applicant's original expression of interest. Incongruent salary expectations, falsification of information on the application, shift requirements, or type and location of work can all be considered provided that the requirements were consistently and uniformly applied to all applicants.

RECORDKEEPING REQUIREMENTS

The Internet Applicant Regulations make it very clear that employers must maintain records of any and all expressions of interest made through the Internet or related electronic data technologies, for all individuals considered for a particular position, even if those individuals do not ultimately meet all four criteria of an Internet applicant[11]. For internal resume databases, the employer must maintain:

- A record for each resume added to the database;

- A record of the date each resume was added to the database;

- Corresponding to each search: 1) A record of the position for which each search for the database was made, 2) the substantive search criteria, and 3) the date of the search;

- Records identifying job seekers contacted regarding their interest in a particular position.

For external databases, the employer must maintain:

- A record of the position for which each search of the database was made;

- Corresponding to each search: 1) the substantive search criteria used, 2) the date of the search, 3) the resumes of any job seekers who met the BQ for the particular position who are considered by the employer;

- Records identifying job seekers contacted regarding their interest in a particular position.

It is important to note that the recordkeeping requirements not only relate to hiring, but also to assignments, promotion, demotion, transfer, layoff or termination, rates of pay or other terms of compensation, selection for training or apprenticeship, and other requests for reasonable accommodations. The results of any physical examination, job advertisements and postings, applications, resumes, BQs, and any and all expressions of interest through the Internet or related electronic data technologies are also included. These records must be maintained for a period of no less than two years from the date of making the record or personnel action involved, whichever occurs later (regardless of whether the individual qualifies as an Internet Applicant)[12].

SOLICITING GENDER AND RACE/ETHNIC INFORMATION

Obtaining gender and race/ethnic information from applicants is not a new requirement. In fact, there are several provisions already in the regulations requiring employers to solicit this information. The Internet Applicant Regulations state that employers are required to gain this information from only those who are applicants, or Internet Applicants (whichever definition is applicable to the particular position)[13]. It is apparent that employers can obtain this information at any time using the same traditional methods they have always used (e.g., tear-off sheets, postcards, etc.), as well as other methods such as web-based input and automated bulk emails. The commentary to the Internet Applicant Regulations as well as an OFCCP directive on employer data tracking responsibilities (dated April 21, 2004) reiterates that self-identification is the preferable and most reliable method for collecting this information. However, since self-identification is always voluntary, if an individual declines to identify a visual assessment may be made. With that said, the OFCCP directive on employer data tracking responsibilities continues to state:

> When contractors are unable to elicit or ascertain specific information regarding an applicant's gender, race or ethnicity, contractors should not guess or assume. Rather, if, after making reasonable efforts to identify applicant gender, race and ethnicity information, the contractor is unable to obtain such information, the contractor must record race or gender as "unknown" in its applicant flow log. A contractor is not

required to "guess" as to the gender, race or ethnicity of an applicant. Adverse impact determinations should be based on the pool of applicants where gender, race or ethnicity is known.

In short, conflicting guidance currently exists. A visual assessment may be made, but employers should not guess or assume and should only conduct adverse impact analyses with known demographic information provided by the applicant.

When the OFCCP evaluates if an employer has maintained information on impact and conducted adverse impact analyses per 41 C.F.R. § 60-3 in relation to Internet hiring, the OFCCP will only require those records relating to the impact of selection procedures on Internet Applicants. However, if employment tests are administered by employers as part of the selection process, data on the impact of those tests will also be required regardless of whether the tests were administered to Internet Applicants[14]. As a result, it is important for employers to understand that the sequence in which they administer selection tests greatly affects whether it is necessary to solicit demographic information from applicants. For example, if an employment test is administered online prior to an assessment of BQs, then employers are required to solicit demographic information from all who take the test. However, if only those who possess the requisite BQs take the test, then employers are only required to solicit demographic information from those who met the BQs and took the test.

RECOMMENDATIONS

The following are procedural and system recommendations to help employers address the Internet Applicant Regulations. Procedural recommendations refer to the "best practices" employers can implement to bolster the defensibility of their policies and procedures in light of the Internet Applicant Regulations. System recommendations refer to features and functionality that internal applicant tracking systems should include to address the Internet Applicant Regulations. These recommendations can also be used to evaluate external databases for compliance. Employers who follow these recommendations will realize increased defensibility and reduced exposure related to their hiring practices.

Procedural recommendations

1.   Allow for the collection of applications and responses via electronic means to all job openings (this way the Internet Applicant Regulations will apply).

2.   Create an "Active Consideration Period" for applications for all positions (i.e., "We will consider an application active for XX days after receipt, after which time you will need to re-apply if you wish to be considered for employment").

3.   Establish policies regarding unsolicited resumes. Ensure they are uniformly and consistently applied across the employer.

4.   Review job postings for BQs. Ensure they are:

    a.   Non-comparative;

    b.   Objective;

    c.   Relevant to the performance of the particular position and enable the employer to accomplish business-related goals.

5.   If BQs have adverse impact, validate them using the steps outlined in this chapter or other similar process that provides a clear connection between the BQ and job requirements that are needed "day one" on the job.

6.   Pre-define approved search criteria and data management techniques in advance of accepting applications.

7.   Ensure search criteria are specific to the particular job and not "generic."

8.   Ensure all recruiting/staffing personnel have been trained on the proper use of queries, search criteria, and data management techniques.

9.   Collect gender and race/ethnic data after the individual meets basic qualification.

10.   Do not administer employment tests until after BQs have been assessed. Otherwise, employers will be required to solicit demographic information from all applicants who took the test, even those who are later deemed to have not been basically qualified for the position.

System recommendations

1.   The applicant tracking system, or associated applicant tracking protocol, should include a search "log" linked to each individual job opening (i.e., requisition), including:

   a.   the position for which the search was made;

   b.   substantive search criteria;

   c.   search date(s);

   d.   ability to store and/or replicate results of the search for later verification.

2.   In addition, applicant tracking systems must:

   a.   retain each resume added and the date each was added;

   b.   retain records of applicants contacted regarding their interest in a position;

   c.   be able to identify if/when applicants voluntarily withdraw from the selection process and why;

   d.   be able to document where exactly the applicant is within the process and whether they passed/failed each step in the process;

   e.   retain all records for two years from the date of action (e.g., hire, requisition closing, etc.);

   f.   not include for consideration or analysis purposes those records that are beyond active consideration period (described above);

   g.   retain all expressions of interest submitted via electronic data technologies that are considered even if the individual does not meet all criteria to become an Internet applicant.

NOTES

1   41 C.F.R § 60-1
2   41 C.F.R. § 60-1.3(1)
3   41 C.F.R. § 60-1.3(2)
4   US Department of Commerce: "Falling Through the Net?" The Economist (24 June, 2000), p. 24. Although these differences may have reduced somewhat over the past several years, it is likely that they are still apparent to varying degrees.
5   Uniform Guidelines, Questions and Answers 15.
6   69 Fed. Reg. March 4, 2004 at 10155 (in proposed draft form)
7   41 C.F.R. § 60-1.3(3)
8   41 C.F.R. § 60-1.3(4)
9   Located on the Internet at: http://www.dol.gov/esa/regs/compliance/ofccp/faqs/iappfaqs.htm
10   41 C.F.R. § 60-1.3(5)
11   41 C.F.R. § 60-1.12
12   41 C.F.R. § 60-1.12(a)
13   41 C.F.R. 60-1.12(c)(ii)
14   41 C.F.R. 60-1.12(c)

Seven Steps for Developing a Content Valid Job Knowledge Written Test

Stacy L. Pilchard

INTRODUCTION

Job knowledge can be defined as, "...the cumulation of facts, principles, concepts and other pieces of information that are considered important in the performance of one's job" (Dye, Reck, & McDaniel, 1993, p. 153)[1]. Applied to written tests in the personnel setting, knowledge can be categorized as: declarative knowledge—knowledge of technical information; or procedural knowledge—knowledge of the processes and judgmental criteria required to perform correctly and efficiently on the job (Hunter, 1983; Dye et al., 1993)[2].

While job knowledge is not typically critical for many entry-level positions, it clearly has its place in many supervisory roles where having a command of certain knowledge areas is essential for job performance. For example, if a Fire Captain, responsible for instructing firefighters who have been deployed to extinguish a house fire, does not possess a mastery-level of knowledge required for the task, the safety of the firefighters and the public could be in jeopardy. It is not feasible to require a Fire Captain in this position to refer to textbooks and determine the best course of action, but rather they must have that particular knowledge memorized.

As Chapter 3 describes, there are a variety of steps that should be followed to ensure that a job knowledge written test is developed and utilized properly. Depending upon the size and type of the employer, they may be faced with litigation from the EEOC, the DOJ, the OFCCP (under DOL), or a private plaintiff attorney. Each year employers accused of utilizing tests that have adverse impact spend millions of dollars defending litigated promotional processes[3].

An unlawful employment practice based on adverse impact may be established by an employee under the 1991 Civil Rights Act only if:

A(i) a complaining party demonstrates that a respondent uses a particular employment practice that causes a disparate impact on the basis of race, color, religion, sex, or national origin, and the respondent fails to demonstrate that the challenged practice is job-related for the position in question and consistent with business necessity; OR,

A(ii) the complaining party makes the demonstration described in subparagraph (C) with respect to an alternate employment practice, and the respondent refuses to adopt such alternative employment practice (Section 2000e-2[k][1][A][i])

In litigation settings, addressing these standards is typically conducted by completing a validation study (using any of the acceptable types of validity). This Appendix is designed to provide seven steps for developing a job-related, and court-defensible, process for creating a content valid job knowledge written test used for hiring or promoting employees.

SEVEN STEPS FOR DEVELOPING A CONTENT VALID JOB KNOWLEDGE WRITTEN TEST

The seven steps below are designed to address the essential requirements based on the Uniform Guidelines (1978), the Principles (2003), and the Standards (1999)[4]:

1.   Conduct a job analysis;

2.   Develop a selection plan;

3.   Identify test plan goals;

4.   Develop the test content;

5.   Validate the test;

6.   Compile the test;

7.   Conduct post-administration analyses.

STEP 1: CONDUCT A JOB ANALYSIS

The foundational requirement for developing a content valid job knowledge written test is a current and thorough job analysis for the target position. Brief 1-2 page "job descriptions" are almost never sufficient for showing validation under the Uniform Guidelines unless, at a bare minimum, they include:

•   Job Expert input and/or review;

- Job duties and KSAPCs that are essential for the job;

- Operationally defined KSAPCs.

In practice we find that where validity is required, updated job analyses need to be developed. Ideally creating a Uniform Guidelines-style job analysis would include the following ratings for job duties (see Chapter 2 for a complete discussion on completing job analyses).

Frequency (Uniform Guidelines, Section 15B3; 14D4)[5]

This duty is performed (Select one option from below) by me or other active (target position) in my department.

1. Annually or less often

2. Semi-annually (approx. 2 times/year)

3. Quarterly (approx. 4 times/year)

4. Monthly (approx. 1 time/month)

5. Bi-weekly (approx. every 2 weeks)

6. Weekly (approx. 1 time/week)

7. Semi-weekly (approx. 2 to 6 times/week)

8. Daily/infrequently (approx. 1 to 6 times/day)

9. Daily/frequently (approx. 7 or more times/day)

Importance (Uniform Guidelines, Section 14C1, 2, 4; 14D2, 3;
15C3, 4, 5; 15D3)

Competent performance of this duty is (select one option from below) for the job of (target position) in my department.

1. Not important: Minor significance to the performance of the job.

2. Of some importance: Somewhat useful and/or meaningful to the performance of the job.

    - Improper performance may result in slight negative consequences

3. Important: Useful and/or meaningful to the performance of the job.

- Improper performance may result in moderate negative consequences

4.   Critical: Necessary for the performance of the job.

- Improper performance may result in serious negative consequences

5.   Very critical: Necessary for the performance of the job, and with more extreme consequences.

- Improper performance may result in very serious negative consequences

Creating a Uniform Guidelines-style job analysis requires that each KSAPC has the following ratings:

Frequency (Uniform Guidelines, Section 15B3; 14D4)[5]

This KSAPC is performed (select one option from below) by me or other active (target position) in my department.

1.   Annually or less often

2.   Semi-annually (approx. 2 times/year)

3.   Quarterly (approx. 4 times/year)

4.   Monthly (approx. 1 time/month)

5.   Bi-weekly (approx. every 2 weeks)

6.   Weekly (approx. 1 time/week)

7.   Semi-weekly (approx. 2 to 6 times/week)

8.   Daily/infrequently (approx. 1 to 6 times/day)

9.   Daily/frequently (approx. 7 or more times/day)

Importance (Uniform Guidelines, Section 14C1, 2, 4; 14D2, 3; 15C3, 4, 5; 15D3)

This KSAPC is (select one option from below) for the job of (target position) in my department.

1.   Not important: Minor significance to the performance of the job.

2.   Of some importance: Somewhat useful and/or meaningful to the performance of the job.

   •   Not possessing adequate levels of this KSAPC may result in slight negative consequences

3.   Important: Useful and/or meaningful to the performance of the job.

   •   Not possessing adequate levels of this KSAPC may result in moderate negative consequences

4.   Critical: Necessary for the performance of the job.

   •   Not possessing adequate levels of this KSAPC may result in serious negative consequences

5.   Very critical: Necessary for the performance of the job, and with more extreme consequences

   •   Not possessing adequate levels of this KSAPC may result in very serious negative consequences

Differentiating "Best Worker" Ratings (Uniform Guidelines, Section 14C9)

Possessing above-minimum levels of this KSAPC makes (select one option from below) difference in overall job performance.

1.   No

2.   Little

3.   Some

4.   A significant

5.   A very significant

Note: Obtaining ratings on the "Best Worker" scale is not necessary if the job knowledge written test will be used only on a pass/fail basis (rather than ranking final test results).

When Needed (Uniform Guidelines, Section 5F; 14C1)

Possessing (select one option from below) of this KSAPC is needed upon entry to the job for the (target position) position in your department.

1.   None or very little

2.   Some (less than half)

3.   Most (more than half)

4.   All or almost all

In addition to these four KSPAC rating scales, we recommend that a mastery level scale be used when validating written job knowledge tests. The data from these ratings are useful for choosing the job knowledges that should be included in a written job knowledge test, and are useful for addressing Section 14C4 of the Uniform Guidelines, which require that job knowledges measured on a test be "... operationally defined as that body of learned information which is used in and is a necessary prerequisite for observable aspects of work behavior of the job." We suggest using an average rating threshold of 3.0 on the mastery-level scale for selecting job knowledges to be included on job knowledge tests. A sample mastery level scale is listed below:

Mastery Level (Uniform Guidelines, Section 14C4)

A (select one option from below) level of this job knowledge is necessary for successful job performance.

1—Low: none or only a few general concepts or specifics available in memory in none or only a few circumstances without referencing materials or asking questions.

2—Familiarity: have some general concepts and some specifics available in memory in some circumstances without referencing materials or asking questions.

3—Working knowledge: have most general concepts and most specifics available in memory in most circumstances without referencing materials or asking questions.

4—Mastery: have almost all general concepts and almost all specifics available in memory in almost all circumstances without referencing materials or asking questions.

Finally, a duty/KSAPC linkage scale should be used to ensure that the KSAPCs are necessary to the performance of important job duties. A sample duty/KSAPC linkage scale is provided below:

Duty/KSAPC Linkages (Uniform Guidelines, Section 14C4)

This KSAPC is _____ to the performance of this duty.

1. Not important

2. Of minor importance

3. Important

4. Of major importance

5. Critically important

When Job Experts identify KSAPCs necessary for the job, it is helpful if they are written in a way that maximizes the likelihood of job duty linkages. When KSAPCs fail to provide enough content to link to job duties, their inclusion in a job analysis is limited. Listed below are examples of a poorly written and a well written KSAPC from a firefighter job analysis:

Example of a poorly written KSAPC:

Knowledge of ventilation practices.

Example of a well written KSAPC:

Knowledge of ventilation practices and techniques to release contained heat, smoke, and gases in order to enter a building. Includes application of appropriate fire suppression techniques and equipment (including manual and power tools and ventilation fans).

STEP 2: DEVELOP A SELECTION PLAN

The first step in developing a selection plan is to review the KSAPCs from the job analysis and design a plan for measuring the essential KSAPCs using various selection procedures (particularly, knowledge areas). Refer to the Selection Plan section in Chapter 2 for specific criteria for selecting KSAPCs for the selection process. At a minimum, the knowledge areas selected for the test should be important, necessary on the first day of the job, required at some level of mastery (rather than easily looked up without hindrance on the job), and appropriately measured using a written test format. Job knowledges that meet these criteria are selected for inclusion in the "Test Plan" below.

STEP 3: IDENTIFY TEST PLAN GOALS

Once the KSAPCs to be measured on the test have been identified, the test sources relevant for the knowledges should be identified. To do this, review relevant job-related materials and discuss the target job in considerable detail with Job Experts. This will focus attention on the job specific information for the job under analysis. Review the knowledges that meet the necessary criteria and determine which sources and/or textbooks are best suited to measure them. It is imperative that the selected sources do not contradict each other in content.

Once the test sources have been identified, determine whether or not preparatory materials will be offered to applicants. If they are to be used, ensure that the materials are current, specific, and released to all applicants taking the test. In addition to preparatory materials, determine if preparatory sessions will be offered to the applicants.

Use of preparatory sessions appear to be beneficial to both minority and non-minority applicants, although they do not consistently reduce adverse impact (Sackett, Schmitt, Ellingson, & Kabin, 2001).[6] If study sessions are conducted, make every attempt to schedule them at a location that is geographically convenient to all applicants and that they are offered at a reasonable time of day. Invite all applicants to attend and provide plenty of notice of the date and time.

Following the identification of the knowledge areas and source materials to be used to develop the job knowledge written test, identify the number of test items that will be included on the test. Be sure to include enough items to ensure high test reliability. Typically, job knowledge tests that are made up of similar job knowledge domains will generate reliability levels in the high .80s to the low .90s when they include 80 items or more.

Consider using Job Expert input to determine internal weights for the written test. Provide Job Experts with the list of knowledges to be measured and ask experts to distribute 100 points among them to obtain a balanced written test. See Table A.1 for a sample of a knowledge weighting survey used to develop a written test for certifying firefighters (this type of test would be used by fire departments that hire only pre-trained firefighters into entry-level positions).

Attempt to obtain adequate sampling of the various knowledges and ensure that there are a sufficient number of items to effectively measure each knowledge at the desired level. Note that some knowledges will require more items than others for making a "sufficiently deep" assessment. The test should be internally weighted so that they ensure a sufficient measurement of the relevant knowledge areas.

Firefighter Certification Test Development Survey	
Job Expert Name: _____ Date: _____	
Instructions: Assume that you have $100 to "buy" the perfect **Firefighter** for your department (based only on job knowledge qualifications--assume other important areas such as physical abilities and interpersonal skills have already been tested). How much money would you spend in the following areas to ensure that you have bought the most qualified **Firefighter** for your department?" Be sure that you're your allocations equal exactly $100.	
Knowledge Sources to Choose From	**Amount of Dollars you would spend to buy the Perfect Firefighter**
Pumping Apparatus Driver/Operator Handbook (1st Ed.)	
Principles of Vehicle Extrication (2nd Ed.)	
Fire Department Company Officer (3rd Ed.)	
Fire and Emergency Services Instructor (6th Ed.)	
Aerial Apparatus Driver/Operator Handbook (1st Ed.)	
Essentials of Firefighting (4th Ed.)	
Rapid Intervention Teams	
The Source Book for Fire Company Training Evolutions (2nd Ed.)	
Fire Inspection and Code Enforcement (6th Ed.)	
Hazardous Materials (2nd Ed.)	
Ability to Compute Hydraulic Equations	
TOTAL (must equal $100)	

Table A.1   Firefighter Certification Test Development Survey

Following the determination of the length of the test and the number of items to be derived from each source, determine the types of items that will be included on the test. One helpful tool is a process-by-content matrix to ensure adequate sampling of job knowledge content areas and problem-solving processes. Problem-solving levels include:

- Knowledge of terminology

- Understanding of principles

- Application of knowledge to new situations

While knowledge of terminology is important, the understanding and application of principles may be considered a primary importance. The job knowledge written test should include items that ensure the applicants can define important terms related to the job and apply their knowledge to answer more complex questions. Job Experts should consider how the knowledge is applied on the job (e.g., factual recall, application, etc.) when determining the types of items to be included on the final test form (see Table A.2 for a sample process-by-content matrix for a police sergeant written test).

Process-by-Content Matrix: Police Sergeant				
Source	Definition	Principle	Application	Total
1. Essentials of Modern Police Work	4	10	20	34
2. Community Policing	3	7	13	23
3. Rules of Evidence	3	10	17	30
4. Department Rules & Regulations	1	3	6	10
5. State Criminal Code	4	5	9	18
6. State Vehicle Code	4	6	10	20
7. City Ordinances	2	2	6	10
8. Performance Appraisal Guidelines	0	1	1	2
9. Labor Agreement with the City	0	1	2	3
Total	21	45	84	150

Table A.2 Process-by-Content Matrix: Police Sergeant

STEP 4: DEVELOP THE TEST CONTENT

After the number and types of test items to be developed has been determined, select a diverse panel of four to ten Job Experts (who have a minimum of one year experience) to review the test plan to ensure compliance with the parameters. Have each Job Expert sign a "Confidentiality Form." If the Job Experts are going to write the test items, provide item-writing training (see Attachment C in the TVAP® User Manual on the Evaluation CD for item-writing guidelines) and have Job Experts peer review the items.

Once the Job Experts have written the items to be included in the test, ensure proper use of grammar, style, and consistency. Additionally, make certain that the test plan requirements are met. Ensure that the items address the criteria on the TVAP Survey (see the Evaluation CD for the TVAP Software and corresponding survey for rating/validating test items). Assume that 20-30% of the test items will not meet the requirements of the TVAP Survey and account for this attrition by developing a surplus of test items. Once the bank of test items has been created, provide the final test version to the panel of Job Experts for the validation process (the next step).

STEP 5: VALIDATE THE TEST

Use the TVAP Survey to have Job Experts assign various ratings to the items in the test bank. Additionally, have the Job Experts identify an appropriate time limit. A common rule-of-thumb used by practitioners to determine a written test cutoff time is to allow one minute per test item plus thirty additional minutes (e.g., a 150-item test would yield a three hour time limit).[7] A reasonable time limit would allow for at least 95% of the applicants to complete the test within the time limit.

STEP 6: COMPILE THE TEST

Evaluate the Job Expert ratings on the TVAP Survey and discard those items that do not meet the criteria (see TVAP User Manual). Once the Job Experts have assigned the various ratings to each of the test items, analyze the "Angoff" ratings identified by the Job Experts. Discard raters whose ratings are statistically different from other raters by evaluating rater reliability and high/low rater bias. Calculate the difficulty level of the test (called the pre-administration cutoff percentage).

STEP 7: POST-ADMINISTRATION ANALYSES

Following the administration of the job knowledge written test, conduct an item-level analysis of the test results to evaluate the item-level qualities (such as the point-biserial, difficulty level, and Differential Item Functioning [DIF] of each item). Use the guidelines in Chapter 3 for deciding which items to keep or remove for this administration (or improve for later administrations). In addition to the guidelines proposed in Chapter 3 for evaluating when to discard an item due to DIF, consider the following excerpt from Hearn v. City of Jackson (Aug. 7, 2003)[3] where DIF was being considered for a job knowledge test:

Plaintiffs suggest in their post-trial memorandum that the test is subject to challenge on the basis that they failed to perform a DIF analysis to determine whether, and if so on which items, blacks performed more poorly than whites, so that an effort could have been made to reduce adverse impact by eliminating those items on which blacks performed more poorly. Dr. Landy testified that the consensus of professional opinion is that DIF modifications of tests is not a good idea because it reduces the validity of the examination. Dr. Landy explained: "The problem with [DIF] is suppose one of those items is a knowledge item and has to do with an issue like Miranda or an issue in the preservation of evidence or a hostage situation. You're going to take that item out only because whites answer it more correctly than blacks do, in spite of the fact that you'd really want a sergeant to know this [issue] because the sergeant is going to supervise. A police officer is going to count on that officer to tell him or her what to do. So you're reducing the validity of the exam just for the sake of making sure that there are no items in which whites and blacks do differentially, or DIF, and he's assuming that the reason that 65 percent of the blacks got it right and 70 percent of the whites got it right was that it's an unfair item rather than, hey, maybe two or three whites or two or three blacks studied more or less that section of general orders."

Certainly this excerpt provides some good arguments against discarding items based only on DIF analyses. These issues and the guidelines discussed in Chapter 3 should be carefully considered before removing items from a test.

After conducting the item-level analysis and removing items that do not comply with acceptable ranges, conduct a test-level analysis to assess descriptive and psychometric statistics (e.g., reliability, standard deviation, etc.). Adjust the unmodified Angoff by using the Standard Error of Measurement or the Conditional Standard Error of Measurement where applicable (see Chapter 6 for a complete discussion on this subject).

SUMMARY

Developing a content valid job knowledge written test for hiring/promoting employees (where the job requires testing for critical job knowledge areas) is the safest route to avoid potential litigation. If the test has adverse impact, validate. Pay particular attention in addressing the Uniform Guidelines, Principles, and Standards (in that order, based on the weight they are typically given in court), and remember that a house is only as strong as its foundation. Be sure to base everything on a solid job analysis.

NOTES

1 Dye, D. A., Reck, M., & McDaniel, M. A. (1993, July). The validity of job knowledge measures. International Journal of Selection and Assessment, 1 (3), 153-157.

2 Hunter, J.E. (1983). A causal analysis of cognitive ability, job knowledge, job performance and supervisory ratings. In F. Landy and S. Zedeck and J. Cleveland (Eds.), Performance measurement theory (pp. 257-266). Hillsdale, NJ: Erlbaum.

3 For example, see Bouman v. Block (940 F2d 1211, 9th Cir 1991); Hearn v. City of Jackson, Miss. (110 Fed. 242, 5th Cir 2004); Isabel v. City of Memphis (F.Supp.2d 2003, 6th Cir 2003); Paige v. State of California (102 F.3d 1035, 1040, 9th Cir 1996).

4 The steps outlined in this Appendix are based on the requirements outlined by the Uniform Guidelines (1978), the Principles (2003), and the Standards (1999). The proposed model is not a one-size-fits-all process, but rather a generic template which could be employed in an ideal setting. While it is not guaranteed that by following these steps litigation will be avoided, implementing the practices outlined in this Appendix will greatly increase the likelihood of success in the event of a challenge to a written testing process.

5 The Uniform Guidelines do not require frequency ratings for content validity; however, obtaining frequency ratings provides useful information for addressing the 1990 Americans with Disabilities Act (ADA) and can also help when developing a test using content validity.

6 Sackett, P. R., Schmitt, N., Ellingson, J. E., & Kabin, M. B. (2001). High-stakes testing in employment, credentialing, and higher education: Prospects in a post-affirmative-action world. American Psychologist, 56(4), 302-318.

7 This rule-of-thumb time limit is only applicable for conventional multiple-choice tests. Where many calculations are needed for each test item (e.g., hydraulic items on a Fire Engineer test), obtain input from Job Experts to ensure an appropriate time limit.

References

Agresti, A. (1990), *Categorical Data Analysis*. New York: Wiley.

American Educational Research Association, the American Psychological Association, and the National Council on Measurement in Education (1999), *Standards for Educational and Psychological Testing*. Washington DC: American Educational Research Association.

Anastasi, A. & Urbina, S. (1997), *Psychological Testing* (7th ed.; pp. 199–200). Upper Saddle River, NJ: Prentice Hall.

Angoff W. H. (1971), Scales, norms, and equivalent scores. In Thorndike RL, *Educational Measurement* (pp. 508–600). Washington, DC: American Council on Education.

Anrig, G. (1987), Golden rule: Second thoughts, *APA Monitor* January, 3.

Association Against Discrimination in Employment, Inc. v. City of Bridgeport (479 F. Supp. 101, 112-13 D. Conn., 1979).

Bloom, B. S. (Ed.) (1956), *Taxonomy of Educational Objectives: The Classification of Educational Goals*, Handbook I, *Cognitive Domain*. New York, Toronto: Longmans, Green.

Boston Chapter, NAACP Inc. v. Beecher (504 F.2d 1017, 1021, 1st Cir. 1974).

Breslow, N. E. & Day, N. E. (1980), *Statistical Methods in Cancer Research*, Vol. I. *The Analysis of Case-Control Studies*, WHO/IARC Scientific Publication No. 32. Oxford: Oxford University Press.

Cascio, W. (1998), *Applied Psychology in Human Resource Management*. Upper Saddle River, NJ: Prentice-Hall.

DeGroot, M. H., Fienberg, S. E., & Kadane, J. B. (1985), *Statistics and the Law*, New York: Wiley.

Feldt, L. S., Steffen, M., & Gupta, N. C. (1985), A comparison of five methods for estimating the standard error of measurement at specific score levels, *Applied Psychological Measurement*, **9**(4), 351–361.

Gastwirth, J. L. & Greenhouse, S. W. (1987), Estimating a common relative risk: Application in equal employment, *Journal of the American Statistical Association*, **82**, 38–45.

Gatewood, R. D. & Feild, H. S. (1994 [1986]), *Human Resource Selection*, Orlando, FL: The Dryden Press.

Golden Rule Life Insurance Company v. Mathias (86 Ill.App.3d 323, 41 Ill. Dec. 888, 408 N.E.2d 310, 1980)

Guardians Association of the New York City Police Dept. v. Civil Service Commission (630 F.2d 79, 88, 2d Cir., 1980; cert. denied, 452 U.S. 940, 101 S.Ct. 3083, 69 L.Ed.2d 954, 1981).

Guion, R. M. (1998), *Assessment, Measurement, and Prediction for Personnel Decisions*. Mahwah, NJ: Lawrence Erlbaum Associates.

Hazelwood School District v. United States (433 U.S. 299, 1977).

Kolen, M. J., Hanson, B. A., & Brennan, R. L. (1992), Conditional standard errors of measurement for scale scores, *Journal of Educational Measurement*, **29**(4), 285–307.

Lord, F. M. (1984), Standard errors of measurement at different ability levels, *Journal of Educational Measurement*, **21**(3), 239–243.

Louv, W. C. & Littell, R. C. (1986), Combining one-sided binomial tests, *Journal of the American Statistical Association*, **81**, 550–554.

Mehrotra, D. & Railkar, R. (2000), Minimum risk weights for comparing treatments in stratified binomial trials, *Statistics in Medicine*, **19**, 811–825.

Mosteller, F., Rouke, R. E. K., & Thomas, G. B. (1970), *Probability with Statistical Applications* (2nd ed.). Menlo Park, CA: Addison-Wesley.

Neisser, U., Boodoo, G., Bouthard, T. J., Boykin, A. W., Brody, N., Ceei, S. J., Halpern, D. F., Loehlin, J. C., Perloft, R., Sternberg, R. J., & Urbina, S. (1996), Intelligence: Knowns and unknowns, *American Psychologist*, **51**, 77–101.

OFCCP (Office of Federal Contract Compliance Programs) (1993), *Federal Contract Compliance Manual*. Washington, DC: Department of Labor, Employment Standards Administration, Office of Federal Contract Compliance Programs (SUDOC# L 36.8: C 76/1993).

Peng, C. J. & Subkoviak, M. (1980), A note on Huynh's normal approximation procedure for estimating criterion-referenced reliability, *Journal of Educational Measurement*, **17**(4), 359–368.

Qualls-Payne, A. L. (1992), A comparison of score level estimates of the standard error of measurement, *Journal of Educational Measurement*, **29**(3), 213–225.

Sackett, P. R., Schmitt, N., Ellingson, J. E., & Kabin, M. B. (2001), High stakes testing in employment, credentialing, and higher education: Prospects in a post-affirmative action world, *American Psychologist*, **56**, 302–318.

SIOP (Society for Industrial and Organizational Psychology, Inc.) (1987, 2003), *Principles for the Validation and Use of Personnel Selection Procedures* (3rd and 4th eds). College Park, MD: SIOP.

Subkoviak, M. (1988), A practioner's guide to computation and interpretation of reliability indices for mastery tests, *Journal of Educational Measurement*, **25**(1), 47–55.

Tarone R. E. (1988), Homogeneity score tests with nuisance parameters, *Communications in Statistics*, Series A; **17**, 1549–1556.

Thorndike, R. L. (1951), Reliability. In E. F. Lindquist (Ed.). *Educational Measurement* (pp. 560–620). Washington DC: American Council on Education.

Uniform Guidelines – Equal Employment Opportunity Commission, Civil Service Commission, Department of Labor, and Department of Justice (August 25, 1978), *Adoption of Four Agencies of Uniform Guidelines on Employee Selection Procedures*, 43 Federal Register, 38,290-38,315, referred to in the text as; Equal Employment Opportunity Commission, Office of Personnel Management, Department of Treasury (1979), *Adoption of Questions and Answers to Clarify and Provide a Common Interpretation of the Uniform Guidelines on Employee Selection Procedures*, 44 Federal Register 11,996-12,009.

US Department of Labor: Employment and training administration (2000), *Testing and Assessment: An Employer's Guide to Good Practices*. Washington DC: Department of Labor Employment and Training Administration.

List of Cases

Anderson v. Premier Industrial Corp. (62 F.3d 1417, 1995 WL 469429, 6th Cir., 1995) (unpublished opinion).

Arnold v. Postmaster General (Civil Action Nos. 85-2571, 86-2291, US Dist. Ct. for the District of Columbia, 667 F. Supp. 6, 1987).

Bouman v. Block (940 F.2d 1211, C.A.9, Cal., 1991).

Bradley v. Pizzaco of Nebraska, Inc. (926 F.2d 714, C.A.8, Neb., 1991).

Brown v. Delta Air Lines, Inc. (522 F.Supp. 1218, 1229, n. 14, S.D., Texas, 1980).

Brunet v. City of Columbus (1 F.3d 390, C.A.6, Ohio, 1993).

Castaneda v. Partida (430 U.S. 482, 496, 1977).

Chang v. University of Rhode Island (606 F.Supp. 1161, D.R.I., 1985).

Cicero v. Borg Warner Automotive (75 F.Supp.2d 695, November, 1999).

Clady v. County of Los Angeles (770 F.2d 1421, 1428, 9th Cir., 1985).

Contreras v. City of Los Angeles (656 F.2d 1267, 9th Cir., 1981).

Cooper v. University of Texas at Dallas (482 F. Supp. 187, N.D. Tex., 1979).

Covington v. District of Columbia (Nos. 94-7014, 94-7015, 94-7022, 94-7107, U.S. Ct of Appeals, 313 U.S. App. D.C. 16; 57 F.3d 1101, 1995).

Csicseri v. Bowsher (862 F.Supp. 547, D.D.C., 1994).

Dees v. Orr, Secretary of the Air Force (No. Civil S-82-471 LKK, U.S. Dist. Ct., Eastern District of California, 1983).

Dennis L. Harrison v. Drew Lewis (Civil Action No. 79-1816, U.S. Dist. Ct. for the District of Columbia, 559 F. Supp. 943, 1983).

Donnel v. General Motors Corp (576 F2d 1292, 8th Cir., 1978).

Dothard v. Rawlinson (433 U.S. 321, 1977).

EEOC v. Federal Reserve Bank of Richmond (698 F.2d 633, C.A.N.C., 1983).

EEOC v. United Virginia Bank (615 F.2d 147, 4th Cir., 1980).

Franks v. Bowman Transportation Company (495 F. 2d 398, 419, 8 FEP, 66, 81, 5th Cir., 1974; and 12 FEP 549, 1976).

Gault v. Zellerbach (172 F.3d 48, 1998 WL 898831 at 2, 6th Cir.,1998) (unpublished opinion).

Griggs v. Duke Power Co. (91 S. Ct. 849, 1971).

Hogan v. Pierce, Secretary, Housing and Urban Development (No. 79-2124, U.S. Dist. Ct District of Columbia, 1983).

Hoops v. Elk Run Coal Co., Inc. (95 F.Supp.2d 612, S.D.W.Va., 2000).

Johnson v. Garrett, III as Secretary of the Navy (Case No. 73-702-Civ-J-12, U.S. Dist. Ct. for the Middle District of Florida, 1991).

Manko v. U.S. (No. 79-1011-CV-W-9, U.S. Dist. Ct. for the Western District of Missouri, 636 F. Supp. 1419, 1986).

Martin v. United States Playing Card Co. (172 F.3d 48, 1998 WL 869970, 6th Cir., 1998) (unpublished opinion).

McKay v. U.S. (Civil Action No. 75-M-1162, U.S. Dist. Ct. for the District of Colorado, 1985).

Moore v. Summers (113 F.Supp.2d 5, D.D.C., 2000).

Mozee v. American Commercial Marine Service Co. (940 F.2d 1036, C.A.7, Ind., 1991).

Osborne v. Brandeis Machinery & Supply Corp. (1994 WL 486628, 6th Cir., June 15, 1994) (unpublished opinion).

Ottaviani v. State University of New York at New Paltz (679 F.Supp. 288, D.N.Y., 1988).

Paige v. California Highway Patrol (No. CV 94-0083 CBM [Ctx], U.S. District Court, Central District of California, Order Entered August 12, 1999).

Palmer v. Shultz (815 F.2d 84, C.A.D.C., 1987).

Police Officers for Equal Rights v. City of Columbus (644 F.Supp. 393, S.D.Ohio, 1985).

Shutt v. Sandoz Crop Protection Corp. (934 F.2d 186, 188, 9th Cir., 1991).

Tinker v. Sears, Roebuck & Co. (127 F.3d 519, 524, 6th Cir.,1997).

Trout v. Hidalgo (Civ. A. Nos. 73-55, 76-315, 76-1206, 78-1098, U.S. Dist. Ct. of Columbia, 517 F. Supp. 873, 1981).

US v. Commonwealth of Virginia (569 F2d 1300, CA-4 1978, 454 F. Supp. 1077).

US v. South Carolina (434 US 1026, 1978).

Vuyanich v. Republic National Bank (N.D. Texas 1980, 505 F. Supp. 224).

Watson v. Fort Worth Bank & Trust (487 U.S. 1977, 1988).

Williams v. Owens-Illinois, Inc. (665 F2d 918, 9th Cir, Cert denied, 459 U.S. 971, 1982).

Waisome v. Port Authority (948 F.2d 1370, 1376, 2d Cir.,1991).

Zamlen v. City of Cleveland (686 F.Supp. 631, N.D. Ohio, 1988).

Index

80% test 3–5, 21
  selection rate comparisons 13–15

abilities xiv, 98
ADA (Americans With Disabilities Act
    1990) xiii, xxvii
adverse impact xx
  analysis 5–6
  Availability Comparisons 5–6
  definition xiii, 1, 4
  history of 2–5
  reasons for 1–2
  Selection Rate Comparisons 5–6
Adverse Impact Toolkit ® xxv
aggregation of data, selection rate
    comparisons 18–20
aggregation techniques 7–8
Americans With Disabilities Act (ADA)
    1990 xiii, xxvii
Anderson v. Premier Industrial Corp. (1995)
    10
Angoff method 106–10
ANOVA tables 134–5, 144, 147
Arnold v. Postmaster General 20
Association Against Discrimination in
    Employment, Inc. v. City of
    Bridgeport (1979) 9
Availability Comparisons 5–6
  adverse impact 22–4
  data aggregation 24–5
  gross disparity 26
  gross under-representation 26
  multiple events 24–5
  single event 20–24
  statistical significance tests 21–2

banding in selection procedures 111–12
barriers analysis 26
Basic Qualifications (BQs) 153–9
  validation 155–9
behavioral questions 84
Best Worker
  job duties 41

KSPACs (Knowledge, Skills, Abilities
    and Personal Characteristics) 45
  Physical Requirements 45
  ratings 45–6, 169
Bloom's Taxonomy 62
Boston Chapter, NAACP Inc. v. Beecher
    114
Bouman v. Block (1991) 14, 119, 176
Bradley v. Pizzaco of Nebraska, Inc. (1991)
    9
Breslow-Day test 19, 24
Brown v. Delta Air Lines, Inc. (1980) 12
Brunet v. City of Columbus (1993) 114

California Fair Employment Practice
    Commission (FEPC) 2–4
California Guidelines on Employee
    Selection Procedures 2–5
cases
  Anderson v. Premier Industrial Corp.
    (1995) 10
  Arnold v. Postmaster General 20
  Association Against Discrimination
    in Employment, Inc. v. City of
    Bridgeport (1979) 9
  Boston Chapter, NAACP Inc. v. Beecher
    114
  Bouman v. Block (1991) 14, 119, 176
  Bradley v. Pizzaco of Nebraska, Inc.
    (1991) 9
  Brown v. Delta Air Lines, Inc. (1980) 12
  Brunet v. City of Columbus (1993) 114
  Castaneda v. Partida (1977) 14
  Chang v. University of Rhode Island
    (1985) 12
  Cicero v. Borg Warner Automotive
    (1999) 10
  Clady v. County of Los Angeles (1985)
    115
  Contreras v. City of Los Angeles (1981)
    14, 16, 56, 66
  Cooper v. University of Texas at Dallas
    (1979) 25

Covington v. District of Columbia (1995) 20

Csicseri v. Bowsher (1994) 12

Dees v. Orr, Secretary of the Air force (1983) 20

Dennis L. Harrison v. Drew Lewis (1983) 20

Donnel v. General Motors Corp. (1978) 26

Dothard v. Rawlinson (1977) 26

Edwards v. City of Houston (1996) 79

EEOC v. Federal Reserve Bank of Richmond (1983) 12

EEOC v. United Virginia Bank (1980) 25

Evans v. City of Evanston (1989) 79

Forsberg v. Pacific Northwest Bell Telephone (1988) 55

Franks v. Bowman Transportation Co. (1974, 1976) 9

Frazier v. Garrison I. S. D. (1993) 26

Gault v. Zellerbach (1998) 10

Gilbert v. East Bay Municipal Utility District (1979) 55

Golden Rule Life Insurance Company v. Mathias (1980) 68–9

Griggs v. Duke Power Company (1971) 2, 154–5

Guardians v. CSC of New York 119

Hearn v. City of Jackson (2003) 175, 176

Hogan v. Pierce, Secretary, Housing and Urban Development (1983) 20

Hoops v. Elk Run Coal Co., Inc. (2000) 12

Houston Chapter of the International Association of Black Professional Firefighters v. City of Houston (1991) 79

Isabel v. City of Memphis (2003) 176

Johnson v. Garrett, III as Secretary of the Navy (1991) 20

Lanning v. Southeastern Pennsylvania Transport Authority (1999) 55

Manko v. US (1986) 20

Martin v. United States Playing Card Co. (1998) 10

Martinez v. City of Salinas 55

McKay v. US (1985) 20

Moore v. Southwestern Bell (1979) 26

Moore v. Summers (2000) 12

Mozee v. American Commercial Marine Service Co. (1991) 12

Officers for Justice v. Civil Service Commission (1993) 119

Osborne v. Brandeis Machinery & Supply Corp. (1994) 10

Ottaviani v. State University of New York (1988) 13

Paige v. California Highway Patrol (1999) 20

Paige v. State of California (1996) 176

Palmer v. Shultz (1987) 12

Parks v. City of Long Beach 55

Police Officers for Equal Rights v. City of Columbus (1985) 13

Sanchez v. City of Santa Ana 55

Shutt v. Sandoz Corp. (1991) 9

Simmons v. City of Kansas City 55–6

Tinker v. Sears, Roebuck & Co. (1997) 10

Trout v. Hidalgo (1981) 20

US v. City of Torrance 56

US v. Commonwealth of Virginia (1978) 16

US v. South Carolina (1978) 56, 66, 109–10, 119

Vuyanich v. Republic National Bank (1980) 25

Waisome v. Port Authority (1991) 16

Watson v. Fort Worth Bank & Trust (1977, 1988) 9

Williams v. Owens-Illinois, Inc. (1982) 26

Zamlen v. City of Cleveland (1988) 115

Castaneda v. Partida (1977) 14

Chang v. University of Rhode Island (1985) 12

Cicero v. Borg Warner Automotive (1999) 10

Civil Rights Act 1964 (Title VII)
litigation costs 25
seniority systems 104

Clady v. County of Los Angeles (1985) 115

compensation
metrics 147
multiple regression analysis 121–46
t-tests 121

competencies xxiv

competency-based questions 84–6

Conditional SEM (Standard Error of Measurement) 75–7, 79, 109–10

construct validity 31–2
content validation
    selection procedures 47–9
    studies 33
content validity 27–8, 31–2
    Uniform Guidelines on Employee
        Selection Procedures 176
    written tests 165–76
Content Validity Checklists xxvii
Contreras v. City of Los Angeles (1981) 14,
    16, 56, 66
Cooper v. University of Texas at Dallas
    (1979) 25
Covington v. District of Columbia (1995) 20
criterion-related validity 28, 31–2, 50–55
    bias 55
    concurrent studies 54
    corrections 55
    cross validation 54
    expectancy tables 54
    predictive studies 53
    ranking in selection procedures 114–15
    selection procedures 52–4
    statistical power 52
    weighting of selection procedures
        116–18
Cronbach's Alpha test 74
cross validation, criterion-related validity 54
Csicseri v. Bowsher (1994) 12

Decision Consistency Reliability (DCR)
    xiii, 78
Dees v. Orr, Secretary of the Air force
    (1983) 20
Dennis L. Harrison v. Drew Lewis (1983) 20
descriptive test analyses 73
Differential Item Functioning (DIF) 68–72,
    175–6
    definition xiii
    item removal 71–2
    KSPACs (Knowledge, Skills, Abilities
        and Personal Characteristics) 70–71
    sample size 70
disparate impact see adverse impact
Donnel v. General Motors Corp. (1978) 26
Dothard v. Rawlinson (1977) 26

education see TEE (training, education and
    experience)
Edwards v. City of Houston (1996) 79
EEO (Equal Employment Opportunity) xiii

EEOC (Equal Employment Opportunity
    Commission) xiii
    guidelines 4
EEOC v. Federal Reserve Bank of
    Richmond (1983) 12
EEOC v. United Virginia Bank (1980) 25
effect size 7
80% test 3–5, 21
    selection rate comparisons 13–15
Equal Employment Opportunity
    Commission (EEOC) xiii
    guidelines 4
Equal Employment Opportunity (EEO),
    definition xiii
Evans v. City of Evanston (1989) 79
Exact Binomial Probability Test 22
Excel (Microsoft), multiple regression (MR)
    analysis 139–46
expectancy tables 54
experience see TEE (training, education and
    experience)

Federal Executive Agency (FEA),
    guidelines 4
FEPC (California Fair Employment Practice
    Commission) 2–4
Fisher Exact Test 15
Fisher's Method 25
Forsberg v. Pacific Northwest Bell
    Telephone (1988) 55
Franks v. Bowman Transportation Co.
    (1974, 1976) 9
Frazier v. Garrison I. S. D. (1993) 26

Gault v. Zellerbach (1998) 10
Generalized Binomial test 25
Gilbert v. East Bay Municipal Utility
    District (1979) 55
GOJA (Guidelines Oriented Job Analysis)
    xiii, xxvi–xxvii
Golden Rule Life Insurance Company v.
    Mathias (1980) 68–9
Griggs v. Duke Power Company (1971) 2,
    154–5
gross disparity 26
gross under-representation 26
Guardians v. CSC of New York 119
Guidelines Oriented Job Analysis (GOJA)
    xiii, xxvi–xxvii

Hearn v. City of Jackson (2003) 175, 176

Hogan v. Pierce, Secretary, Housing and
    Urban Development (1983) 20
Hoops v. Elk Run Coal Co., Inc. (2000) 12
Houston Chapter of the International
    Association of Black Professional
    Firefighters v. City of Houston
    (1991) 79

inexorable zero 9
Internet Applicant Regulations 149–64
    applicants
        considered for employment 152–3
        definition 151
        removing themselves from
            consideration 159–60
    Basic Qualifications (BQs) 153–9
    electronic data technologies, examples
        151–2
    ethnic information 161–2
    gender information 161–2
    internet access 151
    procedural recommendations 162–3
    race information 161–2
    recommendations 162–4
    recordkeeping requirements 160–61
    submission of an expression of interest
        150–52
    system recommendations 163–4
interviews 81 see also structured interviews
Isabel v. City of Memphis (2003) 176

JAS see Job Analysis Survey
job analysis 34–43
    Basic Qualifications (BQs) 155–9
    KSPACs (Knowledge, Skills, Abilities
        and Personal Characteristics) 37–9,
        168–71
    Other Requirements 37–9
    Physical Requirements 37–9
    situational questions 86
    Standards 37–9
    structured interviews 86
    supervisors 41–3
    TEE (training, education and
        experience) requirements 98
    Tools & Equipment 37–9
    written tests 166–71
Job Analysis Survey (JAS) xiii
    Job Experts 40–41
job duties 36–7
    Best Worker 41

KSPACs (Knowledge, Skills, Abilities
    and Personal Characteristics) 171
    rating 38–43, 167–8
    TEE (training, education and
        experience) requirements 104
Job Experts
    Basic Qualifications (BQs) 156–8
    definition xiii
    Job Analysis Survey (JAS) 40–41
    sample size 35
    selection of 34–6
    selection procedures 106–10
    situational questions 86–8
    weighting of selection procedures
        117–18
    Work History Evaluation (WHE) 102–3
    written tests 63–5, 172–4
job knowledge xiv, 98
    definition 165
    rating 167–71
    written tests 165–76
Johnson v. Garrett, III as Secretary of the
    Navy (1991) 20

Kappa Coefficients 78
KSPACs (Knowledge, Skills, Abilities and
    Personal Characteristics) xiv
    Basic Qualifications (BQs) 156–8
    Best Worker 45
    Bloom's Taxonomy 62
    job analysis 37–9, 168–71
    job duties 171
    rating 38–43, 168–9
    situational questions 86–90
    structured interviews 86–90
    TEE (training, education and
        experience) requirements 98–9
    tests 47–9
    weighting of selection procedures
        116–17
    written tests 58–63
Kuder-Richardson formulae 74

Lanning v. Southeastern Pennsylvania
    Transport Authority (1999) 55

manifest imbalance 22
Manko v. US (1986) 20
Mantel-Haenszel test 19
Martin v. United States Playing Card Co.
    (1998) 10

Martinez v. City of Salinas 55
mastery-based tests 77–8
mastery levels 170
McKay v. US (1985) 20
Microsoft Excel, multiple regression (MR) analysis 139–46
Minimum Risk Weights test 20
minimum time-in-grade requirements 101
Moore v. Southwestern Bell (1979) 26
Moore v. Summers (2000) 12
Mozee v. American Commercial Marine Service Co. (1991) 12
multiple regression (MR) analysis 121–46
  age variable 147
  coding of variables 126–7
  cohort analysis 146
  compensation metrics 147
  conduct of 124–46
  correlation of variables 123
  grouping of employees 128–30
  identification of data 124–6
  interaction terms 145–6
  Microsoft Excel 139–46
    Analysis ToolPak 139
    ANOVA table 144, 147
    conduct using 139–43
    interpretation of results 143–6
  Multiple R Squared (R2) 123
  outputs 123–4
  preliminary data analysis 127–8
  R2 123
  R2 Change 123
  review of data 124–6
  sample size 130
  Similarly Situated Employee Groups (SSEGs) 128–30
  SPSS software 131–9
    ANOVA report 134–5
    Coefficients Report 135–7
    collinearity 137–8
    conduct using 131–2
    interpretation of results 132–9
    model summary 132–4
    multicollinearity 137–8
    regression diagnostics 132
    supplemental statistical procedures 132
  statistical power 129–30
  variables 122
    correlation 123

Office of Federal Contract Compliance Programs (OFCCP) xiv
  guidelines 4
Officers for Justice v. Civil Service Commission (1993) 119
one-tail statistical tests 11–13
Osborne v. Brandeis Machinery & Supply Corp. (1994) 10
Ottaviani v. State University of New York (1988) 13

p-values 6
Paige v. California Highway Patrol (1999) 20
Paige v. State of California (1996) 176
Palmer v. Shultz (1987) 12
Parks v. City of Long Beach 55
pattern consistency 24–5
personal characteristics xiv
Physical Requirements
  Best Worker 45
  job analysis 37–9
  rating 38–43
point biserial correlations 67–8
Police Officers for Equal Rights v. City of Columbus (1985) 13
Pooled Two-Sample Z-Score test 26
practical significance tests 15–16
Principles for the Validation and Use of Personnel Selection Procedures 30–31, 96–7
psychometric analyses 73–4

ranking in selection procedures 112–15
  criterion-related validity 114–15

sample size
  Differential Item Functioning (DIF) 70
  Job Experts 35
  minimum 9
  multiple regression (MR) analysis 130
  small 9–11
  statistical power 7–11
Sanchez v. City of Santa Ana 55
SED see Standard Error of Difference (SED)
selection plans 44–6, 171
selection procedures 45–6, 105–18
  Angoff method 106–10
  banding 111–12
  combined scores 115–18

Conditional SEM (Standard Error of
     Measurement) 109–10
content validation 47–9
criterion-related validity 52–4, 114–15
cut-off scores 105–11
   definition xv
   ranking 112–15
   Standard Error of Difference (SED)
      110–11, 111–12
   standardizing scores 118
   strict rank ordering 111, 112–13
   weighting 115–18
Selection Rate Comparisons 5–6
   adverse impact 16–17
   aggregation of data 18–20
   80% test 13–15
   multiple events 17–20
   practical significance tests 15–16
   Simpson's Paradox 17–18
   single event 13–17
   statistical significance tests 15
SEM see Standard Error of Measurement
Shutt v. Sandoz Corp. (1991) 9
Similarly Situated Employee Groups
     (SSEGs) 128–30
Simmons v. City of Kansas City 55–6
Simpson's Paradox 17–18
situational questions 83–4, 86–90
   job analysis 86
   Job Experts 86–8
   KSPACs (Knowledge, Skills, Abilities
      and Personal Characteristics) 86–90
skills xiv, 98
SPSS software, multiple regression analysis
     131–9
SSEGs see Similarly Situated Employee
     Groups
Standard Error of Difference (SED) xiv
   selection procedures 110–11, 111–12
Standard Error of Measurement (SEM)
     xiv–xv
   conditional 75–7, 79
   written tests 74–7
standard scoring selection procedures 118
Standards, job analysis 37–9
Standards for Educational and Psychological
     Testing 29–30
statistical power 7, 147
   aggregation techniques 7–8
   criterion-related validity 52
   effect size 7

multiple regression analysis 129–30
   sample size 7–11
   minimum 9
   small 9–11
statistical significance 6–13
   p-values 6
   statistical power 7
   testing 4–5, 5–6, 15, 21–2
statistical tests 11–13
   Breslow-Day 19, 24
   Exact Binomial Probability 22
   Fisher Exact 15
   Fisher's Method 25
   Generalized Binomial 25
   Mantel-Haenszel 19
   Minimum Risk Weights 20
   Pooled Two-Sample Z-Score test 26
   practical significance 15–16
   Treatment by Strata Interaction 19
statistically significant underutilization 22
strict rank ordering, selection procedures
      111, 112–13
structured interviews 81–91
   administration 90–91
   improvement methods 81–3
   job analysis 86
   KSPACs (Knowledge, Skills, Abilities
      and Personal Characteristics) 86–90
   questions
      behavioral 84
      competency-based 84–6
      situational 83–4, 86–90
   rating 90–91
   scoring 90–91
supervisors, job analysis 41–3

t-tests, compensation practices 121
Technical Advisory Committee on Testing
      (TACT) 2–4
TEE (training, education and experience)
      requirements 93–103
   job analysis 98
   job duties 104
   KSPACs (Knowledge, Skills, Abilities
      and Personal Characteristics) 98–9
   minimum time-in-grade 101
   professional standards 96–7
   promotion
      closed 100–103
      open 98–100
   rating 100

selection
    closed 100–103
    open 98–100
    surveys 98–9
    Uniform Guidelines on Employee
       Selection Procedures 93–7
    validation 93–7
    Work History Evaluation (WHE) 101–3
    work seniority 100
Test Analysis Workbook xxvi
test validation xx
Test Validation & Analysis Program ®
    (TVAP ®) xxv–xxvi
Test Validation Workbook xxvi
Thorndike method 76–7, 79
Tinker v. Sears, Roebuck & Co. (1997) 10
Title VII (Civil Rights Act 1964)
    litigation costs 25
    seniority systems 104
Tools & Equipment, job analysis 37–9
training see TEE (training, education and
    experience)
Treatment by Strata Interaction test 19
Trout v. Hidalgo (1981) 20
TVAP ® see Test Validation & Analysis
    Program ®
two-tail statistical tests 11–13
    Fisher Exact 15

Uniform Guidelines on Employee Selection
    Procedures 3, 27–8
    80% test 4–5
    content validity 176
    strict rank ordering 112
    TEE (training, education and experi-
       ence) requirements 93–7
    validation 31–3
US v. City of Torrance 56
US v. Commonwealth of Virginia (1978) 16
US v. South Carolina (1978) 56, 66, 109–10,
    119

validation
    benefits 28–9
    definition 27
    professional standards 29–31
    studies 27–8, 33
    Uniform Guidelines on Employee
       Selection Procedures 31–3
validity xxiv
    construct 31–2

content 27–8, 31–2, 33
criterion-related 28, 31–2, 50–55
definition 30–31
Vuyanich v. Republic National Bank (1980)
    25

Waisome v. Port Authority (1991) 16
Watson v. Fort Worth Bank & Trust (1977,
    1988) 9
weighting of selection procedures 115–18
    content validity methods 116–18
    criterion-related validity methods 116
    Job Experts 117–18
    KSPACs (Knowledge, Skills, Abili-
       ties and Personal Characteristics)
       116–18
    unit weighting 116
WHE see Work History Evaluation (WHE)
Williams v. Owens-Illinois, Inc. (1982) 26
Work History Evaluation (WHE) xv, 101–3
    Job Experts 102–3
work sample tests 47–9, 119
written tests 57–78
    analysis 66–78
       item-level 67–72
       test-level 73–4
    analysis of results 175–6
    applicant preparation 172
    compilation 175
    content 63–4, 174
    content valid 165–76
    Cronbach's Alpha test 74
    Decision Consistency Reliability (DCR)
       78
    descriptive test analyses 73
    Differential Item Functioning (DIF)
       68–72
    item difficulty 68
    job analysis 166–71
    Job Experts 63–5, 172–4
    job knowledge 165–76
    Kappa Coefficients 78
    KSPACs (Knowledge, Skills, Abilities
       and Personal Characteristics)
       Bloom's Taxonomy 62
       determination 58
       test plans 58–63
    Kuder-Richardson formulae 74
    mastery-based 77–8
    point biserial correlations 67–8
    psychometric analyses 73–4, 77–8

reliability 74
Standard Error of Measurement (SEM)
    74–7
    conditional 75–7, 79
test plan goals 172–4
time limits 174
validation 64–6, 174

Zamlen v. City of Cleveland (1988) 115